The Colonial Caribbean

The Colonial Caribbean is an archaeological analysis of the Jamaican plantation system at the turn of the nineteenth century. Focused specifically on coffee plantation landscapes and framed by Marxist theory, the analysis considers plantation landscapes using a multiscalar approach to landscape archaeology. James A. Delle considers spatial phenomena ranging from the diachronic settlement pattern of the island as a whole to the organization of individual house and yard areas located within the villages of enslaved workers. Delle argues that a Marxist approach to landscape archaeology provides a powerful theoretical framework to understand how the built environment played a direct role in the negotiation of social relations in the colonial Caribbean.

James A. Delle is Professor of Anthropology and Chair of the Department of Anthropology and Sociology at Kutztown University of Pennsylvania. He is former chief editor and current member of the *International Journal of Historical Archaeology* editorial board and currently is an associate editor of *Historical Archaeology*. He is a member of the executive board of the Council for Northeast Historical Archaeology. Delle is the author of *An Archaeology of Social Space*; coeditor of *Lines That Divide: Historical Archaeologies of Race, Class, and Gender* and *Out of Many, One People: The Historical Archaeology of Colonial Jamaica*; and editor of *Limits of Tyranny: Archaeological Perspectives on the Struggle against New World Slavery*. Delle has published articles in the *Journal of Social Archaeology*, *Historical Archaeology*, *Northeast Historical Archaeology*, *International Journal of Historical Archaeology*, and *Archaeologies*.

T0371083

The Colonial Caribbean

Case Studies in Early Societies

Series Editor
Rita P. Wright, New York University

This series aims to introduce students to early societies that have been the subject of sustained archaeological research. Each study is also designed to demonstrate a contemporary method of archaeological analysis in action, and the authors are all specialists currently engaged in field research.

The books have been planned to cover many of the same fundamental issues. Tracing long-term developments and describing and analyzing a discrete segment in the prehistory or history of a region, they represent an invaluable tool for comparative analysis. Clear, well organized, authoritative, and succinct, the case studies are an important resource for students, and for scholars in related fields such as anthropology, ethnohistory, history, and political science. They also offer the general reader accessible introductions to important archaeological sites.

Other Titles in the Series Include:

Ancient Mesopotamia
Susan Pollock

Ancient Oaxaca
Richard E. Blanton, Gary M. Feinman, Stephen A. Kowalewski, and Linda M. Nicholas

Ancient Maya
Arthur Demarest

Ancient Jomon of Japan
Junko Habu

Ancient Puebloan Southwest
John Kantner

Ancient Cahokia and the Mississippians
Timothy R. Pauketat

Ancient Middle Niger
Rod McIntosh

Ancient Egyptian Civilization
Robert Wenke

Ancient Tiwanaku
John Janusek

The Ancient Indus
Rita P. Wright

Ancient Inca
Alan L. Kolata

Ancient Central China
Rowan K. Flad and Pochan Chen

The Colonial Caribbean

*Landscapes of Power in the
Plantation System*

James A. Delle
Kutztown University of Pennsylvania

CAMBRIDGE
UNIVERSITY PRESS

CAMBRIDGE
UNIVERSITY PRESS

University Printing House, Cambridge CB2 8BS, United Kingdom

One Liberty Plaza, 20th Floor, New York, NY 10006, USA

477 Williamstown Road, Port Melbourne, VIC 3207, Australia

314-321, 3rd Floor, Plot 3, Splendor Forum, Jasola District Centre, New Delhi - 110025, India

79 Anson Road, #06-04/06, Singapore 079906

Cambridge University Press is part of the University of Cambridge.

It furthers the University's mission by disseminating knowledge in the pursuit of education, learning and research at the highest international levels of excellence.

www.cambridge.org
Information on this title: www.cambridge.org/9780521744331

© James A. Delle 2014

First published 2014

A catalogue record for this publication is available from the British Library

Library of Congress Cataloging in Publication data
Delle, James A.
The colonial Caribbean : landscapes of power in the plantation system / James A. Delle.
    p. cm. – (Case studies in early societies)
Landscapes of power in the plantation system
ISBN 978-0-521-76770-5
1. Plantations – Jamaica – History – 19th century. 2. Landscape archaeology – Jamaica. I. Title. II. Title: Landscapes of power in Jamaica's plantation system. III. Series: Case studies in early societies.
HD1471.J3D45 2014
306.3′49–dc23   2013043768

ISBN 978-0-521-76770-5 Hardback
ISBN 978-0-521-74433-1 Paperback

Contents

Figures

Tables

Preface

In following the format for Case Studies in Early Societies, this volume explores a former civilization, the plantation society of colonial-period Jamaica, framing the analysis of fieldwork within a coherent theoretical structure. The theory that structures this book, Marxism, has a long history of use by Anglo-American archaeologists, dating from at least the work of V. Gordon Childe through to the twenty-first century. Some readers may enter this book from a frame of reference dismissive of Marxism, its basis in materialism, and its focus on the development of class structure and dialectical conflict; others may be curious about how Marxist theory can be used to create understandings of the archaeological past. It is on this latter audience that I have focused my writing. It was my intention when starting out on this book to simultaneously present a thoughtful analysis of the archaeology of plantation Jamaica and to provide an introduction to Marxist archaeology. Knowing that many readers will have had only a cursory introduction to Marxist theory, I have endeavored to explain some of the primary concepts that inform Marxist archaeology without overly depending on jargon. I hope those with a deeper understanding of Marxism will forgive my occasional definition of terms with which they may already be familiar.

There are many people to whom I owe a debt of gratitude for the completion of this book. First and foremost of these is Rita P. Wright, the series editor for Cambridge University Press's Case Studies in Early Societies series. I was flattered that Rita asked me to contribute this volume to the series, and I thank her for her patience while I wrote it. I am also grateful to the editorial staff at Cambridge, including Beatrice Rehl, Anastasia Graf, and Isabella Vitti. Two colleagues whom I hold in the highest regard, Tom Patterson and Chuck Orser, read and commented on a complete draft of this manuscript, and, as always, I learned a great deal from their thoughtful comments, which helped guide and refine my thinking through the process of revision.

The analysis contained herein is based on fieldwork conducted in Jamaica over the course of more than twenty years. The list of people who assisted me in the collection and analysis of field data is long indeed; I would like to especially thank all of the one-time graduate students from a variety of universities with whom I have had the privilege of working over the years, including Elizabeth Clay, Kristen Fellows, Patrick Heaton, Lizzie Martin, Jordan Pickrell, Janet Six, Ashley Tupper, and Mike Volmar. Field school students too numerous to mention, from both Franklin and Marshall College and Kutztown University, contributed a great deal to the projects discussed here. A number of colleagues in archaeology and other fields contributed a great deal to both the fieldwork and analysis behind this work; my thanks go to Doug Armstrong, Mark Hauser, Ken Kelly, Jack Rossen, Chris Sacchi, Rob Sternberg, Norman Stolzoff, and, of course, Mary Ann Levine. Several administrators of my former employer, Franklin and Marshall College, especially John Campbell and Bruce Pipes, were instrumental in helping my work in Jamaica move beyond the dissertation. My current employer, Kutztown University, provided me with a sabbatical leave during which I began writing this book. My thanks go to President Javier Cevallos, Dean Anne Zayaitz, and Provost Carlos Vargas. Funding for this project was provided by Franklin and Marshall College, Kutztown University, the Keck Foundation, and three separate grants from the Wenner-Gren Foundation for Anthropological Research. My thanks to the grants administrators at both Kutztown University and Franklin and Marshall for helping secure and administer these funds.

In Jamaica, I owe a debt of tremendous gratitude to my friend and colleague Dorrick Gray and the staff of the Jamaica National Heritage Trust. Several landowners provided me with virtually unlimited access to their properties, including Charles Deichman, owner of Sherwood Forest, and the Sutton family – the late Arthur and late Robert, and Ann – owners of Marshall's Pen. The Jamaica Forestry Department was kind enough to allow me access to Clydesdale, a property they maintain as a forest preserve. The Earl of Crawford, descendant of the Earl of Balcarres, has generously allowed me to conduct research on his family papers at the National Library of Scotland. My thanks to Kenneth Dunn, keeper of manuscripts at the National Library of Scotland, who has always been extremely helpful to my research efforts there. One of the requirements for inclusion in this series was a discussion of a comparative case study. I would like to thank the many colleagues who helped me form my ideas about seventeenth-century Virginia, including Kelley Deetz, Chuck Downing, Jillian Galle, Chris McDaid, Fraser Neiman, and Matt Reeves. Although they may not necessarily agree with the approach I take in the analysis of early colonial Virginia, I hope they each find this comparative analysis interesting and informative.

I would like to thank those who helped prepare the images presented here. The GIS images that appear in Chapter 2 were generated by my friend and colleague Richard Courtney of the Department of Geography and GIS Lab at Kutztown University. I could not have done the analysis without his help. Nick Stover, an undergraduate student in Kutztown's Department of Communication Design, completed many of the images you will see here. He did an outstanding job completing graphic work begun by my late friend John Svatek, who unexpectedly passed away during the preparation of the images for this volume.

Finally, I would like to thank my family, Mary Ann Levine and Lily Delle-Levine, for their patience and understanding as I hauled versions of this manuscript around with me, taking every advantage of the moments in between family events to revise my writing and clarify my thoughts.

1 Landscapes of Power in the Colonial Caribbean

On the morning of May 23, 1832, Samuel Sharpe was hanged in the Jamaican town of Montego Bay. The hanging of black men was a tragically common event in the colonial Caribbean, and this particular execution may well have slipped unnoticed into the annals of history had it not been for the fact that Sam Sharpe was the condemned leader of an uprising of Jamaica's enslaved population. Although insurrections of the enslaved working class were common in colonial Jamaica, the scale of this particular event was unprecedented in British West Indian history. The insurrection led by Sharpe, known alternately as the Baptist War, the Christmas Rebellion, and the Great Slave Rebellion, involved tens of thousands of people who took up arms, not against the planters who enslaved them, but against the sugarcane fields and industrial buildings in which they worked. During the two-week period between December 27, 1831 and January 5, 1832, some 100 plantations in the western parishes of Jamaica were destroyed; yet only about 17 white people were killed. The uprising was quickly suppressed by the well-armed Jamaica militia, and reprisals against the rebels were swift and brutal, resulting in more than 300 executions, including that of Sam Sharpe (Blackburn 1988; Hart 2002; Holt 1992; Reckford 1968; Watts 1990).

Although the events of 1831–1832 shed considerable light on the social world of colonial Jamaica, what that light reveals is complex and sometimes difficult to comprehend from a twenty-first-century frame of reference. On the surface, the uprising can be seen as a mass release of pent-up anger against the oppressive nature of the slave-based plantation economy of the colonial Caribbean. The system *was* brutal and the common use of dehumanizing corporal punishment *did* foment great resentment against the white planters. Yet little violent retribution was focused on the men and women responsible for the cruel infliction of those punishments. If one looks deeper into the colonial world of 1831, one can interpret the conflict that erupted that Christmastide as a microcosmic manifestation of ongoing and broader historical changes shaking the colonial order of the British Empire. By 1831, the global influence of the British West Indies, even

1

Jamaica, was receding as the focus of British colonialism shifted steadily east, to the consolidation of British interests on the Indian Subcontinent and, eventually, Africa (James 2000; Judd 2004). In England, industrialized production using wage labor was becoming commonplace, resulting in rapid urbanization as more and more people were employed in briskly developing factory towns (Hobsbawn 1999; Polanyi 2001). Urban dwellers, industrialists, and liberals successfully agitated for Parliamentary reform, a process that resulted in a great expansion of the franchise in Britain, a shift in the distribution of Members of Parliament as industrial cities received representation for the first time, and, in 1832, the election of a reform-minded Whig government at Westminster (Evans 1994, 2008; Phillips and Whetherell 1995). Industrialists, religious reformers, and republicans all agitated for an end to slavery in the British Empire, organizing boycotts and propaganda campaigns against the use of slave labor, especially in the production of West Indian sugar (Oldfield 1992, 1995). In Jamaica, Sam Sharpe and his many colleagues were aware of these global developments and, as many working people in Europe were doing, demanded the rights of free people, particularly the right to be paid fair wages for their work (Drescher 2004; Green 1976). In effect, the thousands of people who rose up against the system of unfree labor were seeking to put an end to what Tom Brass and Henry Bernstein have characterized as capitalism's general trend to limit workers' rights to their own labor (Brass and Bernstein 1992). The Baptist War did not go unnoticed in Britain, and Parliament quickly acted first to inform itself about what was happening in Jamaica, and then to legislate the end of slavery in the British West Indies (Bulter 1995; Draper 2010).

When Sam Sharpe was executed, he was hanged as a man who had organized a general strike demanding the end of slavery and the institution of wage labor for the Jamaican working class (Hart 2002). He lived, and died, at a crucial moment of change in the Western Hemisphere; within fifteen months of his death, the British Parliament had abolished slavery in its New World colonies, a labor and social system that had been in place in British America for the better part of two centuries. The British Empire, and the European colonial world more generally expressed, was experiencing a long moment of epochal change during which old colonies in the New World – including the unified Republic of Haiti under President Jean-Pierre Boyer – were establishing themselves as independent republics without any formal monarchical head of state (Hobsbawn 1996; Middlekauf 2007). Economists, industrialists, and statesmen had begun to seriously reconsider the long-standing use of price-controlling tariffs to support colonial production in places like Jamaica. Britons had begun contemplating the era of what would be variously called free trade or laissez-faire capitalism (Polanyi 2001). Great political, economic, and social change was emerging as the nineteenth century blossomed, change brought on by the actions of people like Sam Sharpe.

The purpose of this book is to interpret Jamaican colonial society during this moment of epochal change through the lens of Marxist-informed landscape archaeology. Viewed from this perspective, the opening decades of the nineteenth century can be seen as a moment of dialectical change for the British Empire. In the British Caribbean, eighteenth-century colonial society had been built on the success of agricultural production (Tomich 1990). In Jamaica as elsewhere in the Caribbean, that success was dependent on the social and physical realities of a mode of production driven by open access to enslaved labor (Dunn 2000; Holt 1992; Sheridan 2000; Tomich 1990). A goal of this analysis of Jamaican plantation landscapes as they existed at the turn of the nineteenth century is to better understand the material and social realities of the slave-based plantation system and to consider why, in the end, it failed.

This book interprets the historical realities of colonial Jamaica through an archaeological analysis of Jamaica's plantation landscapes. Based on archaeological fieldwork conducted between 1990 and 2012, this book analyzes plantation landscapes at multiple scales, from the island-wide settlement pattern of plantations across Jamaica, to the development of internally coherent regions in which enclaves of planters formed their class relations and social realities, to the plantation as a material component of a mode of production that mediated the negotiation of social relations between planters and the enslaved, to individual house yards located within the cramped plantation villages that were home to hundreds of enslaved men, women, and children. The methodologies of landscape archaeology allow for analyses at each of these scales; however, landscape archaeology is but a set of methodologies that needs to be structured by a theoretical framework through which we can endow the remnants of the past left to us – the archaeological record – with meaning. The theoretical framework used here to interpret those landscapes of colonial Jamaica is what is commonly referred to as Marxist Archaeology (McGuire 1992, 2008; Patterson 2003; Trigger 1989).

On Marxism and Archaeology

Archaeologists and historians of the Caribbean have utilized a variety of theoretical frameworks to understand the complex social realities of the plantation system, ranging from feminist approaches to understanding the gender dynamics of the slave system (e.g., Bush 1990; Morgan 2004; Reddick 1985) to adaptationalist perspectives defining ongoing evolutionary processes (e.g., Galle 2011). The focus of research is similarly diverse. For example, some archaeologists of the colonial Caribbean have looked at the complexities of the informal economy developed by the enslaved (e.g., Hauser 2011, 2008; Reeves 2011; see also Mintz and Hall 1960), the emergence of Creole identities (e.g., Delle 2000; Loftfield 2001; Wilkie 1999, 2001), the development of interisland trading networks (e.g., Armstrong 2003; Curet and Hauser 2011), and the organization of colonial enterprise (e.g., Barka 2001; Kelly and Hardy 2011). Others have focused on understanding the dynamics of maroon resistance to the plantation system (e.g., Agorsah 2007; Goucher and Agorsah 2011; Orser and Funari 2001). Each of these approaches and foci has its merits and has made a significant contribution to our understanding of the colonial Caribbean.

As a work of landscape archaeology, this book is concerned with understanding how plantation landscapes were created and how those landscapes actively shaped human action under the colonial regime of early-nineteenth-century Jamaica. By the turn of the nineteenth century, the "plantation" was a well-defined locus of monocrop production of agricultural commodities, destined to be exchanged in global markets. The plantation was a privately owned, capitalized operation, often using enslaved or other forms of coerced labor to maximize the profits realized by its proprietor (Genovese 1989, 15). The work presented here focuses on plantation landscapes. Although many theoretical approaches to the past can be applied to understanding plantation landscapes, perhaps none is more effective in understanding the relationship between spatial structure and human agency than the dialectical approach essential to Marxist archaeological theory.

Although Marxist analysis has sometimes, and spuriously, been dismissed as simultaneously being "totalizing" and narrowly focused (e.g., Hicks and Horning 2006; Wilkie and Bartoy 2000), Marxist theory actually provides a robust and compelling framework for understanding the development and operation of class-stratified social systems, and has informed the practice of Anglo-American archaeology for decades (see Adams 1965; Brumfiel 1980; Childe 1936, 1950; Delle 1998, 1999; Gilman 1981; Kohl 1981; Leone, Potter, and Shackel 1987; Matthews 2005; McGuire 1992, 1993, 2008; Patterson 1986, 2003; Rosenswig 2012; Spriggs 1984; Tosi 1976; Trigger 1989, 1993). Far from being a fundamentalist philosophy of history, Marxist archaeology, as McGuire (2008) has noted, is a diverse tradition of thought emerging from a philosophy of history and practice that is simultaneously a way to know the world, a way to critique the world, and a way to change it.

One of the main tenets of Marxian thought that applies specifically to archaeological analysis is the idea that the material conditions under which people live shape not only their own lives but the very nature of social interaction within their given society. Marxist thought contends that there is a direct relationship between the tools and technologies used to make a living and the nature of the social relationships operating within a given society; changes in either – for example the invention of new technologies or a rapid increase in the number of people needing to be fed – could result in historical change that rapidly reconfigures how people live and relate to each other (Marx 1979).

Marx and Engels used an architectural metaphor to explain how the material realities of making a living shape the overall structure of a given society at any historical moment, a theoretical construct known as a "mode of production" (Engels 2007; Marx 1979, 2011, 1992). To Marx and Engels, the economy formed the base of a society and other manifestations of social interaction – religion, ideology, social consciousness, political organization – were built on the foundation of the economic base to form a social superstructure. The economic base of any society defined its mode of production and emerged from the interplay of contextually dependent historical phenomena and events. Despite this historic diversity, the essential components of all modes of production include what are known as the forces of production, which include the means of production (raw materials, tools, and knowledge necessary to use them). What are called the "relations of production" (social relationships within a society) determine what roles people play in the manufacture and use of material objects.

Another important concept within Marxism that has influenced archaeological theory is what is known as the "labor theory of value" (McGuire and Reckner 2002; Paynter 1999). This idea holds that anything that is produced by a society will have a value equal to the cost of the materials required for its production plus the value of the labor expended to produce it. If a manufactured object is sold for more than it costs to produce, the difference is known as surplus value (Marx 1984, 2000). Class relations develop when someone other than the worker who made something, sometimes called the primary producer, systematically collects the surplus value resulting from the exchange of goods. Under capitalism, workers are said to be alienated from the means of production, which means that they do not own the tools and raw materials they use to manufacture objects, nor do they own the final products of their labor (Marx 1961). In describing capitalism as a mode of production, Marx used the term "bourgeoisie" to describe the class of people who built the factories and owned the raw materials (e.g., cotton, iron, coal) required to produce commodities for sale. In the capitalist mode of production, the social relations of production are such that society allows the bourgeoisie to own the surplus value derived from the sale of commodities. This results in the development of an unequal class structure in which the bourgeoisie and workers are in dialectical conflict with each other, which means that members of the two classes have their own specific set of interests existing in opposition to each other. Members of the bourgeois class wish to lower costs of production, including the cost of building and maintaining factories, and will thus try to avoid incurring surplus expenses. It is also in their best interest to minimize labor costs so as to maximize the extraction of surplus value (sometimes known as profit). Members of the working class, which Marx called the "proletariat," have a diametrically opposed interest to retain as much surplus value as possible through the receipt of high wages, investment in better and safer working conditions, pensions, health care benefits, and so forth. Significant structural change, including the emergence of new modes of production, can result when the conflict between classes reaches a crisis point and the society is no longer stable. To many Marxists, such dialectical conflicts between social classes are the engines of historical change (Marx 1992). In colonial plantation contexts like Jamaica, enslaved workers are further alienated from what Marxists refer to as their labor power – a commodity that workers sell for wages, but which enslaved workers are prohibited from owning, and thus from exchanging for wages (Brass and Bernstein 1992).

These key elements of Marxist thought have informed archaeological theory over the past four decades: (1) social and material forces work to construct and reproduce unequal social relations; (2) societies can be interpreted using the concept of the mode of production; (3) social stratification is a process based on class formation and struggle; and (4) relationships between social classes are dialectical in nature (see Adams 1966; Gilman 1981, 1984; Kohl 1981; Kus 1984; Leone 1995; McGuire 1992, 2008; Patterson 1986, 1991; Paynter 1982; Wurst 1999, 2011). Shaped by this tradition of archaeological thought, this book begins with the premise that material culture – objects fashioned, exchanged, and used by people – actively create and mediate social relations within a given historical context. The form of material culture analyzed here is the landscape, specifically coffee plantation landscapes in colonial Jamaica, a complex and dynamic form of material culture that can be analyzed on a range of analytical scales, from the settlement pattern of the island as a whole to individual houses within enslaved villages.

Each of the subsequent chapters of this book explores a primary theme within Marxist thought by archaeologically analyzing Jamaican plantation landscapes from a different point on the spectrum of landscape analysis. Chapter 2 examines the historical context within which the social relations of production formed in colonial Jamaica, by reviewing the island-wide settlement pattern history of Jamaica as it relates to the shifting realities of the colonial experience. Chapter 3 explores the plantation mode of production as it existed in Jamaica at the turn of the nineteenth century, when large-scale coffee production was first introduced to the island. In so doing, this chapter examines landscapes at the local plantation scale of analysis. Chapter 4 analyzes the development of class consciousness among the planters, exploring how regional landscapes between plantations were active agents in the development and maintenance of class consciousness and solidarity among planters in the early nineteenth century. Chapter 5 explores the nature of dialectical relations between the planters and the enslaved from the perspective of the households located within enslaved workers' villages, and Chapter 6 expands from the preceding chapters to explore how dialectics can be used to understand historical change, while emphasizing the totality of the lived experience of the people of colonial Jamaica. Following the comparative Chapter 7, which considers the plantation complex of seventeenth-century Virginia, the main arguments of the book are summarized in the concluding Chapter 8. Before delving into the specifics of the analysis, however, it might be best to explain the theoretical framework used for each of the chapters in a bit more detail.

The Material Context of Colonial Jamaica (Chapter 2)

In the opening decade of the nineteenth century, Jamaica – an island about equal in landmass to the American state of Connecticut or to Britain's East Anglia – led the world in the production of both sugar and coffee (Higman 2005). The eighteenth century had been a time of great prosperity for Jamaica's planters. Although it was occasionally threatened by military action, Jamaica had not been successfully invaded since the British conquest of 1655. In contrast to Jamaica, many of the smaller Caribbean islands had changed colonial hands multiple times as a result of the many colonial wars fought between the British, French, Dutch, and Spanish (Dunn 2000; Sheridan 2000). Similarly, although there had been numerous uprisings within Jamaica's enslaved population, before 1831 none had significantly threatened the colonial regime on the island (Hart 2002). Although there was a significant population of sovereign black people, known as Maroons, living in Jamaica's interior, the colony was on peaceful terms with them at the conclusion of the eighteenth century. A series of guerrilla wars fought against the Maroons in the hinterlands had resulted in a truce; in return for the guarantee that the white Jamaicans would not threaten their independence, the leaders of Jamaica's Maroon communities agreed not to fight against the plantation system and, perhaps more significantly, to return any escaped slaves that sought refuge in Maroon communities (Campbell 1988; Dallas 1803; Price 1996). In contrast, the wealthiest of all the Caribbean colonies, the French colony of St. Domingue, had witnessed a successful revolution of the enslaved against the planters that could not be suppressed even by Napoleon's expeditionary forces; by the opening decade of the nineteenth century, St. Domingue's plantation society had been destroyed and replaced by the black republic of Haiti (Blackburn 1988). Jamaica was, from the perspective of Caribbean planters, a relatively peaceful and stable place to grow vast fortunes.

And grow they did. By the middle of the eighteenth century, slave-based agro-industry, based primarily on sugar production, was an engine that drove the accumulation of great wealth – for those who controlled the means of production (Dunn 2000). Higman proposes that by the middle of the eighteenth century, investment in sugar production had made the largest Jamaican planters among the wealthiest men in the world (Higman 2005: 5). The agricultural system they developed was very complex and resulted in the formation of a diverse society of planters, agents, attorneys, merchants, artisans, financiers, and wharfingers – yet this society composed but a small fraction of the population of Jamaica. The vast majority of the population consisted of enslaved Africans – brought to Jamaica against their will to toil for life in servitude – and their island-born descendants who, until 1834, inherited the condition of enslavement.

To contextualize the archaeological analysis of Jamaica's plantation system, Chapter 2 provides a historical overview of the development of plantation society on the island, including a consideration of the island's historical demographics and an overview of the shifting settlement history of the island. In archaeology, the examination of how places are distributed across a broad landscape is usually referred to as settlement pattern analysis (Delle 1989, 1994). Several historical archaeologists have used settlement pattern analysis to interpret how the positioning of settlements within a large area can impact the development of social relationships and give shape to a given mode of production. For example, Robert Paynter (1981, 1982, 1983, 1985) has demonstrated how the historic settlement patterns of rural western Massachusetts served to maximize the flow of surplus value to regional centers known as entrepôts, and thus spatially supported the maintenance of class-based inequality. Although not explicitly concerned with class dynamics, Ken Lewis (1984, 1985) examined the settlement pattern of the colonial South Carolina frontier, concluding that the social structure of colonial South Carolina was dependent on a hierarchically arranged system of frontier towns and settlements. Lewis hypothesized that economic changes – and thus shifts in class relations – would precipitate changes in spatial forms (Lewis 1984: 1–7, 17–27, 107–113).

Archaeological settlement pattern analysis of the plantation era has been conducted on a variety of Caribbean islands, including St. Eustatius, Tobago, and St. John. In each case, archaeologists demonstrated that the shifting location of settlements across island landscapes was directly tied to the historical development of the plantation system. On St. Eustatius, the number and size of plantations fluctuated as many small plantations were consolidated into a relatively few larger and more equally distributed estates, as the local economy of the island shifted. As St. Eustatius declined in importance as a trading port, the number of plantations decreased, as did the overall population of the island, resulting in a rationalization of land use on the island. At the end of the American Revolution, local planters became increasingly focused on the efficient production of sugar, and the distribution and size of plantations shifted accordingly (Delle 1989, 1994). On Tobago, British planters, who did not consolidate control of the island until the 1760s, carefully weighed the resource needs of sugar and rum production (e.g., access to fresh water) as a determinant of both the location of their plantations on the landscape and the internal arrangement of the components of the plantation infrastructure within each plantation (Clement 1997). On St. John, the spatial arrangement of houses within a free black community existing on the fringes of the plantation world was analyzed in the context of a slave-based plantation economy (Armstrong 2003).

Chapter 2 applies settlement pattern analysis to the island of Jamaica, and in doing so draws on the work of one of Jamaica's leading historians and historical geographers, Barry Higman, who has spent decades examining the nature of the Jamaican plantation system (e.g., Higman 1976, 1986, 1987, 1988, 1998, 2005). This analysis considers how the placement of plantations shifted as the plantation economy expanded, specifically considering how the geographic realities of late-eighteenth-century Jamaica allowed for the rapid development of a successful coffee plantation system in areas of the island not developed for sugar production.

The Plantation Mode of Production (Chapter 3)

One of the primary tenets of Marxist historical analysis is that society simultaneously produces and is produced by the relationships that exist between individual people and between people and the material world around them. A distinguishing characteristic of Marxist approaches to social analysis is the contention that the basic relationships that exist between people and nature are primarily economic; people manipulate nature and enter into social relations with other people to meet the basic needs of survival, including finding food and shelter. Unlike most animals, humans have the innate ability to use their intelligence and imagination to manipulate the environment, but in so doing, humans create new needs for themselves, and often create new forms of social relationships to attain those needs. Take, for example, a hypothetical hunting and gathering society that has invented a new weapon to hunt for food – say, the atlatl. The tool increases the efficiency of hunting but requires the use of specific kinds of wood and stone. This hypothetical society has thus created a need for the raw materials required to make elastic spear shafts and lightweight projectile points, and the knowledge and ability to make and use these complex tools. Hunters might enter into new cooperative arrangements for taking down animals and sharing the meat of their quarry; the society might also enter into trade relations with other groups who have a ready supply of the kinds of wood or stone needed to make the new hunting tools. Human innovation, through the invention of this specific tool, can thus have multiple results, changing the way people interact with members of their own group, members of other groups, the animals they are hunting, and the landscapes they must traverse to find both the raw materials they need to make hunting tools and the animals they are seeking to kill.

Marxists define this complex relationship between physical needs (both long-standing and newly invented), the tools and technologies required to fulfill those needs, and the social relations that exist to produce and use those tools and technologies as a mode of production (Marx 1979; Patterson 2003; Rosenswig 2012). Any given mode of production is composed of historically contextual relationships between people, which result in the production and use of objects to fulfill perceived physical and social needs; these relationships are known as the social relations of production (Marx 1979). The second set of components of a mode of production includes the forces of production, sometimes called the productive forces (Marx 1976). The forces of production are composed of both objective and subjective factors, the latter including individual mental and physical abilities, training, and skill levels, as well as the technical division of labor. Objective factors include tools, raw materials, industrial buildings, and landscapes. The objective factors are sometimes referred to as the means of production and form the archaeological record of a given mode of production.

Although Marx identified diverse modes of production that had existed in a variety of historical contexts, the one that most interested him was the capitalist mode of production (Marx 1992; Rosenswig 2012). Marx was, among other things, a social critic. He understood that capitalism as it existed in the middle of the nineteenth century was simultaneously generating great wealth for those who controlled the means of production and conditions of dependent poverty for those who had no choice but to sell their labor power to the factory owners for a wage. Wealth and poverty were simultaneously created through the dialectical relationship between worker and factory owner. In drawing off the surplus value of the commodities produced by industrial capitalism, capitalists were growing wealthy, and workers increasingly poor; according to Marx, the condition of labor under the capitalist mode of production assumed and required the existence of the wage relationship to explain this flow of wealth (Marx 1992).

If, however, the social relations of production under the capitalist mode of production are mediated by the payment of wages, how can one account for the existence of slavery, a labor system that operated without a wage relationship? One simple way to explain nineteenth-century slavery is to define it as having been a remnant part of an antiquated mode of production; and indeed Marx did explore the use of slave labor by the Roman Empire in what is sometimes referred to as the Antique Mode of Production (Engels 2010). Interpreting the experience of the Roman Empire does not, however, serve to explain the coexistence of slavery and wage labor at the turn of the nineteenth century. Another way to reconcile the persistence of slavery is to contend that slavery existed as a contradiction within the capitalist mode of production; that the wages due to slaves were being stolen from them, or else the enslaved were being paid a metaphorical wage through the distribution of food provisions, clothing, and housing by the plantation owners (Laycock 1999; Marx 1992). These explanations are satisfactory, however, only if one accepts the unsubstantiated assumption that only one mode of production can be operating at a given time. It is much more likely, particularly given the realities of late-eighteenth-century colonialism, that multiple modes of production were operating simultaneously in the far-flung colonies of the various European empires, unified, though, by colonial capitalism's universalizing mission to impose a class-based social hierarchy designed to maximize the concentration of wealth in the hands of those in control of the means of production (Chibber 2013; Orser 1996; and see Albritton 1993 for a discussion of simultaneously existing "capitalist phenomena"). Each colony would have had its own historical experience resulting in the development of specific manifestations of the relations of production, haunted, however, by what Vivek Chibber has recently referred to as the "specter of capital" (2013). Among the many manifestations of the relations of production under capitalism was the use of unfree labor in plantation contexts, whether enslaved, indentured, or otherwise coerced (Baud 1992).

Colonial Jamaica, then, was operating under its own historically contingent plantation mode of production, operating in the context of globally expanding capitalism (Orser 1996; Williams 1944). Under this mode of production, the relations of production were defined by chattel slavery, a social condition that objectifies the physical abilities of people (i.e., under this mode of production, people themselves were defined as components of the means of production, as saleable commodities with established exchange value). Although the plantation-based economy depended on the production of agricultural commodities for sale in world markets, as Barry Higman has observed, planters' wealth derived from the ownership of slaves, whose values were carefully recorded based on age, gender, ability, and training (Higman 2005: 5). Planters themselves tabulated their wealth by establishing the value of the individuals they enslaved, and indeed, much of the local political apparatus was dependent on taxing planters based on the net value assigned to their enslaved plantation work force.

Chapter 3 examines the development of Jamaican society through the analysis of the plantation mode of production and has several goals. First is an explication of the plantation mode of production examining how the forces and relations of production developed within the context of several coffee plantations operating at the turn of the nineteenth century. Chapter 3 simultaneously analyzes the structure of plantation society through the analysis of some of the few surviving documents recording the daily operations of Jamaican coffee plantations. The daybooks and correspondence from which this analysis draws shed significant light on the division of labor on early-nineteenth-century coffee plantations. The chapter also analyzes the archaeological record of plantation ruins – at the scale of the individual plantation – as remnants of the means of production of the plantation mode of production and considers how plantation lay-outs and landscapes were active components in the negotiation of the social relations of production, particularly between the enslaved laborers and the local planter class.

Influenced by those approaches that seek to link the individual experiences of people to those social and historical processes that work to shape their lives, Chapter 3 concludes with a consideration of how the forces of production and the relations of production were interrelated in spatial reality. This analysis considers plantation buildings and landscapes as conscientiously constructed elements of the means of production under the plantation mode of production. As such, the built environments of Jamaica's plantations were designed and constructed to mediate the relationships between the planters and enslaved workers, not necessarily by display, but through action. Spaces are dynamic phenomena whose nature is experienced only when people move through them. This movement through space helps to shape daily ritual and mediates our experiences and relationships with the physical and social worlds in which we are embedded, a phenomenon defined by the French sociologist Pierre Bourdieu as "habitus" (1977).

A number of archaeologists have used Bourdieu's concept as a theoretical bridge between approaches focused on determinant structures and those based on ahistorical agency (e.g. Dornan 2002; Orser 2007; Paynter and McGuire 1991; Pluckham 2010; Wesson 2008). A difficult term to define, habitus is a social process by which behavioral dispositions are formed within individuals as a result of their constant interaction with their social and physical environments. These dispositions in turn structure the way the individual experiences the world. Bourdieu argued that habitus, though learned, resulted in a largely unconscious understanding of the parameters of behavior possible within given contexts. The structures of a society would help shape habitus, and habitus would create a spectrum of possible action by individuals. Because each individual would experience the world in slightly different ways (even different members of an enslaved community might have a different relationship to an overseer or planter), individual action was not only possible but likely. Although much of the collective habitus might be similar, each individual would develop an idiosyncratic understanding of the world. Actions and behaviors might be constrained by the structures of society that define habitus, but each individual could create new action within the perceived range of the possible (Bourdieu 1977). Charles Orser has applied this concept to archaeological analysis of the process of racialization in North America (Orser 2004, 2007); here I use this concept to interpret the material arrangement of Jamaican coffee plantations.

The Formation and Reproduction of Class Consciousness (Chapter 4)

One of the hallmarks of Marxist theory is the idea that, in some historically occurring modes of production, certain segments of society will be allowed to control access to the forces of production – the tools, raw material, and sometimes complex knowledge required to make objects required by members of their society. According to the labor theory of value, the value of the objects produced is equal to the value of the objective inputs used to produce them; that is, the value of an object is equal to the cost of the extraction, shipment, and manipulation of raw materials into a saleable commodity. If the object is sold at a price greater than this cost, the sale of that commodity produces surplus value. To Marx, it was the appropriation of this surplus value by the bourgeoisie that led to the development and maintenance of the capitalist mode of production. Relations of production emerged that formalized the division of society into several social classes, and, under capitalism, the emergent class of owners manipulated the legal and social superstructure of society to support, maintain, and reproduce the resulting social relations of production. Although individual factory owners might compete against each other to maximize their profit by introducing innovative machinery and more efficient systems of labor extraction, and thus to drive their competitors out of business, these same individuals share a common interest in maintaining a social structure which allows for the wage relationship to continue (Marx 1992).

Marxist analyses of the capitalist mode of production suggest that the appropriation of surplus value by the industrial class was a form of labor exploitation. In this sense of the word, exploitation means that the surplus value generated by the sale of commodities rightly belongs to the laborers whose work produced the commodities. The nature of this relationship – a dominant class extracts value from the work of a subordinate class – leads to conflict within a society. In Marxist thinking, the conflicts between opposing classes foment historical social change, which can be mitigated for a time by members of the dominant class if they are aware of the nature of the operative social relations of production that allow them to extract the surplus value that forms the basis of their ability to accumulate wealth.

This conscientious understanding of the organization and operation of the social relations of production results in the formation of what is known as class consciousness (Lukacs 1972; Marx 1975). Although the full development of class consciousness is not necessary for the successful maintenance of a given mode of production, when a dominant class is able to form a strong sense of why and how their class forms and operates, they are able to deliberately manipulate the legal, political, and military apparatus of their society to defend and reinforce the systems of inequality that underlie the operative relations of production.

Numerous archaeological projects have demonstrated that the manipulation of landscapes was integral to the development of class consciousness. For example, Ed Hood's examination of the twentieth-century colonial revival landscapes of modern Deerfield, Massachusetts demonstrates how an elite class intentionally manipulated the town landscape in the attempt to create a false impression of what the landscapes of the past must have been like (Hood 1996). The sanitized vision of the colonial past that emerged served primarily to reinforce the ideology of early-twentieth-century capitalism by creating a falsely timeless landscape that reflected modern inequality; in so doing, the wealthy classes of twentieth-century Deerfield justified and reinforced the legitimacy of their social class by projecting its presence into the tangible past. Elizabeth Kryder-Reid's study of the Annapolis (Maryland) garden site known as St. Mary's demonstrated that control over eighteenth-century garden space served to reinforce class relations in that colonial city; gardens were powerful media "of the colonial elite to communicate and negotiate their social identity," with other knowledgeable members of their social class (1994: 132). Mark Leone's study of William Paca's garden in colonial Annapolis demonstrated much the same thing. By constructing complex formal gardens, members of the colonial elite class displayed their control over a common understanding of how rational thought could be used to manipulate control over the natural and social landscapes of their colonial world (Leone 1984, 1988, 2005). In each of these cases, archaeologists have demonstrated how landscape manipulation was a key element in the formation of a shared understanding of the social and natural worlds, and how that knowledge contributed to the formation of a common class consciousness.

Archaeologists concerned specifically with plantation contexts have applied the methodologies of landscape archaeology to examine how members of elite classes have deliberately created landscapes to collectively support and advance their class interests (Armstrong and Kelly 1990; Delle 1994; Hudgins 1990; Kelso 1990; Luccketti 1990; McKee 1996; Orser 1988; Pogue 1996). For example, Chuck Orser has demonstrated how landscapes impacted the negotiation of post-emancipation class relations at Millwood, a South Carolina cotton plantation (Orser 1988a, 1991; Orser and Nekola 1985). The owner of Millwood Plantation, James Edward Calhoun, was a well-connected member of the southern elite. With the defeat of the Confederacy at the end of the U.S. Civil War, planters like Calhoun recognized the necessity of reorganizing labor systems, as slavery was no longer legal in the United States. Several new strategies of labor extraction were established, including tenant farming and sharecropping (Orser 1988: 45–51). This restructuring of class relations following emancipation resulted in the restructuring of plantation landscapes. Unlike antebellum plantation settlements which put a premium on direct surveillance of the laborers, postbellum plantation settlements tended to be dispersed; each farmer, whether renter or sharecropper, lived with his or her family near the fields they tended. Significantly, where sharecroppers made up the bulk of the plantation tenants, the settlement form more closely resembled antebellum forms, with barns, sheds, and other outbuildings located near the planter's house to provide the planter class with the capability to directly supervise the sharecroppers (Orser 1988: 92). This study demonstrates that planter elites manipulated the landscape to implement and reinforce a class structure in which they remained in control of land and production, and that these strategies have left an archaeological signature.

Chapter 4 examines the spatial formation of class consciousness among the planter class of colonial Jamaica through the analysis of the regional landscape of the District of Upper St. David. Through the analysis of the records of the parish vestry, and the results of a regional archaeological survey conducted in the Negro River Valley, this chapter explores the structure of Jamaica's planter class, how class consciousness emerged in colonial Jamaica, and how the regional landscape was formed to create and reinforce the social networks on which members of the planter class depended.

Contradictions and Dialectics (Chapter 5)

Marxism is sometimes interpreted as being an evolutionary theory of history, based on the theoretical constructs of historical materialism (Roseberry 1997; Rosenswig 2012). Marx and many of his intellectual progeny argued that all modes of production are inherently unstable and all will eventually transform and be replaced by new modes of production. This instability results from the existence of contradictions within each mode of production. Although the term "contradiction" is somewhat difficult to define, a contradiction can be understood as a systemic flaw in the logic of a particular mode of production. Sometimes these flaws exist between the imagined and the experienced relations of production. For example, in the Declaration of Independence of the United States, Thomas Jefferson famously opined that "all men are created equal and are endowed by their creator with certain unalienable rights, that among these are life, liberty, and the pursuit of happiness." Comparing this statement with the reality that Jefferson, and thousands of men like him, profited not by treating all men as equal, but by the systematic enslavement of hundreds of thousands of people who were deprived of their rights to life and liberty, reveals a contradiction between the ideological superstructure of the early Republic and the operative relations of production in the plantation south. Some historical critics have suggested that slavery itself was a contradiction within industrial capitalism, a mode of production requiring wages to mediate between social classes. When contradictions are not resolved within the operative structure of a given mode of production, they can precipitate dialectical change, as opposing forces pull the mode of production apart along the fault lines created by the unresolved contradictions. A Marxist analysis of the U.S. Civil War, for example, would argue that the conflagration between the North and the South was in actuality a process by which the contradictions emerging within the operating mode of production were resolved, primarily the contradiction between the production of raw materials (e.g., cotton) by slave labor, and the production of finished commodities (e.g., textiles) by wage labor.

The plantation mode of production, like all modes of production, contained contradictions that produced tension within the system. Like wage earners in Great Britain, enslaved workers in Jamaica had no clear control or ownership over the means of production; that is – they were alienated from those means of production. Because laws regulating enslavement in Jamaica prohibited the enslaved from selling their labor power directly, they were not allowed by law to work for wages, even if their work for their master was complete. However, there was a significant contradiction within the plantation mode of production in Jamaica. On most plantations, enslaved people were required to grow their own food in their own time on small farms. Known as provision grounds, these plots of land produced food provisions that were recognized as being the property of the enslaved through the legal concept of "ususfructus" – that is, the enslaved owned what they produced on land that was owned by the planters who claimed them as slaves (Dunn 2000; Hauser 2008). Not only were the enslaved allowed to own the food they produced, many planters across the island purchased food for cash from the people they themselves enslaved. Furthermore, a very thriving internal economy developed among the enslaved population of Jamaica who bought and sold goods from each other in weekly markets held in towns across the island, including the produce being grown in the provision grounds by the enslaved (Hauser 2008).

This practice created a contradiction within the plantation mode of production. The legal apparatus of the plantation, and the nature of the operative relations of production, prohibited the enslaved from being paid wages for the production of export crops. Enslaved people had no right whatsoever to any surplus value derived from the sale of the agricultural commodities they produced in the cane fields or coffee pieces, but held every right to the entire surplus value of food crops they grew in the provision grounds. Thus, a contradiction existed between labor extracted for crop production for export and labor expended for internal consumption in Jamaica. Herein lies one of the great contradictions of Jamaican slavery: two parallel understandings of the rights to labor and surplus value were simultaneously working, one feeding the export market, the other the local market. This contradiction defines much of the nineteenth-century colonial experience, the living in two worlds, the simultaneous exploitation of the working class for export and the payment for local produce; that plantations extract labor to produce commodities, yet purchase commodities from those very same workers. It was the attempt to reconcile this contradiction that led Sam Sharpe and his followers to demand the payment of wages, and thus to organize the great strike of 1831.

Through the analysis of the archaeological record of the slave village at an early nineteenth-century coffee plantation known as Marshall's Pen, Chapter 5 examines the spatial manifestation of this basic contradiction within the plantation mode of production. Inhabited for only a single generation before the end of slavery, the spatial analysis of this village reveals how individual households shaped local landscapes. The analysis includes an architectural analysis of the houses and house compounds located within the village and examines how yard spaces were loci of production for the local markets. In doing so, Chapter 5 explores the nature of the primary contradiction that plagued the plantation mode of production and, indeed, may have been responsible for its downfall.

Dialectics and Culture Change (Chapter 6)

History is not static; it is a process of ongoing change. To Marx, the direction of that change emerged from the contradictions within a system. As members of various classes developed class consciousness, more and more members of a social class began to both comprehend the nature of their exploitation and to work collectively to change the nature of the social relations of production, the reproduction of which led to the rein-forcing of systems of exploitation.

But the direction of historical change is not predetermined. When slavery was abolished in 1834, despite the best efforts of the planter class in Jamaica and Parliamentarians in England, post-emancipation Jamaica developed in unpredicted ways, which emerged from contradictory class interests between the planters and the formerly enslaved (Delle 1998; Holt 1992). On the one hand, the planters wanted to keep the laborers at hand for plantation work, not wanting to pay them every day, but only at those times when labor was required to bring in and process the crop. On the other hand, many members of the working class (as could be seen from the rampant property destruction that marked the 1831–1832 uprising) detested the plantation as an entity and sought to liberate themselves entirely from the Eurocentric export economy that emerged with the plantation mode of production. Many formerly enslaved people sought instead to become self-sufficient small farmers, producing crops for local consumption as they had done under slavery, but free of the limitations that had been imposed on them (Craton 1997; Delle 1998; Holt 1992; Satchell 1990).

Several archaeologists have considered how landscapes were transformed during moments of tension and change in operating modes of
production. For example, Randy McGuire has examined town and community landscapes to analyze changes in the capitalist mode of production as it was manifested in late-nineteenth- and early-twentieth-century
Broome County, New York (McGuire 1988, 1991; Wurst 1991). The
differences in the industrial landscapes constructed by the industrialists
Jonas Kilmer and George F. Johnson demonstrate transformations in
how class relations were materially negotiated through the manipulation
of the social landscape. McGuire documents how in the late nineteenth-
century Kilmer constructed his factories and mansion in such a way as
to exude power, physically demonstrating the social gulf between him
and the working class. In contrast, and in reaction to two generations of
labor unrest, Johnson constructed an industrial landscape that overtly
minimized social distance; in building his house in the same style as that
of his workers, Johnson sought to obscure class differences by manifesting
a sliding scale of relative equality. By constructing an industrial welfare
system through which company profits were used to subsidize the construction of parks, hospitals, and other public monuments, Johnson
attempted to construct an ideology consistent within the framework of
capitalism that emphasized the presumed mutual interests shared by
employers and employees, thus creating an illusion of equality between
classes that served to suppress class conflict (McGuire 1991). Similar
material expressions of the changing ideology of capitalism can be read
in the mortuary architecture, design, and layout of the cemeteries of
Broome County (McGuire 1988; Wurst 1991) and in the urban industrial landscapes of the Boott Mills industrial complex in Lowell,
Massachusetts (Beaudry 1989; Beaudry, Cook, and Mrozowski 1991;
Mrozowski 1991, 2006; Mrozowski, Zeising, and Beaudry 1996;
Mrozowski and Beaudry 1990). Whether in urban, industrial, or plantation contexts, landscapes can be seen as active agents in the negotiation of social relation both among members of a given social class, and
between members of conflicting social classes, particularly at times of
epochal change brought on by contradictions within a given mode of
production.

Chapter 6 explores how Jamaicans attempted to reconcile the contradictions that emerged in the plantation mode of production through the
analysis of post-emancipation spatial changes. For this analysis, we return
to the district of Upper St. David to examine how plantation spatial forms
changed after slavery ended, and how such changes both reflected the
newly emerging social relations of production and provided the material
basis for a newly developing mode of production.

Virginia's Plantation Mode of Production (Chapter 7)

The goals of this series of case studies include the explicit use of a theoretical framework to understand a past society and to illustrate the utility of the approach in comparative context. Although this book is primarily about Jamaica at the turn of the nineteenth century, the comparative case I have chosen to examine is seventeenth-century Virginia. I chose this particular comparison for several reasons. First, it is very easy to assume that all plantation societies developed along a single trajectory, an assumption that does not hold up to the archaeological and historical evidence. By choosing early colonial Virginia as our comparison case, Chapter 7 explores how the trajectories of England's two most important New World colonies differed, despite the economies of both being based on the plantation production of agricultural commodities for the world markets. Second, as a work of historical archaeology, many readers will have some familiarity with the Virginia material, although very few synthetic works on the historical archaeology of plantation Virginia have been published. By interpreting the Virginia material, I hope to demonstrate the power of Marxian theory to analyze what was, for many years, the chaotic and transitory history of plantation landscapes in the Old Dominion.

To this end, the organization of Chapter 7 parallels the overall structure of this book. After a review of the early development of plantation society in Virginia, Chapter 7 considers the development of Virginia's plantation mode of production, the rise of the hegemonic planter class that would come to dominate the colony by the beginning of the eighteenth century, the development of dialectical contradictions in the mode of production that came to head in the year 1676, and how the resolution of those contradictions resulted in the replacement of indentured servitude with chattel slavery as the primary source of labor for Virginia's tobacco plantations.

Conclusion: Landscapes of Power in Colonial Jamaica

A Marxist approach to landscape archaeology contends that elements of the built environment, including plantation landscapes, play a direct role in the negotiation of social relations. This volume explores how this dynamic nature of landscapes was expressed at several scales of spatial analysis: the island, the region or district, the plantation, and the household within the village. In the case study explored here, the region is defined geographically by river valleys and socially by the presence of contemporaneous coffee plantations. Both the enslaved African and the elite European populations that lived and worked in the coffee plantation landscapes viewed the region as a social and political unit; the whites created social networks through which they expressed political power within their region and more expansively on the island colony of Jamaica. Similarly, the black workers who produced coffee created relationships that expanded beyond the boundaries of the specific plantations on which they were enslaved. The plantation was more than an economic unit, but was a dynamic sociospatial landscape that helped to shape the nature of the relations of production within a historically contextual plantation mode of production. The small size of the planter class – and their clearly shared interest in maintaining structures of inequality between themselves and the enslaved – resulted in a coherent class consciousness among the planters. Contradictions occurred within the plantation mode of production; these too were part of a social process through which spaces within villages and provision grounds were created, and in turn served as the basis for the growing internal economy controlled by the enslaved working class. The dialectical conflict that ensued resulted in a redefinition of the relations of production, and a concurrent shift in the physical layout and organization of plantation landscapes. Through a historical-archaeological analysis of Jamaica's plantation landscapes, all of these phenomena are explored in this book.

One must bear in mind, however, that the system in place in colonial Jamaica did not allow for anything near to equality of access to land and power. The enslaved people of Jamaica, and their emancipated descendants, were subject to social norms, laws, and landscapes that were designed to maintain a strict social hierarchy. Power was exerted in many ways by the planters over the enslaved, and the social and physical realities of landscapes worked actively to support the system of inequality. Plantation landscapes, too, were arenas of dialectical conflict in which the enslaved struggled to liberate themselves from their historical oppressions. It is my hope that the chapters that follow elucidate the nature of these landscapes of power.

2   His Majesty's Island

The Colonial World of Plantation Jamaica

Of all the regions around the world that have been at one time or another subject to European colonial rule, none, perhaps, is as diverse in experience and history as the Caribbean. A great archipelago stretching from the south coast of Florida to the east coast of Venezuela, the region has been described as a "continent of islands" (Kurlansky 1993). Comprised of small sand spits, active volcanoes, long white sand beaches, and rugged mountains, over the millennia the Caribbean islands developed geographic, faunal, and botanical diversity that has long inspired the imaginations of visitors (see Figure 2.1).

The human diversity of the modern Caribbean has developed as a consequence of several thousand years of human colonization. Caribbean archaeologists now believe that the indigenous peoples of the Caribbean spread out across the islands in multiple waves of migration, developing complex political and economic relationships within and between islands (e.g., Keegan and Atkinson 2006; Rouse 1992; Wilson 2007). Entering the European imagination in the decades following Columbus's famous landfall in 1492, the Caribbean experienced many waves of European colonial settlement. European adventurers from all of the maritime nations of Western Europe – Spain, Portugal, England, France, Denmark, Holland, Scotland, Ireland, and Sweden – eventually claimed islands for their sovereigns and set out to seek fortunes for themselves. Early on, many of those fortunes were built through the exploitation of local indigenous peoples; by the end of the seventeenth century, those fortunes were nearly uniformly dependent on the exportation of tropical crops including tobacco, cotton, coffee, and above all, sugar (Craton 1997; Dunn 2000; Tomich 1990, 2004; Walvin 1997).

The pursuit of agricultural wealth dramatically changed the demographic, linguistic, social, and cultural landscapes of the Caribbean. When the European colonials began to depend on agricultural exports, they became increasingly dependent on enslaved labor acquired through a massive forced migration of people that has become known to us as the

Figure 2.1. The Caribbean. Image courtesy of Mark W. Hauser

African Slave Trade. Over the 300-year history of this insidious trade, some 10–15 million Africans were taken captive and shipped across the Atlantic to face a life of forced labor (Curtain 1969; Walvin 2008).

The introduction of captive labor into Jamaica played a crucial role in establishing both the social order and settlement pattern of the island. However, the British plantation mode of production was not the first manifestation of colonial rule on the island (Cundall 1911; Padron 2003). In 1509, nearly 150 years prior to the first British settlement of Jamaica, Spanish colonists established settlements on the island. When the British arrived in 1655, Jamaica was already an old colony, and its landscape had been radically transformed to serve the needs of the Spanish colonials who made Jamaica their home. Because landscapes have temporal depth – human landscapes are nearly always built on previously used human landscapes – one needs to understand how the island was transformed by the Spanish before understanding how British plantation landscapes were constructed. In this chapter, I review the settlement patterns created by those Spanish colonists and consider how the introduction of the plantation mode of production changed the island-wide settlement pattern of Jamaica during the eighteenth century. This chapter thus serves to contextualize Jamaican plantation society as it existed at the turn of the nineteenth century through a review of the island's settlement pattern from the initial Spanish colonization of Jamaica through the opening decades of the nineteenth century.

Private Property and Plantation Settlement

Human settlement patterns are defined both by the ecological realities of a given region and the mode of production operating within that region (Steward 1990). The processes of human settlement are reflexive; the ecological realities of a place will define how that land is used by people, and that use will in turn shape the ecological realities of that land. Human history is filled with examples of how human intervention has changed the productive capacity of landscapes from the dry deserts of Mesopotamia and coastal Peru to the flood plains of the Nile and Yellow Rivers (Adams 1965; Billman 2002; Hassan 1997; Lees 1994; Willey 1953). Agricultural technologies, from the irrigation systems of desert Sumer, to the raised field systems of the Central American rainforests, to the highland terracing structures of the Andes, have provided the material base necessary for the creation of vast and complex human sociopolitical systems (Adams 1965; Demarest 2005; Patterson 1991). Such human intervention can, however, lead to the collapse of the same ecological systems vital to the operation of the agricultural economy. Scholars who examine the collapse of civilizations occasionally point to ecological disasters brought on, for example, by climate change or oscillation resulting in extended periods of drought, the salinization of soils precipitated by over irrigation, or the overuse of friable forest soils, as being the vectors of societal failure (Abrams and Rue 1988; Chapdelaine 2011; Clement and Moseley 1991; Dillehay and Kolata 2004; Kus 1984; Lucero 2002; Mosely 1983; Sandweiss et al. 2009).

    Be this as it may, Marxist analyses of settlement patterns contend that, although ecological realities cannot be ignored as variables defining land use, the cultural construction of access to land and other ecological resources (e.g., rivers, aquifers) defines the shape of human settlements and the experiences of people living within them (e.g., Adams 1965; Paynter 1982). As modes of production develop, certain cultural features are created, access to which similarly defines human experience; these include features such as roads, irrigation canals, wells, cultivated fields, bridges, and seaports. When modes of production are designed around the exchange of commodities that can only be produced in specific places (e.g., gold mines, fertile tropical farmland), controlling access to these places can define how labor will be organized, how surplus value will be distributed, and how human settlements will be distributed across the landscape (Mrozowski 1991; Paynter 1985). In the case of colonial Jamaica, by the middle of the eighteenth century, just about every arable piece of land that could produce sugar cane (and many that could not) was defined as the private property of a plantation proprietor (Higman 1988).

The plantation as a unit of space allowed for the expansive ownership of thousands of acres of land by individual landowners who could control access to arable fields and develop land as they saw fit; the resulting spatial patterning of the landscape within plantations defined where enslaved workers lived, and how they would access the productive capacity of the land for their own use.

One of the key concepts explored by Karl Marx in *Capital* is the transformation of what has been alternatively translated as "public" or "collective" property into "private" property (1992). According to Marx, this process was multi-tiered; in some contexts, small producers could claim subdivided parcels of land as their "private" property, and, as owners of their own labor and land, could claim whatever was produced on that land for themselves (see also Engels 2010). As capitalism developed, these smaller parcels of land were consolidated to the point at which agricultural laborers no longer had access to land. According to Marxist thinking, the process by which the resources required to make a living are consolidated into the hands of a relative few, who then use those resources to create commodities for exchange in global markets, is known as capitalization. Marx argued that one of the primary steps to the development of a capitalist mode of production was the capitalization of land. In Marx's view, the capitalization of land resulted in the consolidation of disbursed small landholdings into "socially concentrated ones, of the pigmy property of the many into the huge property of the few" (1992: 714); this process also involved "the expropriation of the great mass of the people from the soil, from the means of subsistence, and from the means of labor to produce their own subsistence" (1992: 714). These two social structures, the consolidation of privately owned estates and the alienation of people from the ability to independently produce the necessities of life, are hallmarks of capitalist agriculture (Adams 1990; Groover 2003; Headlee 1991; Orser 1999; Sayers 2003). In colonial Jamaica, the process of land capitalization was actualized through the construction of the plantation as a privately owned spatial unit, a spatial form that would come to dominate the island's landscape by the middle of the eighteenth century (Dunn 2000: Higman 2005). By that time, the dominant labor system in Jamaica was based on the enslavement of laborers from Africa, and the perpetual captivity of their Jamaican-born offspring (Higman 1995; Walvin 2008). The slave system clearly expropriated the great mass of people from the land and from the ability to make an independent living from that land. Indeed, it can be argued that the labor system was based on human capitalization, as people were defined as the private property of colonial Jamaicans, acquired, used, and valued as saleable commodities exchanged on global markets.

In colonial Jamaica, capitalized, privately owned land was valued not for the use value of the products grown on it, but for the value that could be gained either by exchanging mass quantities of agriculture products in global markets, what Marxists refer to as the exchange value of the commodity (Marx 1992: 54ff) or by the exchange of the land itself, a process generally known as land speculation. In systems in which commodities are produced for their exchange value, capitalized land is put under cultivation not to produce food for those who work the land, but to produce saleable commodities whose surplus value is controlled by the landowner. As the Jamaican plantation system developed in the eighteenth century, vast stretches of land were designated, often simply by a patent granted by the crown, as the private property of members of what developed into a very wealthy oligarchy, comprised of a mix of local planters and British speculators. It was they, the planters both in Jamaica and in Great Britain, who would control the surplus value produced on Jamaican land and would restrict the use of patented but undeveloped land, privately held as an exchangeable asset.

This land use system played a central role in the development of the settlement pattern of Jamaica, the use of land across the island, and the development of a rigidly hierarchical social structure based on land ownership. Even contemporary observers, writing decades before Marx, commented on how the process of privatization of large landholdings was affecting the development of Jamaican society. For example, as early as the 1770s, Edward Long recognized that a small landed oligarchy controlled most of the land base of Jamaica. By the middle of the eighteenth century, nearly the entire landmass of Jamaica had been patented. Although most of the best land was under sugar production by Long's day, much of the interior was not cultivated, and could not be so, as it was defined as the private property of the patentees or their descendants, many of whom had little interest in Jamaica as anything other than a place to make investments in land. Long believed this worked to the detriment of the island, as there was limited access to small parcels of land for middle class farmers or planters, without whom, Long thought, Jamaica could not establish a stable class-stratified society (Long 1774).

The monopolization of land by large planters, which Long thought restricted the development of an energetic white middle class, was not the inevitable result of the colonization of Jamaica. Land use patterns could have developed differently, as they had, at least temporarily, in other colonial contexts. For example, in the early seventeenth century, Barbados had been settled largely by former indentured servants, who had received small land grants at the end of their service (Dunn 2000; Watts 1990). The early settlement pattern of colonial Barbados was thus characterized by small farms, of between five and ten acres in extent, dispersed across the island landscape.

This settlement pattern was short-lived, however. When tobacco and cotton production on small farms proved to be difficult and not particularly profitable, those small holdings were consolidated into a fewer number of larger estates, created by wealthy landowners interested in the large-scale, intensive production of sugar using enslaved African labor (Dunn 2000; Higman 1988; Sheridan 2000). In Marxist terms, the scattered small holdings, which provided subsistence and some exchangeable commodities for small farmers, were consolidated into private property worked on by "social labor" – that is, by labor gangs who produced surplus value for the propertied class, the proprietors. This consolidation of the colony's arable land base was facilitated by both ecological and cultural realties: Barbados is a relatively flat island composed of deep limestone deposits, with the central highlands reaching no more than 340 meters above sea level. Culturally, the formerly indentured servants who owned the small ten-acre farms knew little about tropical agriculture, and many were more than willing to sell the land for the more immediately useful cash offered to them by the wealthier planters (Dunn 2000; Watts 1990). The example of Barbados, where the consolidation of land into a relatively few large plantations worked by imported slave labor created great wealth for a small number of planters, became the model for British tropical agriculture throughout the West Indies. It was there, with the consolidation of large plantation estates that exploited the labor of hundreds of enslaved workers, that the British plantation mode of production began within the context of a broader and expanding capitalist system, and it was from there that the plantation model would be exported to Jamaica.

The consolidation of plantations on Jamaica took some time, however, and needed to conform to the geologic and cultural features extant at the time of the English conquest. In contrast to Barbados, the topography of which is relatively flat and featureless, Jamaica is a geologically diverse island. The core of the island was formed during the Early Cretaceous Period, about 100 million years ago, through intensive volcanic activity that lasted for some 45 million years. Followed by an equally intense period of tectonic activity, the landmass that would become Jamaica subsided beneath the sea. As the basal igneous and metamorphic stone that resulted from this birth through fire was subducted beneath the sea for tens of millions of years, thick layers of limestone formed on top of the metamorphic and igneous rock that had resulted from the volcanic and tectonic activity of the Cretaceous Period. This resulted from the deposition of the skeletons of mollusks and corals over millions of years; two-thirds of the current surface area of Jamaica is covered by this limestone

formation. Approximately 12 million years ago, what is now the central
Caribbean region experienced tectonic uplift, which once again exposed
Jamaica as a landmass, featuring high mountain ridges in excess of
2,200 meters above sea level in the eastern part of the island. Over the
past 12 million years, the island has experienced a gradual process of
erosion, which has formed a landscape characterized by dissected limestone plateaus surrounded by extensive valley basins filled with eroded,
and very fertile, terra rossa soils. Outwash resulting from limestone erosion has created a series of alluvial plains, particularly on the south coast of
the island. Extensive chemical erosion has worked to create deeply pocked
karst formations in the center-west of the island (Porter 1990). The coastline, particularly on the north side of the island, is characterized by a
number of small coves and bays, many of which exist at the mouths of
northerly flowing rivers that drain the north slope of the both the eastern
mountains and central plateaus (see Figure 2.2).

  Also in contrast to Barbados, which was not colonized by Europeans
prior to the arrival of the British in 1625, Jamaica was a settled Spanish
possession as early as the opening decade of the sixteenth century (Padron
2003; Sheridan 2000; Woodward 2011). The landscape of Jamaica
was thus already impacted by a century and a half of European colonial
settlement. Although the Spanish transformed the landscape in profound
ways, their system was not based on the privatization and capitalization of
Jamaica's landscape. The Spanish experience did, however, set the stage
for the English conquest, colonization, and capitalization of the island of
Jamaica.

The Settlement History of Spanish Jamaica, 1509–1655

Following Columbus's 1492 landfall in the Caribbean, their Catholic
Majesties, Ferdinand of Aragon and Isabella of Castille, claimed the
islands of the Caribbean archipelago, including Jamaica, as territories of
their emergent American empire. The first Spanish attempt to establish a
permanent presence on Jamaica occurred on the island's north coast in
1509 (Padron 2003; Woodward 2011). The Spanish were attracted to the
north coast not only for its small bays, fresh water rivers, and potentially
gold-rich mountainous terrain within just a few kilometers of the shore-
line, but by its relative proximity to the established Spanish settlements at
Santiago de Cuba and Hispaniola. As was the case with Spanish settlement
in the other islands of the Greater Antilles (Cuba, Hispaniola, and Puerto
Rico), the first Spanish colonists were hopeful of finding profitable mineral
deposits in the Jamaican highlands, and thus exported an early version of
mercantilism to the island. In 1509, eighty Spanish colonists under the

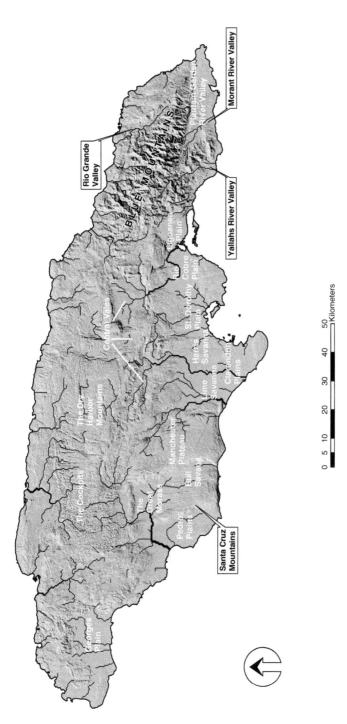

Figure 2.2. Topographic features in Jamaica. Illustration courtesy of Richard Courtney, Department of Geography, Kutztown University.

Figure 2.3. Location of Spanish-era sites in Jamaica. Illustration courtesy of Richard Courtney, Department of Geography, Kutztown University.

leadership of Juan de Esquivel established Jamaica's first European town, Sevilla la Nueva, on the north coast near the modern town of St. Ann's Bay. In the 1510s, under the leadership of Jamaica's second governor, Francesco de Garray, additional settlements were established at Melilla on the north coast and Oristan on the south coast (see Figure 2.3).

Land tenure in Spanish Jamaica was based on Spanish precedents established during the later period of the Iberian reconquest and during the opening decades of Spanish settlement on the American mainland. Spanish colonial policy was based on what was known as the encomienda – a system by which land remained in the hands either of the local indigenous population, or in the absence of such a population, the crown. Settlers granted an encomienda, known as encomenderos, were given the responsibility of "protecting" a specified number of indigenous people, converting them to Christianity, and resettling their lands with Europeans. In return, encomenderos were given the right to extract tribute from the indigenous people within their encomienda, either in the form of gold or other saleable commodities, or in labor. Thus, in theory, the Spanish settlement system in Jamaica was based on the collective ownership of land through the institution of the Imperial State, and a labor system based on coerced labor extracted as tribute. Neither land nor labor were capitalized, however, as individuals could not legally buy or sell land within their encomienda, nor could they buy and sell indigenous people as slaves (Mahoney 2010).

The colonial world of Spanish Jamaica was structured by these systems of land tenure and labor extraction. Jamaica, however, was always a peripheral colony in the Spanish world. No gold was discovered on the island, and thus emergent capitalism did not develop on Jamaica as it had done in other Spanish colonial contexts. The settlement pattern of the island developed largely in the absence of both direct Imperial control and capitalization. Although a sugar mill was established at Sevilla la Nueva as early as 1520 (Woodward 2011), neither the sugar industry nor the north coast of Jamaica was significantly developed by the Spanish. By 1534, the north coast was largely abandoned when the town of Villa de la Vega, today known as Spanish Town, was established on the island's south coast (Robertson 2005). In 1534, the Spanish inhabitants of Sevilla la Nueva abandoned their town to resettle in Villa de la Vega; it is not known whether the surviving indigenous Taino people who labored for the encomenderos accompanied them. From this point forward, most Spanish settlement was concentrated on Jamaica's southern coast (Padron 2003).

The move to the south coast was precipitated by a series of epochal events that unfolded in the 1520s and 1530s. By the early sixteenth century, the relatively modest gold fields of Hispaniola and Puerto Rico had been worked out; as the economy of the Spanish colonies in the West Indies was based primarily on the appropriation of surplus value through mineral extraction within the encomiendas, emergent capitalism began to fail. Simultaneously, labor supplies began to dwindle as the indigenous Taino population rapidly declined as a result of overwork, the appropriation of their farm land by the Spanish encomenderos and the European settlers they recruited, epidemic disease, and cultural upheaval (Rouse 1992; Wilson 2007). Finally, the conquest of the Aztec and Inca empires opened the Spanish Main for colonization; large encomiendas promised great agricultural wealth for Spanish settlers while the lure of mountains of gold and silver from Mexico and Peru drove the expansion of the Spanish Empire in America. As the administrative center of empire shifted from Hispaniola in the Greater Antilles to Cartagena on the coast of mainland South America, the focus of Spanish settlement on Jamaica shifted from the north (facing Cuba and Hispaniola) to the south (facing Cartagena).

Despite this strategic move on the part of the colonists, Jamaica developed into a colonial backwater with a small Spanish population. The primary industry on the island for most of the sixteenth century was based on provisioning passing ships – few of which were Spanish – with meat, water, wood, and other necessary supplies (Padron 2003). As the Spanish crown prohibited trade with any but Spanish vessels, much of the economy of sixteenth-century Jamaica was based on illicit dealings, at least as seen from the perspective of the Spanish crown. However, as few Spanish ships regularly visited Jamaica, the smuggling and contraband trade with French, English, and Dutch corsairs and privateers was an important source of manufactured and other European goods for the colonists (Cundall 1919; Padron 2003).

The settlement pattern of Spanish Jamaica developed in the context of the island's marginal position in the structure of sixteenth-century Spanish colonialism. There was little attempt to establish an export economy on Jamaica, which developed into little more than a provisioning stop for European adventurers. Furthermore, there was little development of "private" property in the Marxian sense of the term, as the Spanish colonial system in the Caribbean was based on the concept of "encomienda." Legally, this system differed from slavery, as the encomenderos could not legally sell the people within their encomienda, nor could they legally buy or sell land. Again, in Marxist terms, Spanish Jamaica did not develop through the consolidation of private property, but through the exploitation of labor to extract surplus value from land owned by, in this case, the state. In this way, the labor and settlement systems of Spanish Jamaica were based on what Marx would call a Feudal Mode of Production (Marx 1964).

The settlement pattern of sixteenth-century Jamaica emerged from this system of land tenure and labor exploitation. The principal settlement form in Jamaica at this time was the "hato," a type of free-range ranch on crown land, controlled by an encomendero, and worked by a small population of impressed Taino people and a few enslaved Africans (Padron 2003). The names and locations of the principal hatos were recorded through the centuries, although little evidence of them remains on the modern landscape of Jamaica. All of the known hatos were located on the alluvial plains of Jamaica's south coast; the hatos included (from west to east) Cabonico, Savanna la Mar, El Eado, Pereda, Yama, Guatibocoa, Guanaboa, Liguaney, Lezama, Ayala, and Morante (see Figure 2.3). The hatos likely included a hacienda for the encomendero or manager of the hato, quarters for the laborers, and a series of corrals, butchering stations, and tanneries for the processing of meat and hides (Blome 1672; Bridges 1828; Cundall 1919; Edwards 1798; Gardner 1873; Hakewell 1825; Long 1774; MacGregor 1847; Woodward 2011). It is thought that in the Spanish Caribbean, hatos encompassed range land within an area with a diameter of approximately sixteen to eighteen miles. Each hato was subdivided into smaller ranching settlements known as estancias, which were populated by the settlers recruited by the encomenderos and their descendants, but – like the hato of which they were a part – were not the private property of the settlers.

Contemporary accounts translated by Irene Wright in the 1910s and 1920s indicate that the cattle on Jamaica were a mix of tame and feral cows introduced to the island with the coming of the Spanish. When needed, the laborers on the hatos and estancias would round up cattle for slaughter. It appears that the hatos had very loosely defined boundaries. The exact number of cattle controlled by each of the hatos is impossible to calculate. It was reported that tens of thousands of cattle were processed during the sixteenth and early seventeenth centuries; Francisco Morales Padron (2003) estimates there were some 40,000 head of cattle grazing on the savannahs of southern Jamaica at the end of the sixteenth century (see also Cundall 1919 and Wright 1930).

The Spanish population of Jamaica likely never numbered more than a few thousand people, and even this figure is likely very liberal. By the end of the sixteenth century, there were somewhere between 100 and 150 Spanish households in Jamaica (Cundall 1919; Robertson 2005), most of which resided in Villa de la Vega. In 1611, the abbot of Jamaica estimated that there were 1,510 people on the entire island of Jamaica, including 523 Spanish men and women, 173 children, 107 free negros, 74 native Indians, 558 African slaves, and 75 foreigners – likely referring in this latter case to Sephardic Jews (Cundall 1919). By this time, it is likely that the majority of the European-descent population was comprised of island-born Creoles; the encomenderos and other settlers becoming increasingly dependent on enslaved African labor as the indigenous population declined. According to Irene Wright's translation of the original Spanish document, the abbot reported that all of the Spaniards were "from only three parentages and are so mixed with one another by marriage that they are all related. This causes many and grave incests to be committed" (Cundall 1919: 34). Because he based his estimates on confessions he had heard, it is possible that the abbot's estimation of the number of Taino people on the island was based solely on household servants and hato laborers who had converted to Catholicism; archaeological work conducted by Kofi Agorsah in the early eighteenth-century Maroon site of Nanny Town suggests that a remnant Taino population was likely living in the mountains in the seventeenth century, apart from the colonial sphere of the Spanish at Villa de la Vega (Agorsah 1994; Goucher and Agrosah 2011). Contemporary Spanish accounts corroborate that some small Taino settlements existed in the Blue Mountains in the early seventeenth century (Cundall 1919). Nevertheless, the native population appears to have been very much reduced by the 1610s.

Although the settlement pattern of southern Jamaica was characterized by dispersed pastoral settlements in the hatos, the majority of the population lived in Villa de la Vega. Several other smaller towns dotted the Jamaican landscape, including Oristan and Parrattee in the west, the port of Esquivel to the south of Villa de la Vega, and the port of Caguay to its east; it is unknown how many people lived in these villages, but the numbers were likely very small. It is also likely that there were some small agricultural settlements outside of the hato-dominated savannas. For example, after the English conquest of 1655, the leader of the Spanish resistance was reported to have stayed in a settlement at Santa Cruz; historians writing in the eighteenth century reported that there were remnants of known Spanish settlements at Porus and Green Pond, both located in the interior of the modern parish of Manchester; Padron reports that during a corsair raid, the abbot of Jamaica took refuge on a ranch on Legua Cay, suggesting that smaller ranches (estancias) existed either as subdivisions of larger hatos, or as independent settlements. Similarly, when assessing the military strength of the island, the town council (Cabildo) of Villa de la Vega reported that it could raise an army of 300 men from the town, accompanied by another 100 drawn from the island's hunters and plainsmen, again suggesting the existence of settlements outside of Villa de la Vega (Padron 2003: 35).

It is also likely that there were some dispersed, and likely impermanent, settlements situated along the north coast. Although the primary focus of settlement was in the south, many small coves and bays on the north coast retain their Spanish place names (e.g., Rio Bueno, Oracabessa, Rio Nuevo). In the early seventeenth century, the Spanish governor of the island, Don Fernando Melgarejo, reported that although there were no settlements on the north coast, nor were there roads connecting the north to the south, the north coast was infested with illicit traders, likely English privateers and French and Dutch corsairs who were raiding Spanish ship-ping and then bartering their booty to the Spanish settlers of Jamaica for hides and provisions. This illicit trading appears to have been occurring in the several ports identified in the early Spanish correspondence translated by Wright; these ports on the north coast included (from west to east) Rio Bueno, Santa Ana (near the location of the abandoned town of Sevilla la Nueva), Las Chorreras, Rio Nuevo, Ora Cabessa, Melilla/Puerto Maria, Rio Espanol, Guayguata, and Puerto Anton. In the west, the bays of Lucea and Manteca (Montego) may also have been the sites of such illicit activity. Melgarejo apparently tried to curtail this activity, much to the chagrin of Jamaica's residents, who apparently were profiting from such trade; Melgarejo was reportedly afraid for his life at the hands of his subjects, so deep ran their resentment against his suppression of the north coast trade. In 1610, made aware both of Melgarejo's apprehension about maintaining such close ties to English and French privateers and the important role this trade had played in the maintenance of the Spanish colony in Jamaica, King Philip III issued a pardon forgiving the Spanish settlers of Jamaica for their role in this illicit trade (Cundall 1919: 33).

The settlement pattern of Spanish Jamaica can thus be seen as a product of an economic system that had isolated the insular colonists of the Greater Antilles from the rest of the Spanish Empire. Provision ships were rare, and so the colonists engaged in illicit trading with French, English, Dutch, and Portuguese ships along the north coast. It is unclear how many Spanish people lived in the contraband ports, but it is likely that there was some semi-permanent presence along the coast. The majority of people lived in a single substantial town, Villa de la Vega, which boasted several hundred buildings framed on a quadrilateral grid; even the encomenderos of the hatos appear to have spent most of their time in town (Robertson 2005; Padron 2003). As the principal town lay inland on an unnavigable river, the residents were dependent on the port towns of Caguay and Esquivel for the legal importation of European goods. The southern lowland savannas were the locations of herds of thousands of semi-wild cattle managed by enslaved African and impressed Taino people stationed at the hatos. The hatos were isolated by dozens of miles from each other, which maximized the amount of grazing land open for the herds, and likely minimized border conflicts between the hatos. A few small villages dotted the coast, and likely a number of people lived in small settlements on the north coast to facilitate illicit trade with the European privateers.

The relatively light presence of Spanish settlers on Jamaica was well-known to those corsairs who plied the waters of the Caribbean, preying on Spanish shipping and selling their ill-gotten goods to the isolated Creole population of Jamaica. The weak military position of the island, with just a few hundred poorly armed, poorly trained, and poorly provisioned men, left the island vulnerable to invasion, an invasion that came to pass in the year 1655, when the English launched an attack on the island, seizing it for their Lord Protector, Oliver Cromwell.

Settlement History of Jamaica, 1655–1690

In 1655, General Robert Venables, veteran of the English Civil War and the Cromwellian invasion of Ireland, accompanied by Admiral William Penn, landed in, and were repulsed from, the island of Hispaniola. Attempting to operationalize Oliver Cromwell's Western Design, which would seize much of Spanish America if successful, Venables and his ragtag force of formerly indentured servants and veterans of Cromwell's New Model Army had embarked from Barbados with the intention of seizing Hispaniola to be the base of command for the Western Design. Suffering a humiliating defeat at the hands of the well-equipped Spanish forces defending Hispaniola, Penn and Venables set sail for Jamaica, easily defeating the poorly garrisoned and sparsely populated Spanish colony (Dunn 2000; Sheridan 2000).

The terms demanded for the Spanish surrender of Jamaica were harsh. Europe in the mid-seventeenth century was experiencing an increasingly brutal series of religious conflicts, both between and within states. In England, a power struggle had broken out between competing factions. On one side was the monarchy and old aristocracy loyal to the Church of England and their Catholic allies; collectively this faction was known as the Cavaliers. Their antagonists were Puritanical Calvinist commoners, known as Roundheads, who had seized control of the English parliament. The ensuing English Civil War was won by the Roundheads; the aftermath of the war witnessed the beheading of King Charles I, the temporary abolition of the British monarchy, the establishment of a republican "Commonwealth" under the leadership of Oliver Cromwell, and the continued suppression of Catholicism in the English world (Braddick 2009; Purkiss 2007). The 1650s were thus a radically intolerant time. Venables and his veterans of the New Model Army, who hoped to settle on Jamaica, did not want to share the island with the Catholic Spaniards. Although nearly the entire population of the island was composed of Jamaican-born Creoles, the Spanish colonists were ordered to abandon their settlements and were forced to leave the island. Although some fled to the interior to engage in internecine guerilla warfare against the English invaders, Jamaica remained a British colony from the 1655 capitulation of Villa de la Vega to the island's declaration of independence three centuries later in 1962.

Human settlements do not appear randomly on landscapes; in choosing where to establish themselves, human groups consider both ecological and cultural variables in deriving their choices of where to live. When the English conquered Jamaica, it was their intention to establish a permanent colony in the central Caribbean; they were thus influenced by the physical topography of the island as well as the existing cultural landscape conditions of Jamaica when they established their first settlements. When the English arrived, they were confronted by a landscape that had been radically transformed during the Spanish occupation of the island. On the southern savannas, hatos and estancias had been established. The low-intensity of human settlement had resulted in a pastoral system in which tens of thousands of cows, and a likely equal number of feral hogs, ranged freely, periodically hunted or rounded up by the "hunters and plainsmen" of the country. Several towns and ports had been established, with an infrastructure (e.g., wells, farm fields, roads) capable of supporting several thousand people. Several harbors had been improved on the south coast for regulated trade, and likely a greater number of smaller harbors were improved on the north coast to facilitate the illicit trade that Governor Melgarejo had tried so hard to suppress. Although the economy of Spanish Jamaica was largely dependent on its pastoral base, several people, particularly in the hato of Liguaney, has established small-scale sugar works (Cundall 1919). The first wave of English colonists thus was confronted with a landscape that had already been sculpted by a century and a half of European activity.

One way to consider how the early English colonists settled within this landscape is to model the early English settlement pattern using Geographic Information Systems (GIS) technology. To do so, one needs to establish the location of those mid-seventeenth-century settlements. This task is a bit more difficult than it may sound, particularly because much of seventeenth-century Jamaica was completely transformed in the eighteenth century as the plantation mode of production developed. Two sources of information exist that provide at least a qualitative understanding of how the English settlements were placed on the landscapes: (1) the historic and documentary evidence of English settlement, which sometimes describes where and how the English established their settlements, and (2) the cartographic record of the island.

From the historic record, we know that the first wave of English settlers was a mix of survivors of Venables's expeditionary force, indentured servants recruited on Barbados for the expedition, and small groups of settlers that had failed to establish themselves on other islands (Beckles 1990; Burnard 1996; Robertson 2002). The first years were very difficult on the English colonists, as the invasion force burned the only sizeable town on the island (Villa de la Vega), quickly decimated the cattle herds and cultivated land around Villa de la Vega, and chased the island's only knowledgeable tropical farmers either off of the island or into the wilderness. It has been estimated that the original expeditionary force of 8,200 men was reduced, largely by disease and malnutrition, to a mere 2,200 by 1660 (Dunn 2000: 153). In these same years, some 1,500 small planters were transplanted to Jamaica from Nevis. Of the approximately 12,000 people who settled on Jamaica in the first years of English settlement, fewer than 3,500 remained in 1661, the rest having died from tropical diseases or else abandoned their attempt at establishing themselves in Jamaica (Burnard 1996).

In 1660, the English monarchy was restored with the return of Charles II from exile. The Restoration period (1660–1688) was one of remarkable growth for the English colony of Jamaica. The dominant political figure in Jamaica during the early Restoration period was Sir Thomas Modyford, who served as the royal governor of the colony from 1664 to 1671. Modyford encouraged plantation settlement by convincing the king to exempt Jamaican planters from paying duty on crops exported back to England, and by issuing liberal land patents to new settlers. Dunn reports that Modyford issued 1,800 patents totaling some 300,000 acres during the 1660s. Many of the patents were relatively small; each new settler was given a land grant of thirty acres for each person he brought to Jamaica. Patents were granted to both small planters who brought their families with them and large entrepreneurs who were able to import dozens or hundreds of enslaved Africans with them; thirty acres would be granted for each slave brought into the island (Dunn 2000:154). During Modyford's term, the consolidation of private property in the form of land and people began to take place; although there were many small farmers on the island at this time, a pattern similar to the early settlement of Barbados, a small class of large planters, holding thousands of acres of the best agricultural land and importing hundreds of slaves, began to form. In the Modyford years, the population of Jamaica increased from a total of 3,470 to approximately 17,000 souls. Significantly, at the end of Modyford's term the enslaved population outnumbered the white population by more than 2,000 people. Modyford's successor, Thomas Lynch, who governed Jamaica on three separate occasions (1663–1664, 1671–1674, and 1682–1684) continued his predecessor's policies of encouraging large plantation settlements. During the time that Modyford and Lynch governed the island, planters from Barbados, Nevis, and Surinam resettled in Jamaica, many with their enslaved workers (Dunn 2000; Sheridan 2000; Watts 1990).

Several maps published during the 1670s provide a fascinating portrait of Jamaica during this period. Of particular note is a 1676 rendering of the island published by John Speed that indicates the location of settlements across the island. At the time this map was published, the dominance of the large sugar planters was not yet assured. The map indicates the locations of some 963 settlements. Many of these were likely the settlements of the small patentees granted land by Modyford. Richard Sheridan has suggested that in the opening decades of the English period in Jamaica, sugar had not yet ascended as the primary crop of the island. Although some large sugar planters (including Modyford and Lynch) were establishing themselves, many more were planting crops that required less capital to start up – such as cacao, indigo, and cotton. Sheridan has demonstrated that cacao was Jamaica's leading export crop until 1670, when a blight destroyed Jamaica's cacao trees (Sheridan 2000: 212). Speed's map likely portrays the areas of the island settled by the small cacao planters.

Even given the limitations of seventeenth-century cartography of a lightly settled island, by transferring the locations identified by Speed into a modern GIS format, one can begin to model how the original plantation settlement pattern of English Jamaica began. Four variables were considered in this analysis – two physiographic and two cultural. The physiographic variables include distance from the coast as expressed in five-kilometer buffer and elevation above sea level expressed in both 100-meter and 250-meter contour intervals. The cultural variables include intersections with the Spanish hatos, and distances from Spanish towns and port settlements. In deriving these cultural variables, hato sizes were calculated with both fifteen- and twenty-kilometer diameters (see Figure 2.4). Both of these diameters are significantly smaller than the recorded diameters of hatos in Hispaniola; but, given the limited range of savanna land in Jamaica and the relatively poor standing of the Spanish settlers in Jamaica, it is likely that the Jamaica hatos were smaller than their counterparts in Hispaniola and Cuba. It should also be noted that the GIS model assumes a circular diameter for the hatos. Although it is more likely that the Jamaican hatos were of irregular shape, conforming to the topographic realities of the island, the actual shape and extent of these land divisions is not now known. Similarly, the five-kilometer buffers from the known towns and the port locations identified in the documentary record of Jamaica is an arbitrary figure, but one that reflects a distance easy to cross by foot within one hour (see Figure 2.5).

The resulting geographic model of the 1670s settlement pattern of Jamaica suggests that 62 percent of the 953 settlements identified by Speed were located within five kilometers of the coast, and that just less than 80 percent were located within ten kilometers of the coast. The elevation model suggests that 80 percent of the settlements were located between sea level and 250 meters above sea level, with 95 percent of the settlements located below 500 meters. In calculating placement within the Spanish hatos, 62 percent of the settlements identified on Speed's map were located within the fifteen-kilometer hato radius. Thus, if we assume that the hatos were approximately fifteen kilometers in diameter, nearly two-thirds of the first English settlements were located within the Spanish hatos; this figure increases to 73 percent if we expand the hatos diameter to twenty kilometers, but this is likely too large a diameter to have been operationalized on the Jamaican landscape. An additional 9 percent of settlements were located within five kilometers of a port identified in the records of the Spanish settlement, mostly on the island's north coast (see Figures 2.6 and 2.7).

The majority of the first English settlers thus established themselves within a short distance of Jamaica's coast, and in lowland areas of the island previously settled by the Spanish. Transplanted settlers from Nevis established themselves in the eastern part of the island, in the former hato

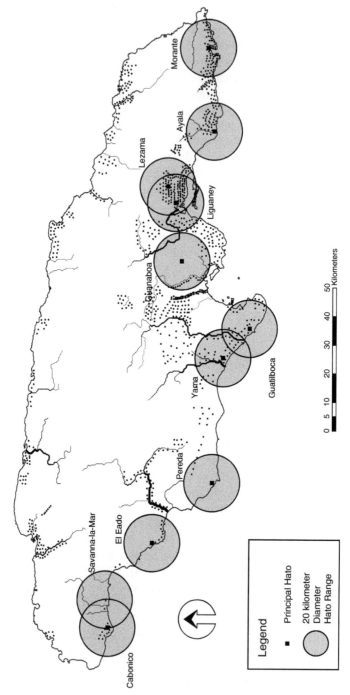

Figure 2.4. GIS model locating plantation sites based on John Speed's 1676 map of Jamaica. The circles indicate 20-km hato diameters. Illustration courtesy of Richard Courtney, Department of Geography, Kutztown University. Illustration courtesy of Richard Courtney, Department of Geography, Kutztown University.

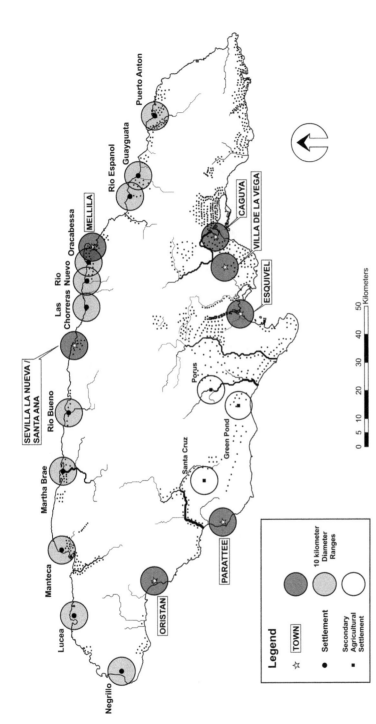

Figure 2.5. GIS model locating plantation sites based on John Speed's 1676 map of Jamaica. The circles indicate 10-km diameters around known Spanish-era towns, port settlements, and secondary agricultural settlements identified in the historic literature. Illustration courtesy of Richard Courtney, Department of Geography, Kutztown University.

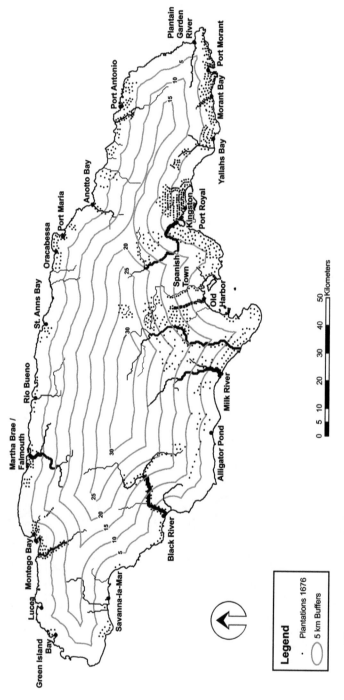

Figure 2.6. GIS model locating plantation sites by distance to coast based on Speed's 1676 map of Jamaica. The buffer lines represent distance to the coast in 5-km increments. Illustration courtesy of Richard Courtney, Department of Geography, Kutztown University.

of Morante, while the Surinam planters established themselves in south-west, in the old hatos of El Eado, Savanna la Mar, Cabonico, and Pareda. The hatos of Liguaney, Lezama, Guanaboa, Ayala, Guatabacoa, and Yama were likely among the first settled and those on what is now known as the Ligueanea Plain (Liguaneya and Lezama) were the most densely settled.

Settlement History of Jamaica, 1690–1750

A series of unfortunate events that transpired between 1690 and 1695 changed the course of plantation settlement on Jamaica. The years follow-ing Modyford's 1671 recall by the king were characterized by insular factionalism. In the 1670s and 1680s, Jamaican society was divided into several interests, including the large planters, the privateers of Port Royal (known as the buccaneers), the small settlers and indentured servants – many of whom were Irish Catholics – and, of course, the enslaved Africans. During the brief ascendancy of Henry Morgan (1674–1675 and 1680–1682) as acting governor and leader of the privateer and small planter party, and that of Governor John Vaughn (1675–1678), the champion of the Irish Catholic indentured servants and small settlers, some of the great planters left Jamaica for England, leaving their estates under the control of agents, later to be known in Jamaica as attorneys; many more joined them to form the culture of absentee proprietors during England's Glorious Revolution of 1688–1689, a conflict that led to the deposing of King James II, and the ascension of his brother-in-law and sister, William and Mary, as monarchs of England (Dunn 2000).

During this flight of the proprietors, it appeared as though much of Jamaica's landscape would remain in the hands of small planters, making short fortunes on sugar, indigo, pimento, and cotton production. However, the cataclysmic earthquake of June 1692, estimated to have been a magnitude of 7.5 on the Richter Scale, caused great damage and loss of life (Kozák and Čermák 2010). It has been estimated that approx-imately 2,000 people perished from the results of the earthquake and subsequent tsunami (O'Loughlin and Lander 2003; Pawson and Buisseret 2002). The town of Port Royal, which served as the de facto capital of the English colony, was destroyed, with some two-thirds of the town's land liquefying and sinking into Kingston Harbor. Most of the houses in the developing town of Kingston and in Spanish Town (the old Villa de la Vega) were destroyed. Many if not most of the small settlements on the island, including the budding sugar plantations, suf-fered major damage. To make matters worse, the English were at war with the French, who launched a raid on the island in 1694. Although the attack was repulsed, the French landed in eastern Jamaica, in the old hato of Morante, and destroyed fifty sugar works in the newly established English parishes of St. Thomas in the East and St. David, carrying away between 1,300 and 1,600 slaves from the island (Dunn 2000: 163; Sheridan 2000). Epidemic diseases followed in the wake of these disasters, causing further contraction of the population. Between 1689 and 1700, the white population of the island had decreased from about 10,000 to about 7,000 (Dunn 2000: 164; Roberts 1957: 33).

As the small planters died or left Jamaica in the wake of these disasters, their erstwhile cotton and pimento plantations, provisioning farms and ranches, were consolidated into larger holdings and transformed into sugar plantations. From the turn of the eighteenth century forward, Jamaica would be, primarily, a sugar island, whose economy was based on consolidated private property – capitalized land actualized through the consolidation of the "pigmy properties" of the small-scale farmers into "the socially concentrated, huge property" of the large plantation proprietors.

Between 1700 – when the white population of Jamaica reached its lowest point since the opening years of the English period – and 1740, the white population of Jamaica stabilized. Although still prone to tropical diseases, low birth rates, and high mortality rates, the white population climbed back to 10,000 by 1740 and never again dropped below that level (Roberts 1957; Watts 1990). During this period, larger planters continued to consolidate land holdings, imported an increasing number of enslaved laborers to work their plantations, and invested in both local and regional infrastructure to support the growing sugar trade. Between 1670 and 1754, the percentage of landowners holding in access of 500 acres had increased from 14 percent to 47 percent. Nevertheless, historian Richard Sheridan has characterized the early part of the eighteenth century as a period of "laggard growth," characterized by conflicts between planters and merchants, planters and royal officials, planters and the South Sea Company which controlled the African Slave Trade at this time, and planters and their fellow planters (Sheridan 2000: 216–218).

Several maps published in the first half of the eighteenth century reflect the changing structure of the plantation landscape of Jamaica. Among the best of these is one published by Emmanuel Bowen in 1747. Using the same methodology employed when considering the 1676 settlement pattern of the island, plantation points were entered into a GIS file and the settlement pattern was modeled using two variables, distance from the coast in five-kilometer buffers, and elevation above sea level in 250 meter contour intervals. The Bowen map identifies approximately 386 plantation settlements in 1747. Just as Speed's map may overestimate the number of settlements in 1676, Bowen's map may underestimate the number in 1747. It is thus prudent, again, to consider percentages of the overall settlements rather than the gross number. Taking this into account, in 1747, 52 percent of identified settlements existed within five kilometers of the coast and 72 percent of the settlements within ten kilometers of the coast. In that year, 88 percent of settlements were located below 250 meters in elevation, and 97 percent were below 500 meters (see Figures 2.7 and 2.8).

The plantation settlement pattern of Jamaica, despite the decrease in the number of settlements identified on the historic maps, thus remained fairly consistent. The great majority of estates were located near the coast and at elevations lower than 250 meters above sea level. This suggests that this period was marked by the consolidation of property into a relatively small number of estates convenient to the coast. If we compare the 1747 percentages of settlements existing within five kilometers from the coast to that of 1676, the spatial data indicates that the highest levels of consolidation were happening in the lowlands. Much of the interior, beyond fifteen kilometers from the coast and higher than 500 meters above sea level, while granted to land owners in patents, remained uncultivated.

Settlement History of Jamaica, 1750–1800

If the first half of the eighteenth century can be considered the formative period of the Jamaican plantation mode of production, the second half can be seen as its florescence. The number and size of sugar plantations increased consistently during this period. It is likely that the plantations consumed all of the island's potentially arable land suited for sugar cane production by the end of the eighteenth century. The Jamaica plantations developed what appears to be an optimal economy of scale, as Jamaica produced more efficiently in terms of per capita output than any other plantation colony in the new world, save French St. Domingue, which Jamaica matched (Higman 2005). When the Haitian revolution toppled the plantation society of St. Domingue, Jamaica was left with no serious rival in the Caribbean for several decades.

Within the British West Indies, Jamaica was clearly the lord of the Caribbean. In 1775, Jamaica exported more to its home country than any other Caribbean colony, again excepting only St. Domingue. The value of the exported produce of Jamaica was triple that of Spanish Cuba, approximately double that of French Martinique and Dutch Surinam, and quadruple that of British Barbados. The value of Jamaican exports was nearly equal that to that of the other ten British West Indian colonies combined (Jamaica Almanac 1788: 152).

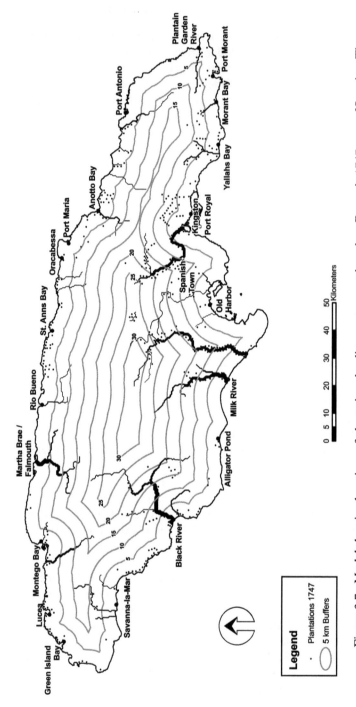

Figure 2.7. Model showing locations of plantations by distance to coast based on Bowen's 1747 map of Jamaica. The buffer lines represent distance to the coast in 5-km increments. Illustration courtesy of Richard Courtney, Department of Geography, Kutztown University.

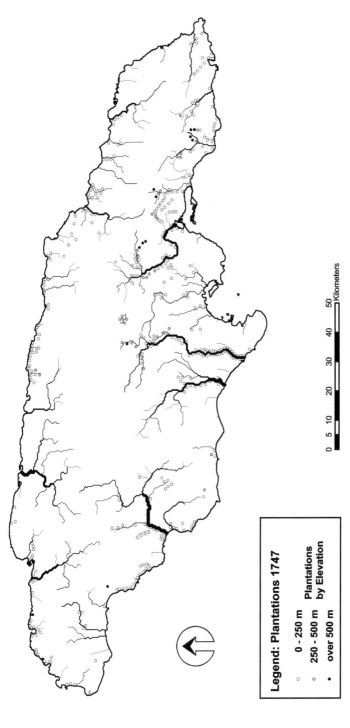

Figure 2.8. Elevation model showing locations of plantations in relation to 100-m contours, based on Bowen's 1747 map. Illustration courtesy of Richard Courtney, Department of Geography, Kutztown University.

Legend: Plantations 1747

○ 0 - 250 m   Plantations
◎ 250 - 500 m   by Elevation
● over 500 m

0 5 10   20   30   40   50
⊢━━━┿━━━┿━━━┿━━━┿━━━┥ Kilometers

The successful capitalization of land and labor in the early eighteenth century precipitated the accumulation of wealth, not only by the planters, but by the merchants and financiers of Jamaica's principle commercial town, Kingston. During the second half of the century, Kingston emerged as a vibrant colonial city. In 1789, Kingston had a population of more than 26,000 people, larger than the city of Boston and nearly equal to that of Philadelphia and New York (Jamaica Almanac 1789: 143). As the commercial center of what would become, by the early 1770s, Britain's wealthiest and most productive American colony (Burnard 2001), Kingston developed as both colonial entrepôt and commercial hub of the colony. Although Spanish Town remained the capital of Jamaica, and was the seat of both the Jamaica Assembly and the governors of the island, the merchants of Kingston commanded great wealth, and the town developed into a cosmopolitan center, attracting even plantation owners as residents. As the eighteenth century progressed, an increasing number of plantation proprietors chose to locate their primary residence in Kingston, becoming increasingly dependent on salaried employees to manage the affairs of their plantations (Burnard 2001; Higman 2005).

Although Kingston was by far the largest and wealthiest of Jamaica's towns, a number of smaller towns developed along Jamaica's coastline during the eighteenth century. These towns were primarily ports for the export of colonial produce. In 1750, the Jamaica Assembly recognized nineteen ports of embarkation in Jamaica, regularly situated along the island's coast line. The Assembly required that a set of standard weights and measures be maintained at each of these ports, and established duties for the use of their harbors. On the north coast, the harbor towns included Lucea, Montego Bay, Martha Brae (known as Falmouth after 1769), Rio Bueno, St. Ann's Bay, Oracabessa, Port Maria, Annotto Bay, and Port Antonio. Eight additional ports of embarkation were established on the south coast, including Kingston, Port Morant, Morant Bay, Yallahs Bay, Old Harbour, Milk River, Black River, and Savanna-la-Mar. Plantain Garden River and Green Island Bay were established on the east and west coasts, respectively. Of these port towns, only Kingston, Montego Bay, Port Antonio, and Savanna-la-Mar were recognized ports of entry for the island (Aikman 1802; Higman 1991).

The relatively large number and wide distribution of ports of embarkation in eighteenth century Jamaica are revelatory of several phenomena. All of the north coast ports were located on harbors or bays identified in the Spanish records of the island, and indeed many retained their Spanish place names (e.g., Rio Bueno, Oracabessa). The location of these ports in the eighteenth century was doubtless the result of a reflexive settlement process. Because ports were established to facilitate the export of crops from plantations, ports were located near concentrations of settlements. Simultaneously, because plantations need to have access to export facilities, they were settled near the ports. The disbursal of these ports along the north coast allowed for the expansion of plantation settlement on the arable lands of the north coast. Similarly, the ports of embarkation on the south coast were established on the old Spanish hatos, and some retained their Spanish place names: Port Morant and Morant Bay (both in the hato of Morante), Yallahs Bay in the hato of Ayalahs, and Savanna-la-Mar. Milk River was located in the hato of Yama, Black River in El Eado, and Kingston in Liguaney. Old Harbour was the English place name given to the old Spanish port of Esquivel. Plantain Garden River and Green Island Bay were likely established to encourage plantation settlement in the eastern and western extremes of the island, but neither developed into a significant port (see Higman 1991 for a discussion of early nineteenth century port towns in Jamaica).

During the second half of the eighteenth century, the population of the island was on an upward trend, doubling from about 85,000 people in 1722 to more than 160,000 by 1762 (Roberts 1957: 33); the population doubled again between 1762 and 1817, when the population reached more than 340,000 people. Of course, as the plantation economy took off, an increasing number and percentage of these people were enslaved. Using information gleaned from the Transatlantic Slave Trade Database compiled by David Eltis and Martin Halbert, Audra Diptee (2010) has calculated that, between 1701 and 1750, some 252,000 people were brought to Jamaica to work as enslaved captives on the island. In the second half of the century, despite significant disruption in the colonial trade precipitated by the American Revolution, the number increased to more than 422,000 between 1751 and 1800 (Diptee 2010: 10). Burnard (2001) reports that 92 percent of Jamaica's population was enslaved during these decades, a figure corroborated by the work of Barry Higman (e.g., 1995) and George Roberts (1957), and the self-reported data appearing in the Jamaica Almanac for 1788. Higman (1995: 61) reports that by 1800 there were 328,000 enslaved people living in Jamaica, an enslaved population greater than that of any one of the several states in the United States, and about equal to half the enslaved population of the entire United States, as recorded in the 1790 U.S. Census.

During the great social and economic upheavals that surrounded the American, French, and Haitian revolutions, the economy of Jamaica began to re-diversify. Whereas most of the expansionary efforts of the mid-eighteenth century were focused on the growth of the sugar industry, the revolution in Haiti created a market vacuum for coffee in Europe. As early as the 1770s, speculators began to acquire land in the mountainous interior of Jamaica, either by buying or by other means acquiring the rights to old, undeveloped patents, or else by patenting mountain land for the first time (Delle 1996, 1998). The late eighteenth century witnessed the first of several boom periods for Jamaican coffee, and a concomitant expansion of plantation settlements into the accessible mountain interior of the parishes of St. Ann, St. Elizabeth, St. George, Port Royal, and St. David.

Several maps produced during the late eighteenth century provide locational data for spatial modeling of this period. A map published in 1775 by Thomas Jeffries identifies the location of approximately 1,020 plantation sites; this may be something of an underestimation as Higman (1988: 10) reports that there were 1,061 sugar estates alone in 1786. Nevertheless, modeling the locations of plantations recorded on the Jeffries map against elevation and distance from the coast provides evidence of settlement trends during this period. In 1775, just more than 50 percent of all estates were located within five kilometers of the coast, and 71 percent were within 10 kilometers (see Figure 2.9). Modeling against 250-meter contours reveals that, in 1775, 78.5 percent of plantations were positioned below 250 meters in elevation; conversely, 21.5 percent were located above 250 meters, with 7.2 percent above 500 meters (see Figure 2.10). A 1798 map published by Bryan Edwards indicates the location of 1295 settlements. Modeling from this map indicates that in 1798 less that 50 percent of Jamaican plantations were located within five kilometers of the coast, and less than 70 percent within ten kilometers (see Figure 2.11). There was a sharp increase in the percentage of sites located above 250 meters in elevation, with just more than 19 percent located between 250 and 500 meters and 6.6 percent between 500 and 750 meters (see Figure 2.12). Movement away from the coast and into the mountainous upland of the island suggests that during the late eighteenth century, the process of land capitalization expanded from the coastal plains and lowland valleys into the highlands. The production of coffee on consolidated plantations was thus able to follow the basic structure established by the sugar plantation complex: most coffee would be produced on large, privately held estates worked by enslaved labor.

Settlement History of Jamaica, 1800–1834

The opening decades of the nineteenth century were a time of great transformation in the Caribbean. The plantation economy of the region, and that of Jamaica in particular, began a decline brought on by several

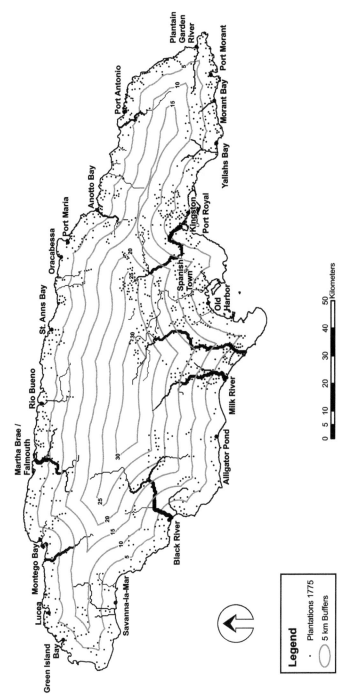

Figure 2.9. Model showing locations of plantations in relation to coast, based on Jeffries's 1775 map of Jamaica. The buffer lines represent distance to the coast in 5-km increments. Illustration courtesy of Richard Courtney, Department of Geography, Kutztown University.

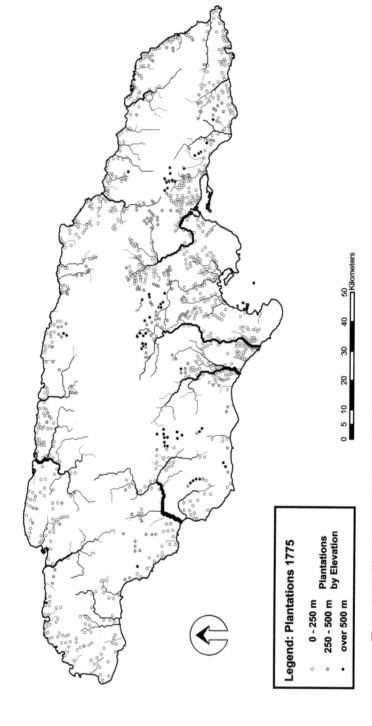

Figure 2.10. Elevation model showing locations of plantations in relation to 100-m contours, based on Jeffries's 1775 map of Jamaica. Illustration courtesy of Richard Courtney, Department of Geography, Kutztown University.

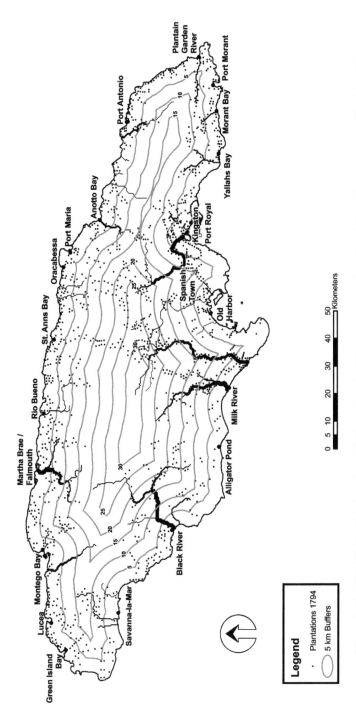

Figure 2.11. Model showing locations of plantations by distance to coast based on Edwards 1798 map of Jamaica. The buffer lines represent distance to the coast in 5-km increments. Illustration courtesy of Richard Courtney, Department of Geography, Kutztown University.

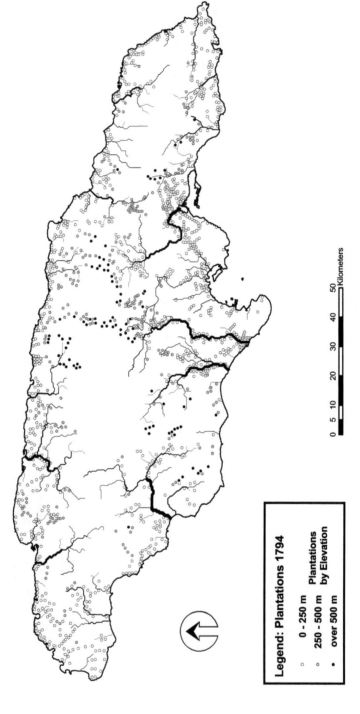

Figure 2.12. Elevation model showing locations of plantations in relation to 100-m contours, based on Edwards 1798 map of Jamaica. Illustration courtesy of Richard Courtney, Department of Geography, Kutztown University.

Legend: Plantations 1794

○ 0 - 250 m
◉ 250 - 500 m   Plantations
● over 500 m   by Elevation

0 5 10 20 30 40 50 Kilometers

coinciding changes in British colonial policy. By the early nineteenth century, European powers began to expand the agricultural economies of newly exploited tropical regions, particularly in the basin of the Indian Ocean. The African Slave Trade, on which the viability of Jamaica's labor system had depended throughout the eighteenth century, was abolished by Parliament in 1807. The curtailing of the trade in human laborers put pressure on the plantation labor system. Despite the fact that hundreds of thousands of African people had been brought to Jamaica to work the plantations, throughout the eighteenth century, Jamaica had experienced an extended period of natural demographic decrease, mitigated only by the incessant re-population of the plantations made possible by the African slave trade. Roberts (1957) calculated that the enslaved population of Jamaica had experienced a very consistent rate of natural decrease throughout the eighteenth century. Between 1722 and 1734, there had been a 3.7 percent natural decrease; the decennial natural decrease of the population hovered between 2 and 3 percent for the rest of the century. These mortality rates were ameliorated only by the continual importation of enslaved laborers, an economy and process that came to a legal end in 1807.

The economy of Jamaica suffered a simultaneous blow during the Napoleonic Wars, particularly after 1806 when Napoleon enforced an embargo on all British imports into Europe. The burgeoning coffee industry was particularly hard hit by the embargo, as much of Jamaica's coffee had been reexported into Europe to take advantage of the market vacuum that had been created when the continent lost its primary source of coffee during the Haitian Revolution. One Jamaica coffee planter, John Mackeson, observed in 1808 that the "present times bear a most gloomy aspect. . . . Numbers in this country must be ruined, many are already so. . . . The present crisis is past all human calculation" (Mackeson mss).

Between 1834 and 1838, the plantation mode of production as it had developed in Jamaica was legislated out of existence with the abolition of slavery in the British West Indies. Although some plantations were able to maintain production using wage labor, many estates, which had relied on a system of credit based on the exchange value of land and slaves as capital assets as well as the approximated value of future commodity production, were unable to maintain the capital flow required to support a regular payroll. Furthermore, many of the previously enslaved laborers had no desire to remain employed on the estates on which they had previously been required to labor, choosing instead to seek their own way on small provisioning farms in the island's interior. In so doing, they abandoned their dependent role in capitalized export production to instead become subsistence farmers tied to a local subsistence economy, rather than a global economy based on the exportation of agricultural commodities.

A map published in 1814 by John Thomson suggests how the settlement pattern of plantations on the island was shifting during these decades of transition. The number of plantations identified on this map is far fewer than those of the late eighteenth century, likely representing the early stages of plantation abandonment that had already begun by the 1810s (Delle 1996, 1998; Higman 1988). Although this map shows fewer than half the number of estates than were represented on Edwards's 1798 map, GIS modeling against the same two variables (distance to coast and elevation) suggests that an equal percentage of estates were located within five kilometers of the coast – that is, 47.4 percent (614 of 1,295 in 1798; 373 of 787 in 1814). The percentages beyond five kilometers (at five to ten, ten to fifteen, and fifteen to twenty) also remained consistent (see Figure 2.13). However, the percentages of plantations modeled by the 250-meter contours show some change, with more than 75 percent of the 1,814 estates appearing below 250 meters in elevation, and significant drops in the percentages of plantations located between 250 and 500 meters (declining from 19.2 percent to 18.3 percent) and between 500 and 750 meters in elevations (declining from 6.6 percent to 5.9 percent; see Figure 2.14). This indicates that plantations in the higher elevations, those more likely to be coffee estates, were more likely to disappear from the cartographic record than those situated on lower elevations, which were more likely to be sugar estates or cattle pens. Higman graphically illustrates that in the post-emancipation period, coffee plantations were much more likely to be abandoned than were sugar plantations (Higman 1988: 12).

Settlement Trends, 1655–1834

Modeling the plantation landscape as we have reveals several diachronic trends about the settlement history of English Jamaica. Having first established themselves in the areas previously cleared by the owners of the Spanish hatos, numerous small planters expanded tropical production by organizing small cacao, cotton, and indigo plantations in the coastal lowlands. In the middle decades of the seventeenth century, the landscape of Jamaica was characterized by small plantations, worked by individual families, with perhaps several enslaved or indentured workers, similar to the settlement pattern observed in Barbados half a century before. This settlement pattern was short lived. The availability of large land grants,

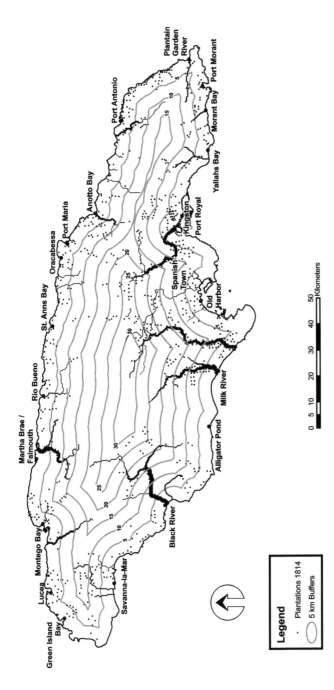

Figure 2.13. GIS model locating plantation sites by distance to coast based on Thomson's 1814 map of Jamaica. Illustration courtesy of Richard Courtney, Department of Geography, Kutztown University.

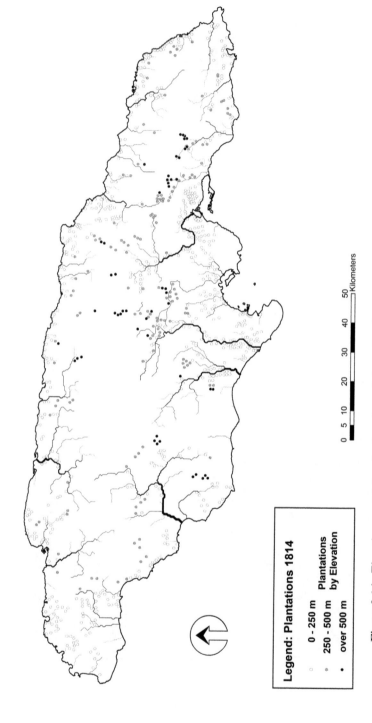

Figure 2.14. Elevation model showing locations of plantations in relation to 100-m contours, based on Thomson's 1814 map of Jamaica. Illustration courtesy of Richard Courtney, Department of Geography, Kutztown University.

Legend: Plantations 1814

0 - 250 m   **Plantations**
250 - 500 m   **by Elevation**
over 500 m

0   5   10   20   30   40   50   Kilometers

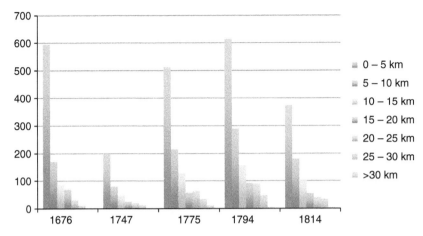

Figure 2.15. Number of plantations by distance from coast, 1676–1814.

the abandonment of small plantations with the deaths of their original owners or by their abandonment of small-scale tropical production, and the introduction of the African slave trade to Jamaica, created the opportunity for wealthy investors to create a sugar monoculture economy based on capitalized land holdings worked by capitalized, enslaved labor. Between the third quarter of the seventeenth century and the second quarter of the eighteenth, the number of plantation settlements contracted as the larger landholders consolidated their estates in the best lowland areas. As this plantation-based settlement pattern expanded throughout the eighteenth century, settlements moved farther from the coast (see Figures 2.15 and 2.16)

As both the number and size of plantations increased in the second half of the eighteenth century, an increasing number and percentage of settlements were established both farther from the coast and at higher elevations. The inland vales in central Jamaica were exploited for sugar, and, in the final quarter of the eighteenth century, coffee was introduced as a secondary crop. Rather than competing for land resources with the sugar estates, coffee was best suited for the highland valleys at higher elevations – areas not well suited for sugar production. By the closing decade of the eighteenth century, more than a quarter of Jamaica's plantations were located at elevations higher than 250 meters above sea level, reflecting both the increased utilization of highland vales for sugar

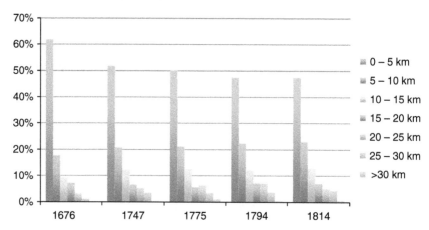

Figure 2.16. Percentage of plantations by distance from coast, 1676–1814.

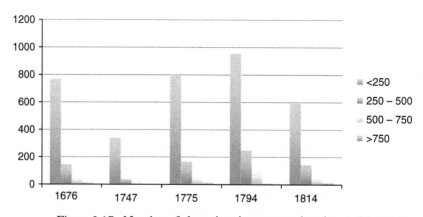

Figure 2.17. Number of plantations by contour elevation, 1676–1814.

production, and the introduction of coffee production into previously undeveloped land.

With the abolition of the slave trade, the expansion of colonial tropical production into the Indian Ocean, and the development of sugar plantations in Cuba and Brazil at a greater economy of scale than was possible in

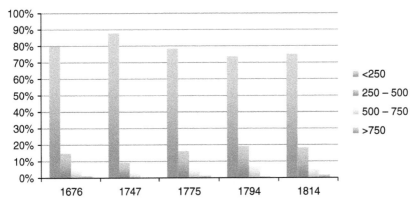

Figure 2.18. Percentage of plantations by contour elevation, 1676–1814.

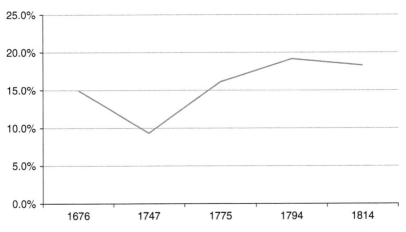

Figure 2.19. Percentage of plantations at 250-m elevation or higher, 1676–1814.

Jamaica, the plantation settlement pattern began to contract. By the 1810s, many of the older coffee plantations were already being abandoned, as were some of the less productive sugar estates. This process would only accelerate following the abolition of slavery between 1834 and 1838 (see Figures 2.18 and 2.19).

Conclusion: Plantation Settlements and Capitalized Space

At the turn of the seventeenth century, the term "plantation" was synonymous with our modern understanding of the word "colony." In sixteenth-century Ireland, both the Munster and later Ulster Plantations were colonial enterprises in which English settlers were "planted" in new lands, collectively known as a plantation. In 1620 in New England, religious dissenters established the Plymouth Plantation and later the Rhode Island and Providence Plantations, names referring to the entire colonial settlement rather than a privately owned estate. By the turn of the eighteenth century, the word "plantation" had taken on a different meaning. In the Caribbean and Southeastern North America, the word "plantation" would connote a privately held agricultural estate, consisting of capitalized land and social labor harnessed for the material gain of the owners of the estates, the plantation proprietors.

The semantic shift in the meaning of the word "plantation" derives directly from the colonial experience of those involved in the agricultural commodities markets of the eighteenth century. In the Caribbean, there was a significant shift in the organization of society brought on in large measure by the capitalization of land and labor, and the development of export economies for sugar and coffee. Land in Jamaica was to be privately owned, transferred by sale or inheritance. Because Marxist analysis contends that material realities shape other elements of culture and society, it follows that the consolidation of private land, and thus the exclusion of non-landowners from a key resource required for agricultural production, impacted the development of colonial society in Jamaica. As we have seen, the landscape of the island was reshaped in the eighteenth century as the structures of plantation production were reproduced and spread across the island, through the river valleys and littoral of the coast where sugar production thrived, to the mountain vales and valleys that were well-suited to coffee production.

As we have seen, a review of the settlement history of colonial Jamaica demonstrates that plantation production of both sugar and coffee dominated the island from the early eighteenth century into the opening decades of the nineteenth. What we have not yet considered is the structure of the social world that developed as the plantation mode of production took root and spread throughout the island. To understand how these historical processes shaped Jamaican society, we now turn to a discussion of the concept of "mode of production," and how Marxist archaeology can use this concept to analyze Jamaica society as it existed at the turn of the nineteenth century.

Box 1: The Atlantic Slave Trade

The rise of the plantation system in the New World was dependent on the importation of enslaved laborers from Africa, a massive forced migration of people that linked the Old World to the New and made vast fortunes for those involved in the buying and selling of human beings. Over the past few decades, several historians of the African Slave Trade have been refining the estimates of the scope of this trans-Atlantic Trade. David Eltis and Martin Halbert of Emory University have spent much of the past two decades refining a database based on primary and published sources of slave trade voyages. Their breathtaking database, available at www.slavevoyages.org, is a compilation of data drawn from the records of more than 35,000 slave trading voyages made between the years 1500 and 1867, which they estimate to be about 80 percent of the actual voyages made. Their estimates of the number of Africans taken to the New World are probably the most accurate ever available.

According to their estimates, approximately 12,521,300 Africans embarked on the Middle Passage across the Atlantic; approximately 1 in 5 perished on route, leaving a total of 10,702,700 who survived to be enslaved in the New World. Almost half of these disembarked into Brazil, by far the largest of the slave-holding regions. The British West Indies follows as the second largest receiver of enslaved workers; some 2,318,300 people were landed in the British slave colonies. Just less than half of these were destined for Jamaica (1,019,596), followed in scope by Barbados (493,200), Antigua (138,00), St. Kitts (134,100), Grenada (128,700), Dominica (110,000), British Guiana (72,700), St. Vincent (58,900), Montserrat and Nevis (46,100), and Trinidad and Tobago (44,000); the smaller possessions totaled another 72,100. In contrast, 388,700 enslaved people were landed in all of mainland North America, only a third of the number landed in Jamaica alone.

3   The Plantation Mode of Production

Most social theorists agree that in any given historical context there exists an underlying logic binding individual human beings into coherent social groups. The nature of this underlying logic has been debated for centuries and, perhaps because social phenomena are so complex, no consensus has yet been reached on just how to define the forces that bind individuals into groups and shape the nature of human relationships within and between recognized groups.

Karl Marx proposed that societies formed when human beings worked together to acquire and distribute the necessities of life; to Marx this meant that human society had a material, or physical, base (Engels 2007; Marx 1979). Because different societies would define different needs for themselves, they would develop both different tools and technologies for the acquisition and use of these necessities and different social structures to facilitate the production, distribution, and consumption of these things. Marx thus argued that a variety of different social formations would historically emerge. Because Marx argued that the production of goods and services was the primary force binding societies together, he defined the various social formations that historically developed as "modes of production" (Marx 1979, 1992).

At the core of Marx's definition of "mode of production" is the idea that any given social structure has a material base; that is, the economic system operating at a given time and place will shape the life experiences of people working in and under that system. A mode of production is defined by the interrelationship between the forces of production, which include the technology, buildings, tools, knowledge, and labor required to make goods for sale, and the relations of production, composed of the social structures and rules which define how people work and relate to each other. The relations of production are largely defined by what is known as the social division of labor and rules governing access to what are called the means of production, which are the material parts of the forces of production that often appear in the archaeological record (Marx 1992).

There has been some considerable debate among Marxists concerning how many different modes of production have historically developed (e.g., Benaji 1977; Siskind 1978; Thorner 1982; van Binsbergen and Geschiere 1985; Wolf 1982). Whereas Marx himself proposed that capitalism was a single mode of production that developed directly out of what is generally referred to as the Feudal Mode of Production (Marx 1979, 1992), some more recent theorists have suggested that multiple variants of the capitalist mode of production developed over time, particularly following the introduction of industrialized production (Bagchi 2004; Cowie 2011; Sen 1984). Some have thus made the distinction between the mercantile capitalist mode of production, under which markets and prices are tightly controlled by the apparatus of the state, and the industrial or competitive capitalist mode of production, under which the power of the state to control and regulate trade is much reduced (Delle 1998; Sen 1984). A variant of Marxist historical analysis, made famous by Immanuel Wallerstein and known as World Systems Theory, contends that multiple variants of the capitalist mode of production can simultaneously exist within a large, coherent system. For example, the economic and social interests of elite classes in a colonial metropolis or core (like London) can differ from the interests of regional elites in the colonial periphery (like Jamaica). In cases such as this, when diverse interests and strategies for organizing society are compatible with the overall structure of the economic and social systems in place, variants of the capitalist mode of production will develop in the periphery, which feature some forms of social organization or technological developments peculiar to the specific colonial context (Wallerstein 1976). Such was the case in much of the New World, including Jamaica, when systems of temporary bondage known as indentured servitude were replaced with chattel slavery (Epperson 1999, 2000), resulting in the formation of the plantation mode of production, a variant of the capitalist mode of production. Both sugar and coffee were produced in great quantity under this mode of production.

This chapter examines how the plantation mode of production was manifested in the coffee producing regions of Jamaica, specifically considering the complex relationship between the tools and technologies required to produce coffee and the social relations that existed to produce and use those tools and technologies within plantation landscapes. Taken together, these elements of Jamaican society, what Marx referred to as the forces of production and relations of production, constituted the plantation mode of production (Marx 1979; Patterson 2003). To better understand how the plantation mode of production shaped early nineteenth century Jamaica society, this chapter first defines the plantation mode of production through a consideration of its constituent parts. Once the forces of production, the relations of production, and the social and technical division of labor of the plantation mode of production are defined, this chapter concludes with a consideration of how coffee plantation landscapes served to bind the material and social forces into a coherent mode of production.

The Plantation Mode of Production

Modes of production arise through a complex, historically contingent process through which humans organize labor and social relations, and develop tools and technologies, to transform what exists in nature into objects that fulfill human needs. Under certain modes of production, this includes the production and sale of food crops through markets, and indeed, it is easy to see how the production and sale of edible food fills a societal need. However, human beings can create needs that go beyond the basics of survival. In the early nineteenth century, for example, there was significant demand for whale oil as factories, shops, and homes "needed" to be illuminated at night by clean burning and sweet smelling fuel, a socially constructed need that stimulated the growth of a huge whaling industry in North America. In the seventeenth and eighteenth centuries, the European colonial powers similarly developed needs for agricultural products that, while addictive, fulfilled socially constructed more than physically defined needs. Tobacco, tea, sugar, and coffee were among the commodities for which significant social need arose, and which were produced on colonial plantations. Those that lived and worked on plantations both created, and were created by, the relations and forces of production operating within the plantation mode of production, which existed to supply the European market with the tropical commodities it demanded.

The Relations of Production

A mode of production is composed both of the tools and techniques used to produce and distribute commodities and by the social relationships that emerge from the production and use of those commodities. In Marxist thought, these relationships are known as the social relations of production (Marx 1979, 1992). Although the social relations of production are often equated with class structure, other operative principles of social organization can be considered as constituent elements of the social relations of production. Under the plantation mode of production, for example, slavery was a key element of the social relations of production.

Although enslavement on plantations was clearly related to the classification of people within the labor structure of the mode of production, and can thus be considered a class relationship, slavery was also, clearly, closely tied to the development of a racialized social hierarchy in colonial Jamaica, which was based in the capitalization of laborers as elements of the means of production. Perceived racial identity, when used to define a person's place within the hierarchy of production, can thus be considered a constituent element of the social relations of production.

Nevertheless, the social relations of production within the plantation mode of production were structured by a strict hierarchy defined by the relationship one had to the productive forces required to produce export crops. Existing at the top of the social pyramid, the members of the agrarian elite who controlled Jamaica's land base and directed the production of commodities referred to themselves as "planters." The planters were not a homogenous group free from internal division, but included members of the landed oligarchy, their estate staff, and other members of Jamaican society involved in the commodities trade and service industries required to maintain it, including merchants, attorneys, and financiers (Butler 1995; Checkland 1957; Davis 1975; Lobdell 1972; Pares 1950; Stinchcombe 1995). In part, because ownership of a plantation allowed one to ascend to the status of "planter," many merchants and attorneys purchased estates, ensuring them access to planter status.

The planter class was subdivided by social ranking, particularly as that ranking applied to an individual's relationship to the means of production. Heuristically, the planters can be divided into three overlapping groups. The most powerful was comprised of proprietors who held legal title to plantations as well as the attorneys who managed the financial affairs of absentee, minor, or deceased proprietors, and often owned plantations of their own. A second group included overseers, who ran the daily operation of the estates, and their assistants (often called "bookkeepers"). The final group included artisans, merchants, doctors, and other professionals, who lived in the urban centers but owned plantations (Roughley 1823; Sheridan 1974).

The social structure of Jamaica, at least until slavery was abolished in 1834, was dependent on enslaved labor. Under this capitalized system of labor organization, enslaved people were not free to sell their labor power in an open market, but were dehumanized and considered commodities, valued both by their potential to provide labor power to commercial agricultural estates and their exchange value as moveable commodities; indeed, at one point, the Jamaica Assembly declared it illegal for the enslaved to hire themselves out for wages (Long 1774). Between 1834 and 1838, most able-bodied workers were required to remain on the estates that had previously enslaved them as "apprentices," a transitional social category created by Parliament as part of the plan to incrementally abolish slavery in the British Empire. The apprenticeship system was designed to teach former slaves the conditions of wage labor; although they were required to work for a certain number of hours each week on the plantations, apprentices were free to sell their labor power at other times. This condition was abolished in 1838 in Jamaica, and the laborers were nominally free to sell their labor power to the highest bidder.

At the apex, there was a significant variance in wealth and power among the proprietors; social standing within the planter class was largely dependent on the type(s) of plantations one owned, the amount of land one held, and the number of laborers one kept in bondage. The most valuable type of plantation was a sugar plantation. In 1823, John Stewart, a Jamaican planter himself, estimated that one would require an investment of approximately £43,000 in Jamaican currency to acquire the land, construct the buildings, and purchase the slaves required to run a profitable sugar plantation; this would amount to approximately £1,280,000 in modern sterling, or about US$2,000,000. Coffee plantations and cattle breeding pens, the second and third most important type of plantations on Jamaica, required a significantly smaller investment (Shepherd 2009). Although many of Jamaica's pens were owned by wealthy planters who operated them in support of their sugar estates, the relatively low start-up costs of a cattle pen or coffee plantation provided opportunities for people of relatively modest means to become proprietors. For example, Thomas Thistlewood, a famous diarist of eighteenth century Jamaica, owned a cattle pen that was worth only £600 in 1789; at the time of his death in 1786, his thirty-four enslaved workers were valued at £1,500. Although £2,100 was a lot of money in the late eighteenth century, it was nothing near £43,000. Thistlewood's example demonstrates that a cattle pen could be established for a fraction of the cost of setting up a sugar estate (Burnard 2004).

Many of the wealthiest plantation owners did not reside on their estates. Some were investors who lived in Great Britain and were known as absentee proprietors. Many plantations were owned by proprietors choosing to live in one of Jamaica's urban centers, or else by a planter who owned multiple plantations and chose one for a principal residence. In each of these cases, the proprietor had little to do with the day-to-day business of the plantation, relying on a manager to run the operation. Such arrangements were common for sugar plantations; for example, in the late eighteenth century, Simon Taylor, a planter who lived in Jamaica and was reputed to be the wealthiest man on the island, owned six sugar estates and three cattle pens. Although he owned estates in the parishes of

St. David, St. Thomas in the East, St. Andrew, and Hanover, Taylor chose to reside for a good part of his life in Kingston, which he represented in the Jamaica Assembly, the island's legislative body, for nearly twenty years (Sheridan 1971). Barry Higman has estimated that in 1834, some 80 percent of Jamaica's sugar estates were managed by someone other than their owners (Higman 1998, 2005).

Absentee proprietors depended on the managerial skills of agents residing on Jamaica, many of whom lived primarily in Kingston (Higman 2005). Such attorneys, or island factors as they were sometimes known, would correspond with the proprietors, and would make their living by taking a percentage of the profits realized by the estates they managed. The more successful attorneys would manage multiple estates, creating great opportunities for the accumulation of wealth through a mixture of good management and clever fraud. According to John Stewart's early-nineteenth-century commentary on Jamaican society, it was customary for attorneys to be paid a commission of 5 or 6 percent of the value of all goods bought and sold by a managed estate. Stewart intimates that merchants who served both as attorneys and importers could sell items to the estates under their management at a 6 percent premium and could over-buy supplies to pad their commissions; he further comments that some unscrupulous attorneys might also overstate the value of an annual crop to fraudulently charge the absentee proprietor a higher fee than was actually due (Stewart 1808). This practice was apparently so common in eighteenth-century Jamaica that the island's legislature, the Jamaica Assembly, moved to curb fraud by passing a law requiring estate managers both to submit reports to the local government tabulating the annual crop for each estate under their care and to sign an oath that their report was true and accurate. Nevertheless, as Stewart notes, "[p]rincely fortunes have been made by men who have had a great number of attorneyships" (Stewart 1808: 129). Richard Sheridan (1971) once concluded that Simon Taylor first acquired his great fortune by managing the estates of absentee proprietors. Sheridan estimated Taylor's income from estate management to be approximately £47,000 per year (about £1.5 million in today's value), and his net worth to have exceeded £1,000,000 (or about £32 million in today's value).

Attorneys like Taylor were able to acquire managerial control over estates through their positions as merchants. Although by the middle of the eighteenth century the Jamaican economy was dominated by sugar production, the management of the estates, to speak nothing of the extravagant lifestyles of the elites, required credit. Many Jamaican planters depended on the island's wealthy urban merchants to provide them with the capital and credit necessary to improve their estates, acquire manufactured and luxury goods from Europe, or to purchase land and slaves. Importing the goods required to run a sugar estate in the style required by the planters, and to lend the money required to purchase such items, made Kingston merchants wealthy. Indeed, according to a study conducted by Trevor Burnard, several Kingston merchants left huge fortunes at their deaths in the 1770s – including such merchants as Aaron Baruh Lousada, a Jewish merchant and moneylender (£151,266); Zachary Bayly (£207,769); and George Paplay, a Kingston merchant who supervised absentees' estates (£176,415). Burnard concludes that successful Jamaican planters and merchants were exponentially wealthier than their counterparts in the thirteen mainland colonies.

It is important to note that, although Jamaica was a wealthy colony, wealth was far more concentrated than in any of the thirteen mainland colonies, including the slave holding colonies of Virginia and South Carolina. On the eve of the American Revolution, there were approximately 210,000 people in Jamaica – of whom 80 percent were enslaved. According to some estimates of comparative wealth, in the thirteen colonies, the top 10 percent of wealth holders owned just more than 50 percent of all wealth during the 1770s. In Jamaica, that top 10 percent owned approximately 66 percent of wealth. As Burnard rightly points out, if the entire population is calculated into this equation, including the enslaved, the top 1 percent of Jamaica's population owned 85 percent of the island's wealth (Burnard 2001).

It is clear that not every white person on Jamaica would be considered wealthy, and indeed there were many Europeans who landed in Jamaica as indentured servants or with very little wealth to their name. Whereas some of these people could secure employment as clerks or artisans in Kingston, many were employed as managers on plantations. The daily operation of a plantation was supervised by an estate employee known as an overseer. An overseer on a Jamaican plantation would be responsible for the day-to-day affairs of the estate, and could earn a salary of as much as £200 per year. Although the majority of overseers probably never rose above this station, some, through a combination of thrift and luck, could accumulate enough wealth to acquire property, Thistlewood being a notorious case in point (Burnard 2004; Hall 1989).

Overseers supervised one or more lower-level plantation managers, known in Jamaica as "bookkeepers." Bookkeepers tended to be young men of modest means trying to get a start in plantation society. Their primary responsibility was in keeping the daily "book," which did not involve accounting as in the modern usage of the word, but instead referred to the plantation daybook which logged daily activities. It was

Box 2: The Diaries of Thomas Thistlewood

Thomas Thistlewood (1721–1786), was an English-born son of a yeoman farmer, who eventually sought his fortune in Jamaica. Migrating in 1750, Thistlewood arrived at a time when the plantation mode of production was in its florescence. Thistlewood quickly gained employment as an overseer, eventually husbanding resources enough to purchase a gang of enslaved workers, which he initially leased to other planters for profit. By 1767, Thistlewood was able to purchase his own estate, a cattle pen known as Breadnut Island Pen.

As an amateur scientist and observer of the world around him, Thistlewood kept a voluminous record of his daily activities. His diary runs to thirty-seven volumes and nearly 10,000 manuscript pages, with entries dating between 1750 and 1786. Among his many daily remarks were notations about his sexual activity with enslaved women; he recorded thousands of encounters including the name of the woman with whom he coupled, and where and at what time of the day the act took place. He recorded nearly 4,000 sex acts with more than 100 women.

Thistlewood's diaries offer an eye-opening look into the life of a "middling planter" at a time when the plantation mode of production was at its peak. They have been abstracted by Douglas Hall (1989) and interpreted by Trevor Burnard (2004). Long the property of the family of William John Monson, Baron Monson, and curated in Lincolnshire, Thistlewood's papers were purchased at auction in 2011 by Yale University and are now available for open research at the Beinecke Rare Book and Manuscript Library at Yale University.

customary for each plantation to record daily operations, including keeping a list of how each of the enslaved workers was occupied that day; bookkeepers were thus responsible for taking daily attendance and keeping track of productive activities on the plantation. Stewart paints a very dreary picture of the bookkeeper's life as being one of lonely toil for little pay; although this may have been the case for some, many bookkeepers could aspire to become overseers after a few years. Burnard has noted that the need for white plantation operatives was so great that bookkeepers of talent and ambition could quickly rise to become overseers (Burnard 2002, 2004).

Social mobility was possible in large measure because the white population of Jamaica was surprisingly transient; Trevor Burnard estimates that as many as 125,000 Europeans migrated to Jamaica between 1655 and 1776, yet according to a census taken on the island in 1774, only some 12,737 remained. Although some of the white immigrant population likely moved on to other colonies, either in the West Indies or the American mainland, much of this demographic discrepancy can be accounted for by, what is to the modern eye, the shocking mortality rate of eighteenth-century Jamaica. Burnard reports that in the Parish of St. Andrew, which today is a suburban parish just outside of Kingston, only 38 percent of white children born in marriages survived to adulthood. Contemporary observers bemoaned the high mortality rates in Jamaica; Edward Long (1774), for example, hoped to create a more stable European presence on the island by the establishment of townships in the interior, at state expense, but Charles Leslie (1740) worried that the island's entire population was replaced every seven years by incoming migrants continually taking the place of those who so quickly died (Burnard 1994).

White society in colonial Jamaica included great proprietors and attorneys, overseers and bookkeepers – all of whom referred to themselves as "planters." In addition to these, the island's white population included merchants, doctors, printers, shop keepers, wharfingers, surveyors, and artisans. Although the greatest wealth was controlled by the proprietors and attorneys of Jamaica's many vast sugar estates, there were also a significant number of small plantation owners, "middling planters," who primarily owned cattle pens or coffee plantations. Although there was a significant minority of wealthy coffee plantation owners holding in excess of 1,000 acres, there were nearly the same number who held less than 100 acres (Smith 2002: 103). At 699 acres, the average size of a coffee plantation was just more than two-thirds the size of the average sugar plantation, and even this number may be skewed by the few truly large estates. Far fewer people were enslaved on an average coffee plantation than on a sugar estate – that is, 128 compared to 223. As a middling class of plantation proprietors, coffee planters tended to live on the island; only about 9 percent of coffee plantations were owned by absentees. In a study of plantation records on Jamaica, S. D. Smith has determined that many smaller coffee planters were engaged in other occupations. Smith relates that, in his sample of small coffee holders, three were professional carpenters, one was a tinsmith, one was a merchant, and two were practicing physicians. Of the forty-nine planters examined in his study, Smith reports that the estates of nineteen small planters were valued at less than £5,000 at the time of their death (Smith 2002: 121). Pen keepers, that is planters who owned cattle pens (sometimes called grass pens) have also been categorized as being of a lower social rank within the planter class, and were sometimes referred to as "small settlers" (Brathwaite 1971; Shepherd and Montieth 2002).

Civil and political rights were granted in colonial Jamaica based on a racial hierarchy created and imposed by the planter class. The European population of Jamaica was not gender-balanced; for much of the eighteenth and early nineteenth century, European men outnumbered European women. This gender imbalance resulted in many sexual unions between European men and women of African descent; the ensuing pregnancies resulted in a large mixed-race population on Jamaica, some of whom remained enslaved, others of whom were either born into freedom or were manumitted by their white fathers. The Reverend Richard Bickel, who lived and preached for a time in Kingston and was a former Chaplain at the Royal Naval station at Port Royal, commented in the 1820s that relationships between European men and women of color were so common as to "looked upon by every person as a matter of course" (Bickel 1825: 105). According to Bickel, few white men of modest means chose to marry, but instead cohabited with a "housekeeper." He further relates that overseers on estates commonly entered into such relationships and would as commonly recognize and raise as their own the children of these unions. Bickel was scandalized that women of the white gentry socialized with such common-law spouses, treating them almost as equals should their men rise to become established proprietors or wealthy attorneys (Bickel 1825: 105).

During the colonial era, this population was known as "free colored" or "free people of color." Gad Heuman has estimated that by 1834, the free colored population outnumbered whites by almost two to one, with about 31,000 free people of color and 16,600 whites living on the island (Heuman 1981: 7).

As the size of the free colored population increased in the eighteenth century, the island's legislature, known as the Jamaica Assembly, acted to limit the economic and social power of this class of people. In the late eighteenth century, the clerk of the Assembly noted that there were four classes of people on Jamaica, including whites, slaves, free people of color having special privileges, and free people of color without special privileges (Brathwaite 1971: 105). The privileges alluded to here were what today we refer to as Civil Rights. For example, in 1761, the Assembly passed an act prohibiting whites from bequeathing real or personal property valued at more than £1,200 sterling, or £2,000 local currency, to a person of color (Heuman 1981: 6; Brathwaite 1971: 170). Only Christian whites were allowed to sit in the Jamaica Assembly, and – after 1733 – free people of color were not allowed to vote. An act passed in 1711 prohibited free people of color from being employed in a public office, and various other laws passed by the Assembly limited the rights of people of color to serve on juries and testify in court. Despite these restrictions, some of the free people of color were able to accumulate wealth and property, and many became planters and owned slaves. Such members of the community were occasionally granted Civil Rights exceptions, resulting in that class who were free people of color "having special privileges," which could include the right to vote or hold public office. Heuman notes that such privileges could only be granted through a specific act of the Assembly, and that such acts became rare after 1761 (Heuman 1981: 6).

Although some free people of color owned small plantations and lived on their estates, the vast majority of the free colored population lived in Jamaica's two largest urban centers: Kingston, the island's primary port city, and Spanish Town, its colonial capital. Several studies have concluded that many free people of color were artisans or worked in or owned shops; many of this latter group included free women of color, who, because of what seems to be a gender-bias on the part of white fathers to free their daughters but not their sons, outnumbered free men of color by a ratio of almost two to one (Heuman 1981: 8). Brathwaithe contends that a few free people of color did serve as overseers or bookkeepers, and some even rose to the status of planter; he cites the example of James Swaby, the mulatto son of John Swaby, who inherited by will his white father's sugar plantations and slaves, owning 217 slaves and 331 head of stock in 1828 (Brathwaite 1971: 172). It was more common for free people of color to own more modest estates, or to work in urban trades as clerks, druggists, schoolmasters, or tavern keepers (Brathwaite 1971: 172). Many women of color owned and operated lodging houses on the island (Heuman 1981: 9).

A key element in the negotiation of this social structure was the planter class's ability to establish and maintain control of surplus production. This involved many social processes, including creating a social division of labor reinforced by a particularly violent form of racism expressed through cruel dehumanization, physical abuse, and denigration of enslaved workers of African descent. "A slave, being a dependent agent," wrote the West Indian planter Dr. David Collins in 1803, "must necessarily move by the will of another, which is incessantly exerted to control his own: hence the necessity of terror to coerce his obedience" (Collins 1811: 197). When Collins wrote these words in the early nineteenth century, he was describing a colonial state that had, for the better part of a century, prospered through the enslavement of hundreds of thousands of people.

Prior to the abolition of slavery, by far the greatest percentage of Jamaica's colonial population was comprised of enslaved Africans and their descendants; in colonial terms, this encompasses both the enslaved black population and those people of color who remained enslaved. Beginning in 1817, British West Indian planters were required to attest to the number of enslaved workers they held in bondage through what are known as the "slave returns;" it has thus been relatively easy to calculate the enslaved population of the island from 1817 forward. Using the slave return data, Barry Higman, the noted demographer of colonial Jamaica, has estimated that there were some 313,000 enslaved people on Jamaica in 1832 (Higman 1995: 16), of which about 90 percent were black and 10 percent people of color (Higman 1995: 142). According to his estimates, just less than half of these 313,000 souls (155,000) were enslaved on sugar estates, 45,000 were enslaved on coffee plantations, 40,000 on cattle pens, and 25,000 were enslaved in the urban centers as domestic servants, artisans, or in other occupations. The remainder of the enslaved population was distributed between minor staple production (e.g., cotton, pimento, tobacco), the wharves, or else were enslaved on "jobbing gangs," groups of enslaved workers whose owners leased them out to other planters for profit (Higman 1995: 16).

Enslavement was not an easy life. One of the very interesting and truly horrifying facts about the slave system in Jamaica is that the enslaved population never experienced what is called "natural increase" by demographers. Simply put, more people died annually than were born. Although measures were mandated by the British Parliament to ameliorate the conditions of slavery, enslaved workers were exposed to deadly diseases and infections, accidents, overwork, poor nutrition, and physical abuse. Contemporary observers, both those who opposed slavery and those who supported and defended it, commented on what we today would consider the violent mistreatment of the enslaved population, which undoubtedly contributed to Jamaica's demographic crisis.

For example, Dr. David Collins suggested to his fellow West Indian colonists that they abandon, or at least significantly curtail, the use of whips to discipline enslaved workers. Collins was concerned with preserving the population following the abolition of the African slave trade in 1807. He estimated that during the slave trade era, at least one-quarter of newly imported workers died within four years of arriving in the West Indies. He attributed this mortality to six causes: disease, change of climate, diet, labor, severity, and suicide. On the issue of diet, Collins remarks that little consideration was given to providing suitable diets for newly arrived captives, as they were not fed "what they were accustomed to eat before they came among us," but instead "what we have" (Collins 1811:51). Collins also complains that the food given was often not of good quality, and "the most frequent error in the feeding of new negroes is not giving them enough" (Collins 1811: 51). When addressing the issue of severity, Collins remarks about the whip, "too frequent use hath been made of this instrument; and that it is often employed to a degree which ... destroys their sensibility, and renders its further application of little avail" (Collins 1811:173). Edward Long (1774) noted that the eighteenth-century black code in Jamaica allowed as many as thirty-one lashes from the whip to be applied for offenses ranging from a slave hiring himself out for wages, to using poison to catch fish, to selling goods without permission from a slave owner. Later works suggest that as many as thirty-nine lashes could be inflicted by an overseer or proprietor, but more could be done only on the authority of a magistrate (Anonymous 1828). A slave could be put to death for practicing a religious tradition known as obeah, having unauthorized weapons in their possession, or attempting to desert the island by hiding on an outgoing ship (Long 1774a: 485–489). Thomas Thistlewood, in his diary, described punishments meted out to three slaves found guilty of theft from an estate; one was hanged and the other two had their faces mutilated by having their "ears cropped" "nostrils slit" and having their cheeks cut to produce scars (Hall 1989: 60).

Although much of this violence was sanctioned by the government of the island, individual overseers could, and would, often inflict cruel and vicious punishments on their own authority. Although it is difficult to determine how representative Thistlewood's punishments were, he did record multiple occasions in which he would have one enslaved person defecate or urinate into the mouth of another. To inflict greater pain following a whipping, Thistlewood was prone to "pickle" the victim of the beating, which he described as rubbing the fresh wounds with "salt pickle, lime juice & bird pepper" (Hall 1989: 72–73). Thistlewood also had an iron collar locked around the neck of at least one woman (Hall 1989: 175), a practice that was commonly used on Jamaica to humiliate and mark people who questioned the authority of the overseers. Writing in the late 1830s, Benjamin M'Mahon, a onetime bookkeeper and overseer in Jamaica, reported seeing the use of such "pothooks" on his very first day as a bookkeeper (M'Mahon 1839: 18). M'Mahon's memoir of his employment in Jamaica is filled with descriptions of floggings, sometimes so severe as to cause death. He also reports on the sexual abuse of enslaved children as young as 10 or 11 years old, and corroborates that it was fairly common practice to force punished slaves to eat their own excrement (M'Mahon 1839).

The maintenance of such an unjust and racist colonial system was complex. The planters developed a number of strategies to maintain order and discipline on the plantations. Clearly, corporal punishment was a key element in all of this; Collins notes that terror underlay the entire system. Thistlewood reported in his diaries that after a slave named Robin had led a mass escape from a plantation, not only was he hanged, but Thistlewood mounted his decapitated head on a pole as a warning to others who might challenge the authority of the plantation system. There were other more subtle means of maintaining order, however. For example, some enslaved men and women known as drivers were given the responsibility of managing the daily work of labor gangs, and were armed with cart whips and given the authority to flog any slave who lagged in their work or disobeyed orders. Drivers were often rewarded with material goods, larger and better houses in the villages, nice clothes, and better plots to grow provisions. White planters, particularly overseers and bookkeepers, often made sexual and romantic links with enslaved women, and although there was a clear imbalance in the power dynamics in such relationships, and rape and sexual abuse were unfortunately all too common, to characterize all such relationships as coercive or a form of rape underestimates the agency women exerted over their own sexual lives and the complexity of the social relations of production which shaped the social world of colonial Jamaica.

The social structure and complex relationships that developed between proprietors, attorneys, overseers, bookkeepers, whites, free people of color, and enslaved workers were products of the organization of plantation production, yet simultaneously worked to shape and reproduce the plantation mode of production. As we have seen, Marx imagined that any mode of production is structured by historically contextual interactions between the forces and relations of production; the social relationships we have explored would not exist outside of the context of the material realities of the plantation system.

The Forces of Production

The materials, tools, knowledge, and techniques used to transform raw materials into saleable commodities are collectively known as the forces of production (Marx 1992). Although human labor can be considered an element of the forces of production, the non-human elements of the forces of production, including land, tools, machinery, and infrastructure, are known as the means of production. The analysis of the means of production is a general goal of archaeological fieldwork, as the means of production tend to leave readable imprints on the archaeological record; this was the goal of a study I conducted in the Yallahs drainage of the Blue Mountains of eastern Jamaica, one of the primary coffee producing regions of the colonial West Indies (Delle 1996, 1998).

Plantation production required a variety of tools, techniques, and knowledge specific to the agriculture needs of tropical produce, as well as tools and technologies of more general application, including coopering (barrel

Figure 3.1. A stonemason's chisel found in situ at Marshall's Pen, a nineteenth-century coffee plantation. Enslaved masons would have used this tool to build and maintain stone structures on the plantation. Photograph by James A. Delle.

making), masonry, and carpentry for the construction and repair of plantation buildings and infrastructure, blacksmithing for the creation and repair of iron tools, transportation technologies for the movement of goods by water and by land, and animal husbandry to raise and care for beasts of burden (see Figure 3.1). Each of these activities required tools and training; each was an integral part of the plantation mode of production.

The techniques used specifically to produce coffee were a key factor in the development of the other means of production specific to Jamaican coffee plantations. Although there was some variation, the primary techniques used to produce coffee were generally similar throughout the island. After acquiring a parcel of undeveloped land, referred to in nineteenth century Jamaica as a "run," that land would need to be cleared for coffee production. This involved clearing dozens of acres of tropical hardwood forests with hand axes and saws; the felled trees were shaped into framing timbers, planks, and shingles for plantation buildings, burned into charcoal for local use, or exported as logwood. Once cleared, the ground would be developed for a series of uses, including coffee fields, known as "pieces," in which the coffee trees would be planted, provision grounds for growing food stuffs for the plantation

Figure 3.2. This tool, known as a socketed bill, was found in situ at Marshall's Pen. This tool would have been used to prune coffee trees. Wooden handles of various lengths would be inserted in the socket to enable enslaved workers to prune branches at various heights off the ground. Photo by James A. Delle.

work force, grass pieces for pasture and fodder for horses, mules, and cattle, residential quarters for the white plantation staff, industrial buildings for the processing and storage of coffee for export, and villages to house the enslaved workforce.

The economic purpose of a coffee plantation was to produce a profitable export crop, which in the case of coffee, quite literally grows on trees. In Jamaica, coffee seedlings would be raised in a sheltered nursery, and then planted in rows accessible for picking. The trees would bear fruit after three to five years, requiring careful pruning done primarily with hand tools (see Figure 3.2). After producing beautiful white flowers, coffee trees bear a red fruit known as a cherry; within the cherry are two seeds that, when processed properly, become coffee beans. Coffee cherries were picked by hand, with each coffee tree needing to be picked more than once per season, as the cherries on a given branch will not all ripen simultaneously; it was thus impossible to strip a branch of its entire fruit without wasting a number of unripe cherries (see Figure 3.3).

Once picked, the coffee fruit would be transformed into an exportable form, a process that required several steps. First, the thick skin of the

Figure 3.3. A branch of a coffee tree with fruit. The darker fruit is ready to pick; the lighter cherries need as much as several additional weeks before they can be picked. Photo by James A. Delle.

cherry needed to be removed, as did a white viscous material surrounding the beans, known as the coffee pulp. Jamaican planters preferred a wet process for pulping which including the use of a mill to break up the skin and pulp; the pulping mill, or "pulper," would separate the pulp and skin from the beans through the action of a perforated copper-sheathed cylinder. The resulting material was then placed in a suspension tank filled with water. The pulp would float to the surface while good beans would sink to the bottom. The pulpy waste product would be skimmed out of the tank, and the wet beans would be collected for curing; deficient beans that floated with the pulp, known as "triage," could be collected for internal use or local exchange.

After pulping, the wet beans would be cured or dried on a large drying platform known as a barbecue (see Figure 3.4). Once laid out, the beans would be turned several times to ensure thorough drying so as to prevent the growth of mold. While the beans were drying, the barbecues would be monitored to ensure the beans would not get soaked by rain. Should the barbecues be threatened by rain, the beans would either be moved into small shelters incorporated into the barbecue complex or else covered by tarpaulins (Laborie 1798; Lowndes 1807; Montieth 2002a, 2002b).

Figure 3.4a. Coffee beans drying on the barbecue at Moy Hall Plantation. This early-nineteenth-century coffee plantation was restored and brought back into production in the 1990s. Photo by James A. Delle.

Figure 3.4b. One of the barbecues at Marshall's Pen. This plantation has not produced coffee in any quantity since the 1840s. Photo by James A. Delle.

Figure 3.5. The long-disused wheel of the grinding mill at Marshall's Pen. Photo by James A. Delle.

The dried beans have a thin membrane called parchment, which is removed by a separate drying process, known as peeling or grinding. The beans would be placed in a grinding mill and a wooden wheel would be lightly turned over the beans to separate them from the dry parchment; once ground, the parchment waste would be winnowed from the beans either by hand or through a fanning mill (see Figure 3.5). The final stage in the process is the separation of beans into qualities. Inferior beans, including those damaged in process, were sold as triage in local markets or consumed on the estate. The majority of the high quality beans were shipped in bags or barrels to any one of the numerous wharves on the Jamaican coast. Fortunate plantations located on or near navigable rivers could send coffee to market by boat or canoe; it was far more common, however, for the coffee to be carried by mule train and by laborers. Once at a wharf or other transshipment point, the crop was consigned to merchants for transport and sale in the European markets.

Market-ready beans were known as "green" beans because of the slight greenish color of the processed coffee beans. Green coffee beans, when kept dry, are very stable and can be stored for several years without overly suffering. Roasting would not take place until point of sale purchases were made, as roasted beans lose their aroma and flavor quite quickly (Laborie 1798; Lowndes 1807; Montieth 2002b).

The means of production on a Jamaican coffee plantation thus included arable land suited for coffee production, a mill complex suited to both the wet process of pulping and the dry processes of grinding and fanning, drying platforms for the pulped beans, a sorting room, and storage facilities to hold the sorted beans prior to shipping. A variety of hand tools would also be required for coffee production, including axes and saws for felling trees while clearing coffee fields, hoes to weed the coffee trees, sharp tools for pruning trees, and baskets and bags for collecting coffee cherries as they were picked from the trees. The means of production would also include the housing required for overseers, bookkeepers, and the enslaved laborers, as well as the tools and knowledge to build and maintain these structures. Technologies required to distribute coffee to market can also be considered part of the means of production; enslaved laborers on plantations built roads within the estate boundaries, and each planter was required to pay a labor tax for maintaining the roads leading from enclaves of plantations to the wharves on the coast. Enslaved artisans on the plantations were skilled in these technologies, from making barrels for storage and transport of coffee beans, to building and maintaining carts, to knowing how to finesse mule trains down the sometimes treacherous mountain roads to the wharves.

Creating the means of production for coffee agriculture was a complex process by which proprietors would first acquire land appropriate for coffee production, survey and establish boundaries between plantations, and create internal divisions of space within each estate. This process required that proprietors and plantation managers arrange for the construction and maintenance of the various components of the means of production, including the clearing and planting of coffee fields and the construction of one or more mills for coffee processing, including the construction of cisterns and water tanks, plus aqueducts or mill races to bring water into the mill for the wet process of pulping, and to allow for the controlled outflow of wastewater. Pastures for working animals, or breeding stock in the case of mixed-use plantations, would also need to be cleared and planted with suitable grass. Although itinerant mill wrights, engineers, and surveyors could be employed by the planters to help organize and design construction projects, the bulk of the work was conducted by enslaved artisans and laborers.

Creating the means of production can sometimes involve transforming what exists in nature into a state that can be utilized to further transform nature into saleable commodities. Coffee plantations required that undifferentiated forest be transformed into privately held, bounded, and

Figure 3.6. The overseer's house at Mile Gulley, a nineteenth-century coffee plantation in the parish of Manchester. Photo by James A. Delle.

compartmentalized runs of land; this was simultaneously a material process through which land was patented and surveyed, and a cognitive process through which places were invented, given a shape, and named. The newly bounded upland forests were then further transformed into coffee fields and other spatial forms useful for coffee production. Once a run of land was defined as a plantation with coffee fields, provision grounds, grass pieces, and plantain walks established, the industrial infrastructure required for coffee production, including housing for the plantation staff, was constructed (see Figure 3.6). The most capital-intensive element of coffee plantation infrastructure was the pulping mill, which required specialized machinery imported from Great Britain, the construction of the means to power the machinery, the development of a mechanism to control the flow of water into and out of the mill, and the erection of a building to house the works.

Now that we have reviewed the nature of the social relations of production that existed under the plantation mode of production and examined the means of production required for coffee production, the question now turns to how people actually experienced the plantation mode of production. We thus now turn to a consideration of the division of labor that defined the specific role a given person would play in the production of coffee under the plantation mode of production.

The Division of Labor

In defining how modes of production were structured, Marx argued that the forces of production could be subdivided into objective forces and subjective forces; the former including the means of production and the latter a variety of socially constructed phenomena, including many forces that are difficult to interpret historically (including such things as the productive aptitude and talents of individual workers). More tangibly, the objective forces of production include strategies for training specific members of the work force to complete specific productive tasks, a process often referred to as the technical division of labor. It can thus be argued that the relations and forces of production converge in the division of labor structuring a mode of production.

The life experiences of people living under a mode of production are largely shaped by the roles they play in the organization of production; as productive tasks become increasingly specialized, the range of actions for workers becomes more and more constrained. Similarly, as the productive process becomes more complex, it is increasingly difficult for workers to control all of the means of production required to produce commodities for sale. As we have seen, one of the primary tenets of Marxism holds that social relationships are in large measure defined by one's position in the hierarchy of productive tasks. This hierarchy of tasks was defined by what Marx called the technical division of labor. The roles and social positions people held in a given society emerging from the technical division of labor are collectively called the social division of labor. The technical division of labor is considered to be part of the forces of production, as it is largely a mechanical division of the tasks needed to be performed as part of the productive process. The social division of labor, on the other hand, is a component of the relations of production, as status and wealth bestowed on individual people is directly correlated with the task they complete within the technical division of labor. In many modes of production, social categories are created or reinforced when members of defined groups are assigned to specific tasks within the technical division of labor. In the case of the plantation mode of production, for example, clearing forests and picking coffee were tasks assigned to enslaved laborers, who were people of African descent. Thus, the social division of labor that emerged was defined by enslavement and racialization of the population, and these categories of social relationship were tied to the specific manifestation of task specialization that emerged in eighteenth-century Jamaica.

As we will see, both the technical and social divisions of labor were based on more than a simple binary opposition between black and white,

African and European, or enslaved and free would allow. Nevertheless, the relationship between task specialization on plantations, and the people assigned to those tasks, played a primary role in the production and reproduction of the plantation mode of production.

The Technical Division of Labor

The technical division of labor is a key element in the organization of any mode of production. Modes of production can be characterized by varying levels of task specialization, which allows for the development of expertise in a specific set of tasks required in the productive process. In Marxist analysis the technical division of labor is considered to be part of the objective forces of production, objective in as much as the range of actions required to complete a specific task are specific but standardized, so can be learned and completed by anyone trained to carry out that task (Marx 1992). In terms of the plantation mode of production, the technical division of labor refers to the way tasks were divided up on the plantation and how specific roles within the labor force were defined. Because the technical division of labor is an objective force of production, this actually referred to the categorization of work, rather than the talents of any specific workers.

The technical division of coffee plantation labor can be interpreted from contemporary printed descriptions of plantation work as well as from the records kept by plantation bookkeepers. In *The Coffee Planter of Saint Domingo* (1798), an instructive treatise written for Jamaican planters by the Haitian émigré P. J. Laborie, the author provided Jamaican coffee planters with a model for the technical division of labor to be established for the enslaved population of a working coffee plantation. Laborie suggested that the labor force be composed of trained artisans, supervisors, and an unskilled labor force, which he calls the gang in general. According to Laborie, the artisan group should include carpenters, masons, and saddlers (Laborie 1798: 164). He also suggested that the unskilled labor force be divided into at least three work gangs. One would be assigned the specialized task of pruning coffee trees. Another gang, composed primarily of adolescents between the ages of 12 and 16, would complete lighter work such as weeding and picking coffee. The bulk of the heavy work was to be done by the third group, the "great gang" (Laborie 1798: 175).

In another treatise designed to instruct plantation managers, *The Jamaica Planter's Guide*, Thomas Roughley (1823) outlines a technical division of labor he thought most effective for the enslaved population of a Jamaican plantation. Roughley suggests that the plantation labor force be organized with a number of skilled and/or supervisory positions, including a head driver responsible for maintaining labor discipline among the field workers. Other supervisory positions recommended by Roughley include mule- and cattlemen, a head boiler to supervise the manufacture of sugar, and head carpenters, coopers, masons, coppersmiths, and watchmen, who should be rewarded with "a quart or two of good rum, some sugar, and now and then a dinner from the overseer's table" (Roughley 1823: 90–91). Roughley notes the importance of employing health care specialists, including hospital doctors, nurses, and midwives. The plantation would also require domestic servants responsible for cooking and cleaning for the white estate staff and proprietor, and would also sew and mend garments for unmarried overseers and bookkeepers.

Like Laborie, Roughly suggests that the labor force be divided into gangs. The strongest and hardest working people would compose the great gang. The second gang should contain weaker adults, nursing mothers, elderly people still capable of working, and adolescents. The third gang, which he also calls the "weeding gang," would be composed of working children, a corps of children from age 5 or 6 "forming the rising generation," in Roughley's words. Opposing common practice, Roughley warns against using children to cut and carry grass (such as that to be used for thatch or for animal fodder), as children were likely to become injured in this occupation (Roughley 1823: 102).

Jamaica plantation managers kept sometimes detailed records of the operations of the estates; a few of these records have survived into the twenty-first century. An analysis of the surviving records of Jamaican coffee plantations indicates that the technical division of labor described by both Laborie and Roughley was in force in early nineteenth-century Jamaica. Among those documents are plantation journals kept by the overseers and/or bookkeepers of Maryland Plantation in the Parish of St. Andrew, New Forest Plantation in the parish of Manchester, and Radnor Plantation in St. David. In addition to these journals, a detailed correspondence between the Earl of Balcarres (a Scottish nobleman and the absentee owner of several Jamaican plantations) and his attorneys in Kingston document the workings of three of his coffee estates, including Martins Hill and Marshall's Pen in Manchester, and Balcarres Plantation in St. George. Two of these six estates had enslaved populations near the 128-person average size for early-nineteenth-century Jamaica (Balcarres with 128 and Marshall's Pen with 116, although this latter number would significantly increase by the end of the 1820s), whereas the other four had somewhat larger enslaved populations (New Forest with 181, Radnor with 216, Martins Hill with 232, and Maryland with 320), but it should be noted that both Martins Hill and Maryland, the largest of the estates considered here, had cattle pens attached to the coffee plantations,

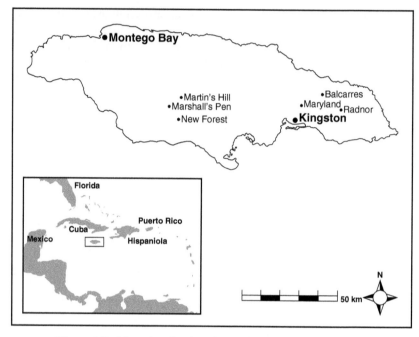

Figure 3.7. Map showing locations of coffee plantations noted in the text. Illustration courtesy of John Svatek.

which may in part explain the larger population of these two estates (see Figure 3.7)

The records of these six early-nineteenth-century coffee plantations indicate that each maintained a technical division of labor similar to that outlined by Roughley and Laborie. In each case, the work force was divided into specific occupation groups, including field work, artisan trades, domestic service, healthcare service, watchmen, and supervisory positions (e.g., drivers or head people). On average, approximately one-half of the population (49.2 percent with a standard deviation of 2.9 percent) were field workers; this percentage ranged but little with a low of 46.6 percent on Martins Hill and a high of 54.7 percent on Balcarres. Field workers on these coffee estates would engage in a variety of tasks from felling trees and clearing fields for coffee production, to picking coffee from the trees, to processing the coffee for export.

The second largest work category on coffee estates was the artisan group. Counted in this group were skilled workers who had learned a trade, including masons, carpenters, coopers, and sawyers. The construction and maintenance of the buildings and other industrial work on a coffee plantation required the skills these workers brought. Some estates would also employ people as wainwrights, who would build and maintain carts, and boatswains, who would move goods up and down navigable rivers and streams on small boats. On average, 6.6 percent (with a standard deviation of 2.2 percent) of the enslaved population of the six estates were artisans, with a low of 4.7 percent on Balcarres and a high of 9.5 percent on Marshall's Pen.

About an equal number of enslaved workers were employed as domestic servants, watchmen, and as stock keepers, with averages of 3.6 percent, 3.2 percent, and 3.1 percent, respectively. Domestic servants were engaged in a variety of tasks, including cooking and cleaning house, primarily in support of the white estate staff. The standard deviation from the average of 3.6 percent was a low 0.8 percent, meaning that each of the six plantations employed nearly the same percentage of people as domestics. Watchmen would be responsible for keeping an eye out for theft and vandalism of the coffee and other plantation stores, both in crop and in the warehouse. The number of watchmen employed likely reflected the incidents of theft, but this is difficult to corroborate; it can be said that some estates had a much higher rate of this kind of surveillance that did others. In our sample of six estates, Maryland had the largest number of watchmen (eighteen, or 6.5 percent of the enslaved population on the estate) followed closely by New Forest (ten, or 5.5 percent) and Radnor (seven, or 3.2 percent). The remaining three estates employed less than 2 percent of the population as watchmen, with Marshall's Pen having only one watchman for the estate, accounting for 0.9 percent of the enslaved population.

Each of the estates also employed people to mind the variety of species of animals on the estates, including poultry, swine, cattle, and horsekind (i.e., horses, donkeys, and mules). Stock keepers would be responsible not only for feeding the stock and moving them to and from pastures, but would also be skilled in veterinary care, and would treat minor injuries to the stock and attend the animals when they gave birth. Not surprisingly, New Forest and Martins Hill, both of which raised livestock for sale, had the highest number and percentage of stock keepers; more surprising is the relatively few number of people engaged in this activity. At New Forest, 12 of the 181 enslaved workers were stock keepers, accounting for 6.6 percent of the population; at Martins Hill, 10 of 232, or 4.3 percent of the people, were engaged in these activities. In contrast, 2.3 percent and 2.5 percent of the population at Balcarres and Maryland, respectively, were stock keepers; at Radnor, only 1.9 percent (4 people) and at Marshall's Pen only 0.9 percent (1 person) were stock keepers.

Health care was an important concern on tropical plantations. Plantation managers would arrange to have a white doctor visit the enslaved population at least once per year. Such doctors would make regular rounds through a number of plantations, being paid by the head for the enslaved workers they visited on each plantation. Despite (or perhaps, because of) these visits, many plantation populations contained health care experts among the enslaved. Most of the larger plantations would have a plantation hospital or "hot house," and some included a specialized quarantine house for people afflicted with yaws, a contagious disease that could leave a victim grossly disfigured and disabled. Many plantations had enslaved doctors and nurses who would minister to the sick and tend to wounds and infections caused by work-related (and other) accidents. Most plantations also counted one or more midwives among the enslaved population, who helped women through pregnancies and childbirth. Some plantations also employed enslaved nurses to care for infants and young children while their mothers were engaged with fieldwork or domestic chores for the estate staff. All of the coffee plantations in our sample, with the exception of New Forest, had between one and five health care specialists among the enslaved population: Balcarres had one, Martins Hill and Marshall's Pen each had two, and Maryland and Radnor each had five.

The Social Division of Labor

When task specialization emerges in a mode of production, the potential exists for this technical division of labor to become a basis both for how people working within these tasks are treated and who is given access to the various jobs. In Marxist terms, the objective technical division of labor is the material basis for the development of social identity through the negotiation of what is called the social division of labor (Marx 1992). Even within working communities, a person's status, position, and overall quality of life can be affected by the job to which they are assigned. Furthermore, in Marxist terms, the technical division of labor in large measure defines these categories. Under the plantation mode of production, the productive process was partitioned into the various tasks we have seen defined as the technical division of labor; who actually performed those specialized tasks led to a subjective division of labor, which nevertheless affected quality of life; this subjective division is what is known as the social division of labor.

The social division of labor on plantations was structured not only by task, but by age, gender, and racial and ethnic assignation. Although it was certainly in the planters' interests to enslave as many able bodied young adults as possible, the realities of life result in babies being born, small children growing up, and young adults growing older and, sometimes, becoming elderly. Plantation communities thus tended to have enslaved members both who were too young or inexperienced to do heavy field work or skilled labor and who were too old or infirm to contribute directly to the productive capacity of a plantation. The plantation work force was comprised of children, adolescents, adults, and the elderly; boys, girls, men, and women; Africans abducted to Jamaica and island-born Creoles; blacks, people of color, and whites.

Age Age is one of the primary structuring principles for most societies, and this was certainly true within the plantation mode of production. On Jamaican plantations, children would be introduced to the workforce at age 5 or 6 (Delle 2000, Higman 1995), often into a separate children's gang. In young adolescence, at about age 12, boys and girls would be elevated from the children's gang to the second gang; and when they reached young adulthood at about age 18, they would become part of the first or great gang, which was responsible for most of the heavy work to be done on a plantation. Although there was no predetermined retirement age for enslaved workers, many would become incapacitated by age, accident, or disease, often by their mid-40s; such people were listed by estate managers as invalids.

The percentage of non-working children at the six coffee plantations examined here was fairly consistent. On average, 17 percent of the plantations' population was composed of non-working children, with a standard deviation of 3.2 percent. Balcarres (15.6 percent), Maryland (16.9 percent), and Martins Hill (16.4 percent) had very comparable percentages, as did Marshall's Pen (20.7 percent) and Radnor (20.4 percent). New Forest, with 12.2 percent of the population being comprised of non-working children, had a relatively smaller percentage of non-working children.

The population of working children on all of the estates was very comparable, with an average of 8.7 percent and with a standard deviation of 1.4 percent. With the exception of Marshall's Pen (11.2 percent) each of the plantations had a population of working children comprising between 7.2 and 8.8 percent of the overall population. There was much greater variance in the size of the invalid population, with Marshall's Pen recording no invalids, and the Maryland plantation book reporting that a full 15.1 percent of the enslaved population was too old, too incapacitated, or too sick to work. Indeed, Maryland had a surprising number of elderly people enslaved on the estate in 1818: twenty-six people aged between 60 and 69; another twenty-six between the ages of 70 and 79; seven between 80 and 89; and four above the age of 90. Age did not necessarily bring incapacity, as several of these elders worked in the field, as cooks, and as artisans during their 60s while others continued to work as watchmen into their 70s.

Looking in more detail at the age structure of Marshall's Pen in the early 1830s gives us a more thorough understanding of the nature of how chronological age was intertwined with the social relations of production. By 1834, the population had tripled from its 1822 level through the purchase and consolidation of labor gangs from other estates. The Marshall's Pen community was divided into age grades through which people would pass; as plantation workers, in the eyes of the planters, members of these age grades were differentially assigned tasks and relative status on the plantation. When first born, any individual was defined as a child; this status was sometimes referred to in plantation documents as "unserviceable children," clearly reflecting that, from the perspective of plantation management, very small children performed no useful service in the organization of production. Members of this age grade were allowed some measure of freedom; no work was expected of them, and social rules separating the various racial groups and genders did not apply. In Jamaica, it was common for white and black boys and girls to socialize freely, generally under the supervision of a black or mulatto nurse; in Jamaica today, members of this age grade are still commonly referred to as "pick-neys" by the African-Jamaican population. At Marshall's Pen, individuals passed out of the "unserviceable children" or "pickney" age grade at age 6 or 7, when they would enter a more highly gendered age grade, which the planters sometimes referred to as "serviceable children;" young African-Jamaicans of this age grade would commonly be considered boys or girls. While a member of this age grade, children were expected to learn gendered behaviors, and social relationships between white, black, and colored children would become more formal and less free. The third age grade was what is commonly referred to as adolescence; boys and girls would usually enter adolescence by age 12; Jamaicans generally refer to members of this age grade as "youth." Adult status was attained between ages 18 and 19, and elder status attained between the ages of 45 and 60.

As was common on Jamaican estates, the age grade structure was used on Marshall's Pen to organize labor gangs and define working status on the plantation. According to the plantation records, the working population at Marshall's Pen assigned to fieldwork was divided into three labor gangs segregated by age grade. The youngest members of the population, the "unserviceable children" or "pickney" age grade (depending on one's frame of reference) were free from work, and minded by an older woman in her 40s or 50s. In 1834, 59-year-old Cecelia Manning minded the weaned children; Peggy Thompson (age 55) supervised nursing children in the field; Susanna Lindsay (age 49) attended the motherless children; and Ann White (age 48) and Jane Hall (age 45) minded children in the nursery. Collectively, these five women supervised forty-seven children aged between 4 months and 6 years old.

Although there was some overlap with the youngest age grade, most children aged 6 to 11 were assigned to the third – or children's – gang, responsible for light work around the plantation, like weeding coffee trees. In 1832, the third gang was composed of forty-three children aged between 6 and 13 years (five 6-year-olds, two 7-year-olds, eleven 8-year-olds, eleven 9-year-olds, seven 10-year-olds, four 11-year-olds, one 12-year-old, and two 13-year-olds). At the age of 11 or 12, most members of the third age grade moved into the second or small gang, where they would work alongside several adults. While in this age grade, gender-specific tasks would reinforce emerging gender identities. For example, while in this age grade, Frances Adams and Peggy Powell became "house girls" or domestics, whereas Joe Logan and William Learmond became apprentice carpenters.

At age 17 or 18, able-bodied people were assigned to the great gang, where they would do the heaviest plantation work, so long as they remained healthy, until their late 40s or 50s. There was no specific age at which elders "retired;" those too infirm or old to work were defined by the crass descriptor of "invalid." In 1834, of the 342 people enslaved at Marshall's Pen, 20 people over the age of 39 were defined as invalids and thus were not assigned work tasks on the estate; these included one woman in her late 30s, six women and two men in their 40s, three women and one man in their 50s, five women and one man in their 60s, and the 86-year-old John Noble, by far the oldest member of the community. Some elders were assigned lighter tasks when they reached their 40s. Older men would become watchmen, and older women would mind small children while their mothers worked in the fields or were cooks for the plantation community.

Gender Although it may seem counterintuitive, the social division of labor on Jamaican coffee plantations was organized such that the majority of field labor was conducted by women. The plantation records of five of the six plantations indicate that the majority of field workers were women or girls (Radnor, 56 percent; Maryland Plantation, 57 percent; New Forest, 58 percent; Balcarres, 64 percent; and Martins Hill, 67 percent). At Marshall's Pen the genders were equally split. Although the numbers are quite smaller, a similar trend can be observed for domestic service at each estate; at both Maryland and New Forest, there were seven female and two male domestics; at Marshall's Pen and Martins Hill the ratios were 3 to 1 and 6 to 1, respectively; Balcarres Plantation employed only one domestic servant who was a woman. At each of the plantations, including Marshall's Pen, there were a greater number of exclusively male occupations. Cumulatively, eighty-two artisans were identified on the six plantations, including blacksmiths, masons, coopers, saddlers, carpenters, and sawyers. All eighty-two were male. Similarly, all forty-five watchmen were male, and twenty-nine of the thirty-six stock keepers were male, with the women generally being assigned to tend fowl while the men tended the breeding and working stock on the estates. Health care and cooking were two occupations that tended to be heavily female. Between the six plantations, eighteen women were identified as midwifes, doctresses, hospital attendants, or nurses, though this last category likely included women tending to young children rather than the sick. Nevertheless, most women born on or purchased by coffee plantations could expect to spend much of their lives doing manual labor in the fields, as 403 of the 474 able-bodied working women and girls on the six plantations in the 1820s, 85 percent of the females, were field laborers. In contrast, only 63 percent of the able males were field laborers, meaning that more than one in three working men were doing something other than manual labor.

Race The division of the world's peoples into taxonomic categories based on physical traits led to the creation of what we now call race and racism. In early-nineteenth-century Jamaica, racial assignation was based on the genealogical distance one had from "whiteness." The terms "negro" and "black" were used to describe a person solely descended from African ancestors; people of mixed African and European heritage were racially defined as "mulatto" (one white parent, one black parent), "sambo" (one mulatto parent, one black parent), "quadroon" (one white parent, one mulatto parent), "mustee" or "mestee" (one white parent, one quadroon parent), "mustifini (one white parent, one mustee parent), "quintroon" (one white parent, one mustifini parent), and "octaroon" (one white parent, one quintroon parent); the child of a white man and octaroon woman was considered legally white. In theory at least, the British West Indian racial structure recognized eight races of African-descent people, regardless of their perceived ethnicity, as well as a variety of other racial groups, including whites, coolies (South Asians), Chinese, and Indians (indigenous people, not those from the subcontinent). John Stewart described the features of women of these various racial groups: "Quadroon and Mestee females are comely ... as they partake chiefly of the European feature; but the Mulattos and Sambos ... retain something of their thick lips and flat noses. ... As for the Africans, their ideas of beauty in the human countenance are almost the reverse of those of an European" (Stewart 1808: 304). This racialized taxonomy was a crucial element used to define the social hierarchy of colonial Jamaica.

This racial hierarchy was clearly evident at Marshall's Pen and Martin's Hill. In 1825, Balcarres's agents forwarded him a combined list of all those enslaved at these two plantations. This so-called valuation list identified people by name, age, "colour," whether African or Creole, occupation, and gender. Of the 441 people enslaved on these two plantations, the vast majority (401) was identified as black; eighteen were identified as mulatto, two as quadroon, fifteen as sambo, and one 18-year-old woman simply as "coloured." Racial assignation had a real effect on the lives of the people. Although a number of blacks (74) held skilled positions (e.g., driver, cooper, mason, midwife, doctress, cook) or were assigned lighter duties (house servants, cattleman, penkeeper, watchman, fowl keeper), the majority, 257, were field hands; the remaining people were either young children or aged or infirm. Thus, of the 351 able-bodied workers recognized as black, 73 percent were field workers. In contrast, none of the eighteen mulattos were field hands; of the seven adults assigned to this category, one was a carpenter, one a stableman, one a mason, three were house servants, and one was sick with yaws. Of those fifteen defined as sambo, one was a driver, one a cattleman, one a house servant, one a penkeeper, five were children, and six – less than half – were field hands. Both quadroons were younger than the age of three and thus had not yet been assigned duties on the plantations.

It should be remembered that of these various racial assignations, mulattos and quadroons were recognized as the children of white men, most likely the estate staff attached to Marshalls' Pen and Martin's Hill, whereas sambos were the children of a mulatto and a black. Although it was often assumed that the white parent would predominantly be male, Hilary Beckles has noted that census data from early-eighteenth-century Barbados suggests that white women were sometimes the mothers of mulattos and quadroons (Beckles 1995: 133), though this was probably more likely to happen in towns and cities than on estates.

In Jamaica, the process of racialization was complex. In the eighteenth century, Jamaican planters used cultural differences to further segment the racialized population of enslaved workers. On one level, the planters recognized a distinction between African-born and Caribbean-born slaves. Those who were transported directly from Africa were sometimes assigned specific ethnic designations, whereas Caribbean-born slaves were universally classified as "Creoles" (Delle 2000b). In the minds of at least some of the white colonial elites, particular ethnic groups were prone to specific character traits that defined a person's usefulness to a plantation. That usefulness was manifested in the occupations to which people would be put to work on the plantation, as supervisors (drivers), field hands, domestics, or artisans. However, this process of racial segmentation became obsolete following the 1807 abolition of the (legal) African slave trade.

Of the six plantations considered here, only Marshall's Pen kept records ascribing specific ethnicities to members of the enslaved labor force. In 1814, all of the adults at Marshall's Pen (over the age of 14) were African-born, and recognized as either "Eboe," "Moco," or "Mungola." These ethnic assignations referred generally to the slave port from whence the captives were originally obtained in Africa. The West Indian historian Bryan Edwards, for example, relates that the term "Eboe" refers to Africans transported from the Bight of Benin, an area encompassing "300 English leagues [900 miles] of which the interior countries are unknown, even by name, to Europeans" (Edwards 1810: 280–281; Delle 2000b). The missionary James Phillippo noted that the "tribes" or "nations" from which captives were taken included the "Mandigoes, the Foulahs, and others from the banks of the Senegal, the Gambia, and the Rio Grande; the Whidahs, or Papaws, the Eboes, the Congoes, the Angolas, the Coromantees, and the Mocoes, from Upper and Lower Guinea" (Phillippo 1843: 239). Of these groups, the "Mandigoes, the Whidahs, and the Congoes, are said, in general, to have been docile, civil, obliging, and peaceable. ... Eboes are described as crafty, frugal, disputative, and avaricious. ... Coromantees ... the tribe that had generally been at the head of all insurrections" (Phillippo 1843: 239–240).

Although the ethnic markers applied to the captive Africans may have had little to do with their actual tribal or national affiliations, Europeans projected physical and personality characteristics onto these groups, in effect creating a racialized hierarchy to rationalize the social order of Jamaican slavery; numerous contemporary observers suggested that members of these assumed groups were better suited for particular kinds of plantation work (e.g., Edwards 1810; Laborie 1798; Long 1774; Stewart 1808: 235–236; see Delle 2000b for a more detailed discussion). For example, Dr. David Collins (1803) characterized the "Cormarantins" and other people originating on the Gold Coast as warlike and prone to "bringing with them into slavery lofty ideas of independence ... [the] history of Jamaica exhibits very sanguinary examples of that disposition" (Collins 1811: 35). Collins noted that the "negroes from Senegal are a handsome race of people, in features resembling the whites. ... They are excellent for the care of cattle and horses, and for domestic service" (Collins 1811: 36). He believed the group called "Congos" to be "a handsome race of Africans, generally very black. ... [T]hey make good domestic servants and tradesmen" (Collins 1811: 37). Collins described the "Mandingos" as "much less ferocious than the Minna and Gold-coast negroes. ... Being reared in the habits of indolence ... though unfit for the labors of the field, they may be employed as watchmen" (Collins 1811: 37). He characterized the "Ebbos, and Ebbo-bees, commonly called Mocos" as "turbulent, stubborn, and much addicted to suicide; yet they are hardy and suscep- tible of labor, the women in particular" (Collins 1811: 37).

The managers of Marshall's Pen used this ethnic taxonomy to identify the ethnicity of the enslaved population, which was apparently used to determine the occupations of the various members of the community, and their overall value to the estate. Whereas members of each of the identified ethnic groups worked as field hands, both drivers were listed as "Eboe," and four of the five artisans were defined as "Mungola," the sole exception being Stephen, a 28-year-old "Moco" sawyer.

The social relations of production on early-nineteenth-century Jamaican coffee plantations were thus structured through the division of the enslaved population into social categories based on age, gender, race, and ethnicity. It was expected that enslaved people would work for the estates to which they were attached from early childhood, as young as 5 or 6. The enslaved community was not homogenous, and the work they performed was varied. Some people became skilled artisans and thus spent much of their working lives using their hands and minds to design, build, and repair houses, mills, water works, and other elements of the built environment of the plantation world. Other people spent much of their time as house servants, cooking, cleaning, and keeping house for the planters, overseers, and bookkeepers, whereas the majority of people toiled in the fields clearing land, planting and caring for coffee trees, and picking and processing coffee. The division of labor was not random; the socially defining concepts of age, gender, ethnicity, and race structured the daily lives of the population, who were, of course, enslaved. As slaves, individual people could express only limited agency in defining how they would work and what the conditions of their employment would be, and, given the violence inherent in the slavery system, were subject to humil- iating punishments for disobedience, which sometimes resulted in death.

Landscapes of the Plantation Mode of Production

One of the most difficult tasks in archaeology is to link the material record of the past with the behaviors that created that record. Over the past several decades, a virtual subfield within archaeology has been dedicated to studying what is called "Middle Range Theory," a contextually defined set of propositions that can be used to explain how the archaeological record was formed. Middle-range theorists can focus on both site formation processes (that is, the natural and human phenomena that combined to shape an archaeological site over time), and the converse (that is, the processes through which the material world shaped human behavior).

Marxian approaches to the past have, sometimes justifiably, been criticized for being normative or merely assuming that the material world shapes other elements of human culture. These critiques largely focus on the ambiguity of the relationship between the means of production and the relations of production, particularly how the material world influences the social rules that shape human relationships.

One of the more useful concepts used to bridge the gap between the means and relations of production was developed by the French sociologist Pierre Bourdieu. In defining what he refers to as a "theory of practice," Bourdieu introduced the concept of "habitus" (Bourdieu 1977). As we briefly reviewed in Chapter 1, habitus is a social process by which behavioral dispositions are formed within individuals as a result of their constant interaction with their social and physical environment – that is, with the means and relations of production. These dispositions in turn structure the way an individual experiences the material and social world, and although actions and behaviors might be constrained by the structures of society defining habitus, each individual has the capacity to create new action within the perceived range of the possible. In exploring the habitus of plantation landscapes, we can get a better idea of how behaviors were constrained, and how the material and social worlds are interrelated.

In our discussion of the means of production, we have considered the various kinds of buildings and other elements of plantation infrastructure that were required by Jamaican coffee planters to produce their export commodity; however, we have not yet touched on how these various elements of the means of production were related to each other. Buildings, machines, coffee fields, and villages did not independently float in space, but were connected physically and cognitively. The network of spaces and objects that tied the various elements of the plantation infrastructure together is what we can call the plantation landscape. Buildings, roads, bridges, coffee fields, provision grounds, slave villages, and overseers' houses were connected together into a unified spatial phenomenon, but one that was experienced differently by the various people who lived, worked, and were bound together within the plantation landscape. It is by examining how the landscapes tied the material and social together – the way that the forces and relations of production were linked – that we can understand how the mode of production operated to create the habitus of coffee plantation landscapes (Delle 2008, 2009).

Because they occupied different positions within their social structure, planters and enslaved workers perceived and experienced the material and social realities of coffee plantations' landscapes differently. The planter class that designed the estate landscapes actively constructed plantation spaces – or more accurately, had enslaved workers create the plantation spaces according to the planters' designs – as an active part of their strategy to control the lives and labor of enslaved workers and thus maximize their ability to accumulate surplus value from the production of plantation commodities. Similarly, those who were enslaved within these landscapes created social meanings of their own, sometimes quite different from those anticipated by the planters when they designed the landscapes.

In the mid-1990s, I archaeologically investigated a series of abandoned coffee estates in the drainage of the Yallahs River in the Blue Mountains of Jamaica with the intention of understanding how the creation of physical space within the landscapes worked to shape relationships between people who lived and worked there. Among the plantations I had the chance to explore were two estates known as Clydesdale and Sherwood Forest. The archaeological evidence of the plantation landscapes of Sherwood Forest and Clydesdale indicates that maximizing panoptic viewscapes over the plantation villages and industrial works was a key element of plantation landscape design. Even a cursory examination of the layout of Blue Mountain coffee plantations clearly indicates that the overseers' houses were a central element of the plantation landscape and served to bind the forces and relations of production together.

Overseer's houses were a key component of the plantation landscape and were frequently tied directly to the productive spaces of the plantation. For example, the Clydesdale overseer's house was located within the industrial complex of the plantation. This is a two-story building. There is no interior stairwell connecting the two stories, however, suggesting that the spaces of the two stories were used for separate purposes; the only access to the second story is an external staircase, originally constructed of wood. The upper story is finished, suggesting that this area was the domestic space of the overseer, where the lower story is not finished, suggesting that this area was used for either the storage of tools and supplies or the storage of coffee (see Figure 3.8).

The upper story is divided into three rooms with a second floor veranda. It is likely that the largest of the three rooms served as a social area in which the overseer would entertain guests and possibly those slaves that had business to discuss with him. One of the smaller rooms was probably a bedroom for the overseer and his wife (if he had one). The second

Figure 3.8. The overseer's house at Clydesdale Plantation. The boarded area was an open veranda in the nineteenth century. Photo by James A. Delle.

bedroom may have been used by their children or perhaps another member of the white estate staff. The veranda overlooks the coffee works, allowing the overseer the ability to supervise the pulping and drying of coffee without having to leave his house. The walls of this structure are cut stone that is two feet thick. Clearly, the overseer had the ability to shut himself and his family into this structure with a significant buffer between them, the elements, and the enslaved workers. With the exterior stairway the only access to the domestic quarters of the upper story, the overseer had a virtually impenetrable fortress.

It has long been thought that the majority of enslaved plantation workers lived in nucleated villages located on the estates to which they were attached. Although the internal arrangement of plantation villages will be addressed in more detail in Chapter 5, the spatial relationship of the village to the other elements of the plantation infrastructure is worth considering here. From the perspective of the planters, villages were a necessary component of plantation infrastructure. Composed of numerous small houses, many villages were abandoned following the abolition of slavery, whereas others developed into towns or villages that are still occupied. In the former case, the small houses located in the villages

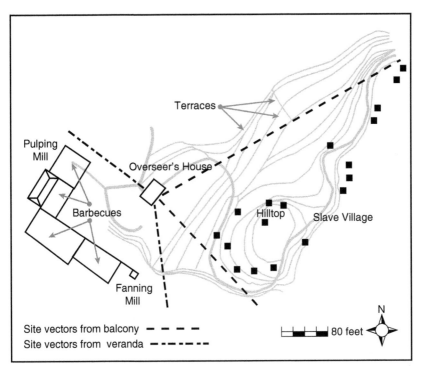

Figure 3.9. The plantation landscape of Clydesdale Plantation. Illustration courtesy of John Svatek.

have become part of the archaeological record and tend to exist now as scatters of artifacts and construction debris. In the latter case, few of the eighteenth- or nineteenth-century houses still exist, having been rebuilt and replaced over the decades.

For Clydesdale, given the superior preservation of the plantation's buildings and the extent of its cartographic record, it is possible to create a composite map that can be used to interpret the plantation landscape (see Figure 3.9). The overseer's house featured two surveillance positions. The first was the entrance door, which probably had a small landing at the top of a wooden stair. From this point, the overseer could monitor the slave village, which was located uphill from the house, within the viewscape of this position. The paths from the village to both the coffee fields and the industrial works passed directly by this point. Thus, without leaving the material confines of his house, the overseer could survey the domestic quarters of the workers and supervise the morning procession to work as the laborers passed below him on their way to the fields and mill.

Figure 3.10. The sprawling overseers house/mill complex at Sherwood Forest, viewed from the site of the slave village. Photo by James A. Delle.

The second surveillance point was the veranda of the overseer's house. The coffee works and barbecues were located downhill and within the viewscape of this vantage point, from which the overseer could supervise the coffee works and any activity occurring on the barbecues. During those times at which the overseer wanted to exert the greatest measure of control over the workers, he could practice panoptic surveillance over the population. This method of social control relied equally on the direct observation of the watcher and on creating the perception that the workers were being constantly observed, whether the overseer was watching them directly or not. By locating the overseer's house in such a way that the overseer could survey both the village and works from the veranda, or even by simply gazing out of one of the house's windows, the workers could never be entirely sure when they were being watched. The purpose behind the construction of this landscape was the construction of an internalized discipline in the work force; the logic of panopticism held that the workers would cooperate if they thought there were a possibility that their behavior at any given moment was under scrutiny, and that severe corporal punishment could be meted out to them if they were seen to be breaking the overseer's rules (Foucault 1979).

A similar spatiality existed at Sherwood Forest (see Figure 3.10). The original pulping mill at Sherwood Forest was located in the overseer's

Figure 3.11. The exterior wall of the original pulping mill/overseer's house at Sherwood Forest. This wall now serves as part of the foundation for the later house. Photo by James A. Delle.

house (see Figure 3.11). The mill was housed in one room of this structure, and the overseer occupied the other. Like the mills at Clydesdale, Sherwood Forest's pulping mill was water-powered. Sherwood Forest, however, is not situated *below* a river, but is instead located *above* the Negro River. To compensate for the lack of river-fed water power, the mill complex is attached to a spring-fed cistern, which serves as a sort of "mill pond." During the pulping process, water from the cistern was channeled to the mill by means of a small aqueduct, which survives today, but is not functional.

The barbecues at Sherwood Forest are terraced into a hill side (see Figure 3.12). Above the terraced barbecues is a series of smaller terraces which are currently used as a coffee nursery, as the current owner of the estate has recently reintroduced coffee production. It is possible that this is the original purpose of these terraces, as coffee plants require careful nurturing for several years before they can be transplanted into the coffee fields. It is likely that each plantation had some kind of nursery facility.

The overseer's house at Sherwood Forest also survives into the twenty-first century. This particular structure exhibits two phases of construction, with the older house actually serving as part of the foundation for the later

Figure 3.12. The barbecues at Sherwood Forest. In the early nineteenth century, the overseer would walk directly onto this barbecue from his veranda. Photo by James A. Delle.

house. As was the case with Clydesdale, the earlier overseer's house is a relatively small structure built with massive stone walls. This structure is divided into two rooms; unlike the overseer's house at Clydesdale, the one at Sherwood Forest contained the domestic space of the overseer as well as the pulping mill. In this case, the overseer would be in direct contact with the first stage of the industrial processing of coffee. The other key architectural feature of this building is a veranda, oriented toward the barbecues. From this vantage point, the overseer would have the capability to be in direct surveillance of the drying beans. At Sherwood Forest, the domestic space of the overseer, at least during the first phase of the plantation's existence, was inseparable from the space of production (see Figure 3.13).

Although no cartographic evidence for the village could be found for Sherwood Forest, an archaeological survey conducted in 1998 confirmed the location of the village. It is likely that the village occupied about three acres of land, and contained between fifteen and twenty-five houses (see Higman 1986).

The plantation landscape at Sherwood Forest, as was the case at Clydesdale, was designed to create a spatiality of control. The original

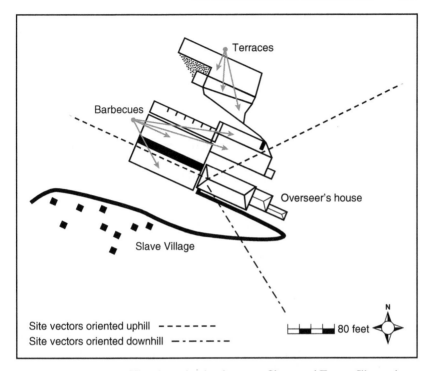

Figure 3.13. The plantation landscape at Sherwood Forest. Illustration courtesy of John Svatek.

overseer's house at this estate was constructed very similarly to the Clydesdale house. From the side entrance to the house, the overseer had a vantage point from which he could survey the flats below the coffee works, where archaeological testing confirmed the village had once been located. As was also the case with Clydesdale, the original overseer's house at Sherwood Forest was massively built with twenty-one-inch thick stone walls. A veranda provided the overseer with a southern view encompassing the coffee barbecues, and an eighteen-inch thick interior wall separated the overseer's room from the pulping mill. Although contained within an imposing fortress-like structure, as long as he was in his room or on his veranda, the overseer could directly supervise the production of coffee. From the veranda, the overseer could monitor the coffee crop as it dried, and – from his room – he could watch the coffee as it was pulped and channeled to the barbecues. This spatial arrangement created an intensive capacity for surveillance over production, while simultaneously socially and physically segregating the overseer from the work force (see Figure 3.13).

The overseer could also view the slave village from the veranda of his house. The coffee works and barbecues were located downhill and within the viewscape of this vantage point. Thus, from the comfort of his veranda, the overseer could supervise the coffee works, and any activity occurring on the barbecues. During those times when the overseer wanted to exert the greatest measure of control over the workers, he could practice panoptic surveillance over the population in the village. By locating the overseer's house in such a way that the overseer could be surveying the village and works from the veranda, or even by gazing out of one of the house's windows, the workers could never be entirely sure whether they were being watched. The purpose behind the construction of this spatiality was the construction of discipline in the workforce; the logic of the panopticon dictated that the workers would cooperate if they thought they were being watched. Through this mechanism, the means of production – that is, the actual physical layout of the plantation – influenced behavior among the enslaved, and thus linked the forces and relations of production into a material and social whole.

Conclusion

The production of agricultural commodities on colonial plantations resulted in the construction of material and social realities that defined how landscapes were built and lived; these plantations landscapes were in turn created to produce export commodities for European markets. Unlike sugar, tea, and tobacco, however, coffee was never consumed in great quantities in Great Britain; at least not as in great a quantity as tea. Nevertheless, by the turn of the nineteenth century, there was a thriving coffee industry in the British West Indies, most notably in Dominica and Jamaica. If, as the historian S. D. Smith argues (Smith 1996), the consumption of coffee in Great Britain remained stagnant until the middle of the nineteenth century, how can one account for the rapid rise and seeming success of coffee planters in pre-emancipation Jamaica?

The answer lies in two places. First, according to Smith's research on the history of coffee consumption in Great Britain, much of the coffee crop that was imported into British ports was reexported to continental Europe, where there was a much greater market for coffee than there was in England (Smith 1996). Prior to 1790, the largest suppliers to the European markets were the planters of the French Antilles, notably the colony of St. Domingue, which was the world's leading exporter of both sugar and coffee in the late 1780s (Geggus 1993). When the Haitian revolution broke out, the export of plantation commodities from the erstwhile colony of St. Domingue came to a screeching halt. The British, having a reexport system already in place, were more than happy to fill the void left by the destruction of the St. Domingue coffee economy. Jamaican coffee planters were able to step into the breach relatively quickly, as Jamaica coffee could fulfill the needs of European coffee drinkers when St. Domingue coffee could not.

Second, because coffee grows best in tropical highlands and thus did not compete directly with sugar for land use in Jamaica, and because coffee plantations require a relatively low initial investment, many would-be planters eagerly invested in coffee production on lands that had not previously been developed for export production. At the turn of the nineteenth century, the number of monocrop coffee plantations sky-rocketed in the highland parishes. The Jamaican historian Kathleen Montieth has calculated that there was virtually no coffee sector in the Jamaican economy prior to 1790. By 1799, a rapid escalation of coffee production resulted in there being 519 coffee plantations on the island; by 1808, there were more than 600 (Montieth 1991: 34–35; Shepherd and Montieth 2002a; see also Delle 1996: 201–208 and Delle 1998). New to the production of coffee, Jamaican planters adapted the existing planta-tion mode of production, which had been thoroughly developed for the production of sugar, to the requirements of coffee cultivation.

Unlike sugar cane, which needs to be replanted each year and produces best on coastal lowlands, coffee grows on trees, which can bear for years and thrive in cool, humid, tropical highlands. Nevertheless, despite these significant differences in the ecology of crop production, Jamaican coffee planters were closely tied into the existing economic and social structures of the island. When coffee production was introduced, it was not intro-duced into an historical vacuum; planters thus adapted the existing planta-tion mode of production that had developed primarily in the sugar industry to the physical and social realities of highland tree husbandry. Although different in many ways from sugar production, coffee produc-tion was organized through the development of a plantation mode of production. The forces of production, like the relations of production, were thus similar in their organization to those developed for sugar production.

The plantation mode of production in operation in Jamaica at the turn of the nineteenth century was complex. It was a web of social relations that defined the nature of class and gender relations, structured relationships between people of various social standings within the hierarchy of the island, and, more than anything, defined who would collect the surplus value produced on the coffee plantations of Jamaica.

Because the mode of production was dependent on the brutal use of enslaved labor to work the land, it was by its nature unstable. Plantation theorists, as well as the actual planters on the ground, developed a series of strategies to ensure that the mode of production would be reproduced from year to year and generation to generation. The key to this for the planter class was to maintain control over the labor force. Violence was commonly used to terrify people into subservience, but other more subtle strategies were employed, including the creation of landscapes within plantations that allowed planters to create and maintain systems of surveillance over the labor force, surveillance that was designed to maintain order, if not full control, over the lives of the enslaved.

To maintain this system, the planters needed to cooperate with each other. It is to the nature of this cooperation – that is, the ways that the various planters were able to define and defend their common interest – that we now turn.

4   A Class for Itself: Regional Landscapes
of the Planter Class

One of the distinguishing characteristics of Marxist analysis is the contention that social class is the primary structuring principle of capitalist society (Marx 1902, 1976, 1992; Wurst 2006). In Marxian thinking, a social class is a group of individuals whose solidarity emerges from their shared economic interest, which is defined by their collective relationship to the means of production. Understanding how economic structures work, and how certain classes benefit from those structures, leads to the development of what is called class consciousness, an understanding of that shared economic interest (Giddens 1973; Lukacs 1972). When members of a group are able to fully develop class consciousness, they are able to use their collective power to organize society to benefit their mutual interest. In so doing, a ruling class can create and control social, political, economic, and military structures to advance and protect their interests (Patterson 1991). Because other social classes with sometimes conflicting interests do exist, the control over social and economic worlds is often a contested process; thus the maintenance of a capitalist social formation will often require the use of force to simultaneously suppress conflicting interests while advancing the interests of the ruling class (Paynter 1989).

The processes of class formation have long been a concern of archaeologists (e.g., Gailey and Patterson 1988; Kohl 1987; Lull and Miko 2011; Patterson 1988). Because archaeologists believe that the material world plays a key part in shaping the social world, it follows that material culture is intertwined into the definition of social class. In historical archaeology the study of these phenomena has often been framed in terms of social status; however, the traditional scope of historical archaeological investigation, which usually focuses on the scale of the individual household, precludes the analysis of the kinds of collective action that result in and from the formation of class consciousness, although there have been some notable exceptions (e.g., Saitta 2007). To complicate matters, some historical archaeologists have misunderstood the concept of "false consciousness" and assume that the formation of class distinction and privilege means that members of subordinate classes uncritically accept the totalizing social formations imposed on them (Hicks and Horning 2006; Wilkie and Bartoy 2000). Rather than a process of duping the subaltern classes, the concept of false consciousness refers to the inability of a social class to understand the totality of the economic system that supports – or suppresses – their class interests. Such historical misconceptions can lead members of social classes to inadvertently act against their own interests by, for example, failing to reform laws regulating banking, securities exchange, and other manifestations of capital flow (as was the case in the Stock Market crash of 1929), or the irrational protection of tax privileges (as was the case in prerevolutionary France, where the aristocracy clung to their traditional non-taxable status, despite a growing fiscal crisis). Ruling classes themselves can fall victim to social and economic crisis when they fail to understand the relationships existing between fiscal reality and socially created privilege, and thus fall victim to false consciousness.

The development of class consciousness is a manifestation of both social and material phenomena. Material culture is often used to symbolically mark class status, as through the creation, purchase, and use of "status symbols." Such symbols can be physical objects, like expensive houses, particular styles of clothing or other personal adornment, automobiles, or works of art, that only members of elite classes can afford to purchase, and thus become markers of class status. Equally important is mastery of the knowledge of how to properly use expensive objects, like complicated tea settings or complex sets of cutlery. The negotiation of class status and the development of class consciousness are also shaped by differential experiences of space and landscape (Delle 1999; Harvey 2006a, 2006b; Lefebvre 1991). On the coarsest level, class segregation of space, that is the isolation or controlled use of specific spaces, reinforces class hierarchies. The existence of gated communities, restricted clubs, private beaches, debutante balls, and servants' entrances and quarters in large houses, exemplify this basic use of the built environment to simultaneously create social separation based on class status, and to promote the development of social bonds and class consciousness between members of the "in" group.

In colonial Jamaica, a very well-defined class consciousness developed among the members of the planter class, consisting primarily of white proprietors, merchants, attorneys, and in many cases, overseers and book-keepers (Higman 2005). Although some free people of color "with special privileges" were able to assimilate into the planter class, white racial solidarity was a social phenomenon that buttressed class status in Jamaica (Burnard 2004). Although there was clearly a great difference in wealth between the largest planter and the meanest overseer, they shared both common interests and knowledge of those interests, and may well have felt more affinity to each other than to members of the working class, primarily of African descent, whom they commonly degraded in servile bondage.

This chapter explores the nature of class consciousness in early-nineteenth-century Jamaica, how race and racialization played a component role in the definition and maintenance of class distinction, and how the built environment on the regional scale worked to create and maintain class consciousness among the coffee planters of an upland valley in the Parish of St. David.

The Development of Class Consciousness in Colonial Jamaica

Although it may sound counterintuitive to describe a racially structured society like colonial Jamaica as being primarily structured by social class, racialization and class hierarchy are not contradictory forces (Orser 2007, 2012). The organization of production in early-nineteenth-century Jamaica was dependent on the objectification of human beings as, essentially, part of the means of production; and planters bought and sold people, valuing them as capital assets. In so doing, Jamaican planters created a working class defined not by the ability to sell labor power on a theoretically free and open market, but by amalgamating identities of African and African-descent people into a small number of races, defined in the opening decades of the nineteenth century as "colors." The planters created distinct social categories defined by social rules that enabled white colonials to compel captives to work for them, on punishment of death for "insolence." In creating a "negro" or "black" race, the planters simultaneously created a "white" race. In the context of early nineteenth century Jamaica, this process of racialization not only created systems of symbolic definition of self, defined by physical characteristics, but used that system to maintain a class-based social structure in which access to the control of the forces of production was mediated by the definition of legal "whiteness" (Burnard 2004).

The process of correlating identity to specific roles within the cycle of agricultural production and distribution led to the development of class consciousness among the white planters. According to American sociologist C. Wright Mills, the construction of class consciousness is dependent on three phenomena: (1) a rational awareness of and identification with one's own class interest; (2) an awareness of and rejection of other class interests; and (3) an awareness of and readiness to use collective political means to the collective political end of realizing one's interests (Anderson 1974: 36; Mills 2000). It follows that any coherent group can be said to have developed class consciousness if there is evidence of a shared understanding of collective interests, a conscientious rejection of the class interests of other groups, and the collective and thoughtful use of political means to realize class interests at the expense of other defined classes (Mills 2000).

Such was certainly the case for the planters in colonial Jamaica. The very fact that wealthy financiers and on-the-ground overseers both referred to themselves as "planters" – and mutually recognized each other as such – demonstrates that wealthy proprietors and salaried employees recognized a shared class interest expressed in the roles they played in the organization of agricultural production. In his consideration of the life of the overseer-turned proprietor Thomas Thistlewood, Trevor Burnard reflects on the thoughts that several contemporary historians of eighteenth- and early-nineteenth-century Jamaica had on this issue. He notes particularly that the West Indian historian Bryan Edwards described a sense of "conscious equality" between wealthy landowners and their white employees (Burnard 2004: 74), a consciousness that developed through a shared understanding that even poor whites in Jamaica could rise to relative wealth and standing, so long as the system of chattel slavery remained in place. It was thus a common relationship to the enslaved working class that shaped this sense of "conscious equality" – or, in our terms here, class consciousness – among the planters of Jamaica.

The planter class in Jamaica quite conscientiously rejected the interests of the agricultural working class. It should be inherently clear that enslavement and the often capricious use of corporal punishment against the enslaved were themselves processes that recognized and suppressed the interests of the working class. The planters recognized that the enslaved were developing a very sophisticated understanding of their own class interests, even within the context of their enslavement. As early as the 1770s, Edward Long noted that enslaved people, through the exchange of produce and other small goods both to the white planters and between each other in Sunday markets, were controlling an increasingly large proportion of the island's coinage (Long 1774). Recognizing that the enslaved were developing some measure of economic power through their participation in the Sunday markets, the planter class acted to limit it. For example, the Jamaica Assembly passed a law prohibiting laborers from the right to "carry about to sell, any goods, wares, or merchandise" saving food provisions, and this only if they had written permission from their slave master (Aikman 1802: 82). Other acts of the Assembly sought to further curtail independent economic activity. For example, slaves were prohibited from hunting with dogs, and they could not legally operate canoes or boats to move cargo for hire, unless in the presence of two white men (Aikman 1802: 22, 53). Statutes in effect at the turn of the nineteenth century further codified this rejection of working class interest by limiting the civil rights and economic and social opportunities of members of the nonwhite working class. For example, by statute, public officials were prohibited from employing "Jews, mulattoes, negroes, and Indians" in their offices (Aikman 1802: 31, 32, 38).

Such statutes codified the process of racialization that was closely tied to class formation in colonial Jamaica. Racial groups are constructed through the process of racialization, a process that defines social difference and creates social hierarchies based on perceived physical or biological differences, as well as a variety of cultural variables such as language, clothing, and cuisine (Orser 2007). In defining "blackness" as being a biological state derived from pure African ancestry, Jamaican planters created two racial poles; those at one end, purely of European descent and defined as "white," were endowed with inalienable rights and privileges bestowed by this very whiteness. Those at the opposite pole, "negro" or "black," existed in the absence of inherent rights and privileges, and were dependent on the legislative process in Jamaica, controlled by the white planters, to grant and protect whatever rights they might be afforded. Access to the ruling class was limited to those on one racial pole, membership in the enslaved working class (at least by the middle of the eighteenth century in Jamaica) was assumed for those at the other pole.

The demographic realities of colonial Jamaica required the legal definitions of racial groups existing between these two poles, including indigenous people ("Indians") native or brought to Jamaica, Jews, and the mixed-race offspring of European and African sexual unions, "by law deemed mulattoes" (Aikman 1802: 88). Theoretically, unencumbered and unlimited access to buying and selling property, holding public office (and thus drawing stipends from the public coffers), voting, and freedom of movement defined the privileges of Jamaican whiteness. Privileges to members of other groups were hierarchically defined by statute. Jews could own property without limit, and many became wealthy merchants and planters; they could not, however, hold public office or even be employed by those that did. Indians were similarly barred from public office and, like the Jewish population, were granted some measure of freedom. Although they were not permitted to be enslaved in Jamaica after 1741, Indians were prohibited from commanding "droggers," small vessels that brought cargo out to merchant ships or plied coastal trade (Aikman 1802: 86). People who were "by law deemed mulattoes" could not hold island-wide public office, could only vote if they were granted the privilege by a specific act of the Assembly, were prohibited from commanding droggers, and, although restrictions were later relaxed, at the turn of the nineteenth century could not inherit more than £2,000, and then only if they were the legal "issue born in wedlock ... and deemed a mulatto" of their white parent (Aikman 1802: 88). Free and enslaved negroes were prohibited from receiving such inheritances.

It is clear from the practice of enslavement and the legislation of property rights and other civil rights that the white planter class, which controlled the political apparatus of the island, conscientiously worked against the interests both of the enslaved class and those who descended from enslaved ancestors but were able to achieve the status of free black or free person of color. It is also clear from the legislative record of the Jamaica Assembly that members of the planter class were consciously aware of their own class interests, defined both by whiteness and unlimited access to the ownership of land and people as part of the means of plantation production. Although the acts of the Assembly allowed for some measure of wealth among the mulatto offspring of the white colonials, the ceiling placed on them prohibited the free people of color from aspiring to join their fathers in the top tiers of the planter class; that they were largely blocked from holding public office is clearly indicative of the planter class's use of the island's political apparatus to further their collective interests at the expense of others. It seems that the planters had a fully developed class consciousness reified by race, and perpetuated by the use of the Jamaica Assembly to create and execute the legal framework necessary to ensure their control over the means of production.

In their consideration of the structure and functioning of corporate cartels in the twentieth century, American sociologists Edward Laumann and David Knoke argue that class consciousness cannot fully develop unless the members of the class in question create active networks between them through which they make and execute decisions impacting the well-being of their group (Laumann and Knoke 1987). Even in a relatively small society like white colonial Jamaica, it would be impossible for the entire population of planters to regularly meet to draw consensus on what defined their class interests. Today, class consciousness is developed in the board rooms and country clubs into which access is restricted to members of the elite class, and through which members of that class create networks to define and execute what is in their collective interest. In late-eighteenth- and early-nineteenth-century Jamaica, the shared interests of the planter class were defined and executed through the political structure of the island, the social world of plantation hospitality (described by contemporary observers in some detail in Carmichael 1833 and Wright 2002), a shared understanding of how to create and exist within plantation landscapes, and the knowledge of how to properly use other forms of material culture (Brown 2011).

The political apparatus of the colonial government was multi-tiered, consisting of public offices (e.g., Island Secretary, Provost-Marshal), parish vestries, and what amounted to a bicameral legislature (the Council and Assembly). Because the population of truly wealthy white males was not sufficient to fill all of the positions island-wide, the wealthy planters had no choice but to allow smaller planters to fill some of these positions. In comparison to England, access to dinner parties and other social events would be far more open to the less wealthy in Jamaica, as the networks of the truly wealthy were so small. The nature of the class structure in Jamaica was thus different from that in the slave-holding colonies on the mainland, where both race and wealth defined entry into the social and political worlds of the ruling class (Burnard 2004: 75ff). As Burnard argues, an "egalitarian tyranny" emerged in Jamaica, where small planters and the occasional overseer would consider themselves to be in the same social stratum as the great proprietors owning thousands of acres and hundreds of slaves. In the words of the Jamaica planter William Beckford, there existed between the white people of Jamaica a "leveling principle" creating a bond between wealthy and relatively poor white Jamaicans, which entrenched on "the duties of society" (Burnard 2004: 74–75). This bond, of course, was a clear recognition of the common relationship all white people held to the enslaved African people which led to the development of a class consciousness emerging from the recognition and rejection of the class interests of the enslaved workers.

The Enclave of Upper St. David

Even in relatively small and insular settings, the development of class consciousness is a phenomenon that takes place through complex networks of social interaction. Even if a social class is comprised of a relatively small number of people who can be in regular personal contact, interaction requires the creation of social networks through which members of a social class can communicate to define and reinforce their shared interests. In the case of colonial Jamaica, the social networks that bound the interests of the individual members of the planter class emerged not only from the well-described predilection that planters had for frequent and costly dinner parties and other entertainments, but from the structure of the colonial administrative system (Delle 2000). In some areas of Jamaica, the planters lived in relative isolation; to understand the dynamics of their social networking, and thus the webs of interaction that allowed for the development of class consciousness among groups of planters, it is useful to consider plantation communities, at least in some parts of Jamaica, as having been colonial enclaves (Trouillot 1988).

The historic political ecology of the island of Jamaica encouraged the development of such plantation enclaves. The plantation economy that developed in eighteenth-century Jamaica resulted in the development of a dispersed settlement pattern as we saw in Chapter 2; prior to the 1790s, and with the exception of a concentration of plantations in the central valleys of the old parishes of St. John and St. Thomas in the Vale, most of these estates were distributed within a short distance of the coast. In his spatial analysis of the growth and contraction of the Jamaican sugar industry, Barry Higman has demonstrated that from its beginnings in the middle of the seventeenth century, through to about the middle of the eighteenth century, Jamaica's landscape was characterized by clusters of plantations, the oldest being in the central valleys and the eastern half of the south coast. During the greatest boom years of sugar production, settlement extended around the arable coast of the island, but contracted again into dispersed and isolated enclaves, with as many as half of all estates being abandoned before 1834 (Higman 1988: 10–16).

The persistence of enclaves, both prior to and following the great boom period of sugar production, can in part be explained by the island's geography. Jamaica is a relatively large island by Caribbean standards – approximately 145 miles in length and 50 miles in breadth at its widest points. Travel from the north coast to the south can be difficult, with mountains exceeding 2,200 meters in elevation rising a mere 16 kilometers from the coast. In the west, the center of the island is characterized by karst

Figure 4.1. The karst topography characteristic of the cockpit country. Photo by James A. Delle.

topography; as ancient limestone eroded over time, thousands of sink-holes and conical peaks formed what is known as the "cockpit country." Difficult to cross, there are few reliable roads through the cockpit country to this day. Unpredictable rivers are prone to flash flooding in both the mountainous east and the limestone plateaus of the center and west, making river crossings often dangerous. Even in the closing decade of the twentieth century, washed out bridges and uncrossable fords occa-sionally left some settled areas of Jamaica nearly inaccessible for days or weeks at a time.

Another West Indian setting, the colonial settlement in the mountainous and sparsely populated island of Dominica, has been characterized by the historian Michel-Rolf Trouillot (1988) as a collection of enclaves: clusters of plantations geographically isolated from other clusters. The archaeologist Mark Hauser has recently used the enclave concept to understand the variable nature of archaeological assemblages recovered from various regions on that island (e.g. Hauser 2011b; Hauser and Armstrong 2012). In Jamaica, Matthew Reeves has considered that shared wharves might be one way to reconstruct colonial plantation enclaves. In his study of how agricultural regimes impacted household consumption patterns, Reeves compares plantations that shared access to the waterfront at Old Harbour, in effect considering those planters sharing that infrastructure as an enclave (Reeves 1997, 2011).

Reeves's approach makes sense, as many plantations shipped their pro-duce to the legal ports of embarkation from small wharves that were best accessed by small boats. The numerous small bays along the coastline of the island provided disbursed transshipment points for sugar and coffee export, as well as the introduction of material goods through small boat traffic through the wharves that existed at many of these small bays. Although some wealthy planters could maintain private wharves should their planta-tion be located directly on the coast, many others would transfer their crops either by cartage or river canoes to the coast, and either consign their crops to merchants at the wharves found at these small bays, or pay droggers to haul their produce from the wharves to ships waiting at anchorage at one of the island's export ports. Sharing access to these specific elements of the means of production – wharves and small boats – would cement bonds between planters, who had a shared interest in ensuring that the droggers charged reasonable rates, that the scales at the wharves were honestly maintained, and that the wharves and roads were in good repair to ensure the easy movement of their product to market. As Reeves's study demon-strated, the system of supplying plantations from these smaller wharves would also encourage the concentration of certain types of imported goods within enclaves, creating a context for localized networks of symbolic interaction through specific forms of material culture distributed within the plantation enclaves.

Some of Jamaica's coffee plantation regions can also be interpreted as having been enclaves, and indeed, the enclave phenomenon was likely more pronounced for coffee planters, as coffee plantations tended to locate along good water sources in the rugged highlands of the eastern Blue Mountains and the eroding limestone plateaus of the central highlands. These areas were largely undeveloped until the very end of the eighteenth century, were geographically isolated from areas of denser and more established settlement, and were connected to the coast by challenging mountain roads. In many parts of Jamaica, the emergence of enclaves was defined by geographic isolation and was reinforced by the structure of the local political apparatus.

One such enclave was located in the northern reaches of the old parish of St. David. Stretching from the southern slope of the Blue Mountains to the sea, St. David was absorbed by the larger parish of St. Thomas (formerly St. Thomas in the East) when the political boundaries of the island were redrawn in the 1860s. Nevertheless, some modern maps still identify the northern, mountainous section of this old parish as the District of Upper St. David.

The Parish of St. David, located to the east of the principle town of Kingston along the south coast of Jamaica, was one of the smallest and least populated of the colony's parishes, comprising only about 2 percent of the island's landmass, and containing about 2.4 percent of the island's pre-emancipation population. Because St. David was located on the southern slope of the Blue Mountains, and stretched across a relatively flat coastal plain to the sea, a variety of different kinds of plantation were established in the parish, including pens, sugar estates, and coffee plantations. Upper St. David was located in the northern highland section of the parish, north of the confluence of the Banana, Negro, and Yallahs Rivers; north of this confluence, large-scale sugar production was infeasible owing to the increasing declivity of the mountainous terrain. River Head Estate, located at the confluence of these three rivers, was the northernmost sugar estate in the parish. Above River Head lay Upper St. David, which was settled at a later date than was Lower St. David, and was primarily a coffee producing region. Lower St. David, well-watered and convenient by road and by sea to Kingston, was a productive sugar producing district.

The number of active plantations in St. David fluctuated over time. In 1796, the vestry minutes of the parish indicated that there were fifty-nine plantation estates or individual landowners in possession of slaves in the parish. Of these, a surprising number, nine, were women, with three being free women of color. Two additional properties were owned by free men of color. Ten of the estates, mostly sugar plantations in Lower St. David, had enslaved populations of more than 150 people, including the largest estate in terms of population in the parish, Albion, which was owned by the plantation grandee Simon Taylor, and to which was attached no fewer than 399 slaves in 1796. The Jamaica Almanac for 1800 reported that the Parish of St. David contained sixteen sugar estates (in Lower St. David) and eighteen coffee plantations (in Upper St. David), as well as fifty other kinds of settlements, which would include cattle pens and small holdings not large enough to be considered a plantation, but may have been producing coffee on a small scale (Jamaica Almanac 1800: 126–128). As coffee production increased in Jamaica in the opening decades of the nineteenth century, more plantations were established in Upper St. David; by 1820, there were twenty-five coffee plantations operating in Upper St. David; between 1801 and 1820, a total of thirty-one Upper St. David coffee plantations appeared at least once in the vestry records (see Figure 4.2).

All but four of the coffee plantations in Upper St. David were located in three valley systems: ten were located in the Green River Valley, which included the tributary Cascade and Fall Rivers; twelve were located in the Negro River Valley, and five were located in the Great Negro River Valley. The rivers forming the last two valleys are parts of separate systems and do not flow into each other. The Negro River flows southerly to its confluence with the southerly flowing Yallahs River, which forms the boundary between Upper St. David and the Parish of Port Royal; and the Great Negro River flows easterly into the Parish of St. Thomas in the East, forming part of the Morant River system. The four outlying plantations, straddling parish boundaries or located on minor streams, were outside of the three valley systems. Those outliers containing land in both St. David and either of the neighboring parishes (Port Royal to the west and St. Thomas to the east) occasionally disappear from the St. David vestry records, likely reflecting the flexibility that planters on parish frontiers had to move between parish enclaves when it suited them.

Enclaves were not without social tension. A grievance forwarded from the St. David's vestry to the parish custos is suggestive of the tensions that existed between resident members of the enclave active in parish politics and those who sat in office primarily for the privilege, likely from plantations that straddled parish lines. In 1801, the parish vestry was having difficulty making quorum for its quarterly sessions, repeatedly having to cancel or postpone the vestry meetings, often, it was recorded, "for want of Magistrates, on account of the non residence of some of the Gentlemen of the Peace in this parish" (SDVM v. 3 f. 38). In July 1801, the vestry ordered the clerk of the vestry to "write in the most respectful manner to

Figure 4.2. The enclave of Upper St. David. Illustration courtesy of John Svatek.

The Honorable the Custos ... requesting the favor of him to appoint as magistrates four or more Gentlemen resident in the parish" to serve as Justices of the Peace (ibid.).

Both this grievance itself and the fact that the vestry often met without a quorum of members is reflective of how small the planter enclave in St. David was. Indeed, the Jamaica Assembly recognized that the parish would have difficulty in filling all required public offices, or even to have enough voters for an election. To vote in Jamaica, one had to be a freeholder. To be recognized as a freeholder in a parish, one needed to be a male of at least 21 years of age, "be possessed" of "negroes of their own liable to be taxed," and to be in possession, either as their own property or that of their wife or through inheritance, of either a house worth £10 per annum, an improved pen [nb: with a house upon it] of at least 10 acres and returning at least £10 per annum, or an improved plantation of at least 8 acres yielding £10 per annum, and of course, be white (Aikman 1802). Those renting estates for at least £50 per annum, as well as parish rectors, were also granted the rights of freeholders, which included the right to sit as a vestryman. However, four parishes, including the urban parish of Kingston and the coffee producing parishes of Port Royal, St. George, and St. David, were granted exceptions to this limitation of rights. Men who did not qualify as freeholders could be vestrymen in these parishes. The exception for St. David was likely granted owing to the small size of the white land-owning population, and thus the limited pool of candidates available to fill the public offices in the parish. This dearth of qualified candidates is likely reflected in the frustration the vestrymen expressed in not having enough resident Justices of the Peace to conduct regular parish business.

The subset of the white population that constituted the planter enclave of Upper St. David was thus a proportionately small segment of the colonial population of Jamaica. A sense of what the enclave was like can be deduced through an analysis of St. David's vestry minutes, which recorded, among other things, the number of people considered white, "coloured," or enslaved on each plantation. The vestry minutes are preserved in the Jamaica Archives in Spanish Town; although the run of vestry minutes is complete for the years 1801–1817, the volumes recording the vestry minutes from 1818 through 1831 are too fragile for public reference. Nevertheless, the 1801–1817 record provides an intriguing look into the social dynamics of the plantation enclave in the opening decades of the nineteenth century.

As discussed in previous chapters, the free white population was a small fraction of the overall population of pre-emancipation Jamaica. In Upper St. David, this was particularly true. In 1801, the enclave consisted of twenty plantations; the aggregate white population on those twenty estates numbered only 43, whereas the enslaved population numbered 1,228. The average number of whites on a plantation was thus 2.15, and the average number of enslaved was 63.32. Calculating percentages from the aggregate population, this means that 3.4 percent of the population consisted of free whites, whereas 96.6 percent of the population was enslaved. In 1802, the white population reached its peak at sixty-five; from that year forward the number of whites living in Upper St. David steadily declined. In 1817, only thirty-two whites were recorded to be living in Upper St. David, less than half the number of 1802; by 1817, 98.7 percent of the population of Upper St. David was composed of enslaved workers on coffee plantations. Although coffee production was a risky enterprise in the early nineteenth century, the declining number of whites does not reflect a contracting industry. On the contrary, the number of coffee estates in the district increased to twenty-five by 1817, and the enslaved population increased to 2,375. As the average number of whites on each plantation decreased from a high of 3.42 in 1802 to only 1.28 in 1817, the average number of enslaved workers on those same estates increased from 63.32 to 95. Thus, although the aggregate numbers and percentages of enslaved people of African descent steadily increased during the first two decades of the nineteenth century, the planter enclave dwindled, both in overall numbers of white people resident in the district and in terms of the ratio of whites to enslaved workers in the total population of Upper St. David. The planter enclave was clearly a small group.

Formation of Class Consciousness in Upper St. David

To understand the social and material dynamics of this small enclave, it might be best first to review the political organization of colonial Jamaica. At the end of the eighteenth century, Jamaica was ruled by a governor, often a British aristocrat or military officer, appointed by the crown. Serving as the chief executive of the island, the governor was advised by the Council, which he appointed from the leading planters on the island. Until 1867, the government of Jamaica, with approval from the crown, was empowered to enact laws governing the management of the island; the legislative body, known as the Jamaica Assembly, was elected by the freeholders of the island. Representation to the Assembly was determined by residence in the various parishes of the island, which served as administrative units. The number of parishes has fluctuated over time. Currently, there are twelve parishes; in 1800, there were nineteen.

Local administrative concerns, including compliance with various laws, the assessment and collection of local taxes, coroners' inquests, and road construction and maintenance, were administered by various public officials elected and appointed from the freeholders within each parish. Appointed by the governor in consultation with the Council, the chief public officer of each parish was known as the Custos, who served as the chief magistrate for the parish. Other parish officers included justices of the peace, coroners, clerks of the vestry, way wardens, parish clerks, constables, (tax) collecting constables, and pound keepers; each of these offices had an attached salary of between 6 and 100 pounds per annum. Each parish had a local council known as the vestry. Elected by the freeholders of each parish, the vestry would appoint and pay public officers, assess and collect local taxes, and conduct the business of the parish.

Parish vestries met quarterly to conduct that business. In the first quarterly meeting of each year, the freeholders gathered to elect the vestrymen for the coming year, who would then appoint the other parish officers, save Justices of the Peace who were appointed by the Custos. During court and vestry sessions, members of the planter class would have the opportunity to socialize and thus create and reinforce bonds of friendship defined by their common interests as property owners – and slaveholders – of the parish. The vestrymen, accompanied by the various parish officers, including the Justices of the Peace, would plan the public events for the quarter, including the assessment of taxes on enslaved people, wheeled vehicles, livestock, and land, the bringing of suits against those property owners in default on their taxes, and the construction and maintenance of roads to be supervised by waywardens.

As was the case with Thomas Thistlewood, planters of relatively limited means had access to public office in the parish of St. David. By means of example, in the year 1796, public offices in St. David included ten vestry-men, two assemblymen (sitting in the Jamaica Assembly), five Justices of the Peace, six waywardens, two churchwardens, two (tax) collecting constables, a vestry clerk, a court clerk, a coroner, a parish clerk, a sexton, and a pound keeper. Twenty men filled these twenty-eight offices, with six filling more than one. Counted among the vestrymen were large planters by St. David's standards, including the sugar planters William Ker, who owned 717 acres at Spring Garden Estate and 123 slaves; James Renny, owner of 2,055 acres at Swamps and Norris estates and 227 slaves; and Lott French, proprietor of the 3,160-acre Creighton Hall estate and owner of 211 slaves. Also counted among the vestry were more modest proprietors like John Tyree who owned 187 acres and 14 slaves, and Thomas Baikie with 42 acres and 51 slaves. Robert Morgan, owner of Radnor Coffee Plantation (600 acres) and ninety-four slaves was also a member of the vestry, as were two overseers, James Harriot of Epping Farm and Patrick Buchanan of Aeolus Valley, who owned 150 acres of his own. The office of Justice of the Peace was likewise filled by men with various levels of wealth. Among the wealthier was William Sutherland who owned 1,057 acres; Robert Telfer of Monklands Coffee Plantation owned 952 acres and thirty slaves, and Thomas Leigh of Whitfield Hall Coffee Plantation who owned 407 acres and forty-eight slaves. A fourth justice, Andrew Deans, owned five slaves and eighty-eight acres at a place called Dry Sugar Work. Although the vestry minutes do not note any property owned by William Vick, it is possible that Vick owned property in another parish. Of these twenty men, Telfer of Monklands, Morgan of Radnor, Leigh of Whitfield Hall, and Harriot of Epping Farm represented the enclave of Upper St. David.

The position of waywarden was what we might consider an entry-level position in the parish political hierarchy. Waywardens were responsible for ensuring that the roads through the parish – including roads that passed through private estates – were maintained and improved. To ensure this, waywardens worked with individual plantation owners, who owed the parish a specified number of days of labor from their enslaved population, based on the size of that population. The waywardens were formed into committees, each of which was assigned a specific stretch of road to maintain, and each of which was given a small budget to pay for any materials required for the job. Although the improvement of roads was clearly meant to improve the ability of the planter class to move their crop to market, much of which was done by mule train from Upper St. David, the planter class – through the actions of the waywardens – required enslaved workers to do the labor; estates were assessed "days" of labor from their enslaved population to work on the roads, once again demonstrating that the collective action of the planter class in the parish of St. David conscientiously advanced the planter's interest at the expense of the enslaved, who were required to do the heavy manual labor of clearing mountain paths, breaking stone, and stabilizing friable soil to create the planters' roads.

The formation of class solidarity was simultaneously a political and social phenomenon. Several contemporary observers noted that white Jamaicans were very fond of hosting elaborate dinner parties and balls (e.g., Long 1774: 265; Wright 2002). Although such events surely would be an arena for conspicuous display, such gatherings were also the opportunity for members of the planter class to cement their social bonds and to discuss local politics. The well-documented case of Thomas Thistlewood indicates that within a short few years of arrival on the island, white emigrants of limited means could aspire to fill parish offices and to socialize with more prominent members of the local elite. Burnard reports that within two years of arriving in Jamaica as an overseer, Thistlewood's diary indicated that he was appointed as a waywarden in Westmoreland parish, was frequently attending dinners at the homes of the parish Custos and other wealthy planters, and was able to eventually rise to the position of Justice of the Peace (Burnard 2004: 77). Burnard considers the frequency, profligacy, and seeming openness of Jamaica dinner parties to be part of a "cult of hospitality." Such hospitality, which networked wealthy planters to small landowners and to overseers, served as a medium to create and perpetuate the planters' class consciousness.

Although no similar diaries detailing the opulence of dinner parties in St. David have yet been discovered, the vestry records for the parish indicate that the planter class was fond of costly entertainments from time to time. As was the case in much of the colonial Atlantic world, the political calendar provided regular opportunities for local men to meet, mingle, dine, and drink. The vestrymen of St. David were apparently fond of the hospitality of Mary Hately, who operated a tavern in Yallahs Bay, at that time the seat of the Parish of St. David. Described by the vestry records as a "free black woman," Miss Hately and her daughter Catherine Logan were granted by order of the vestry "certificates agreeably to the priviledge law in favor of free persons of colour" in 1801, and thus became women of color "with special privileges." Miss Hately regularly hosted the vestry at her tavern. In three of the four quarters of 1816, the parish paid Miss Hately £10 for "Vestry Dinners." For the remaining quarter, she was paid £50 for an "Election Dinner." In this year alone, Miss Hately was paid at least £80; to put this in perspective, in 1822, bookkeepers at Radnor Plantation, located in Upper St. David, were paid £60 per annum, and overseers £160. The annual budget for vestry entertainment was half the annual salary of an overseer, and the election dinner alone nearly the equivalent of a bookkeeper's annual salary. Given that elections were rarely attended by more than ten freeholders, these were likely quite sumptuous entertainments.

The planter class was aware of their distinct privileges in Jamaica, particularly the social division that separated them as a group from the enslaved working class. Nevertheless, St. David's vestry records indicate that the "leveling principle" identified by William Beckford, and the "egalitarian tyranny" defined by Trevor Burnard were operating in the parish at the turn of the nineteenth century. The various laws defining access to public office in Jamaica required that officers be white men who owned property in the parish they represented; however, as Thistlewood's case indicated, white men of relatively modest means could participate in public life through service in local public office. In so doing, class consciousness developed between plantation grandees and, through a shared sense of the "duties of society," small planters and even overseers.

The class solidarity that existed between proprietors and overseers was not only based on racial solidarity and the shared sense of white supremacy that emerged from the slave system. As evidenced by the case of Thomas Thistlewood, thrifty – and possibly ruthless – overseers could marshal the means to acquire or establish plantations of their own. In the opening decades of the nineteenth century, several overseers in Upper St. David used the opportunities open to them to acquire property – in land and enslaved workers – and thus to elevate themselves to the status of "proprietor," much as Thomas Thistlewood had done a generation before. Two cases in particular stand out – those of John Cherrington and John Barclay.

Between 1796 and 1803, John Cherrington was the overseer at Friendship's Retreat, living there with his wife Sarah and the family of the proprietor Richard Croasdale. Cherrington apparently made good use out of the freehold exception granted to the Parish of St. David, as he served as a vestryman in 1801 despite not owning an estate of his own. He apparently left the parish in 1803, but returned in 1807 to work, possibly as an overseer or head bookkeeper, on Abbey Green Plantation. The following year saw Cherrington leave Abbey Green to return to work for the widow of his former employer, Elizabeth Dow Croasdale, at Friendship's Retreat. In 1809, Cherrington became the proprietor of Mount Pleasant, but apparently split his residency between Friendship's Retreat, where he was likely employed as overseer, and his own property at Mount Pleasant.

As proprietor of Mount Pleasant, Cherrington was in possession of twenty-one slaves and a small estate; he likely supplemented his income by "jobbing" or leasing out his enslaved workers. Jobbing was a common way for owners of small or worn out estates in Upper St. David, or overseers who came into possession of a labor gang, to supplement their income. For example, 1821 was a year of declining coffee production at Mavis Bank Plantation, which was located on the west bank of the Yallahs River, on the border between the parishes of Port Royal and St. David. In that year, Mavis Bank shipped 7,012 pounds of coffee; although the price of coffee fluctuated somewhat, the average price in the early 1820s was about 1 shilling per pound (or 100 shillings per hundredweight) in the London market. Mavis Bank's produce for the year was thus worth about £350, from which wharfage and consignment fees would have to be deducted. The owners of the estate would have been lucky to realize £300 from the crop of 1821. In contrast, labor gangs from Mavis Bank were jobbed out to five different plantations that year, both in Upper St. David and neighboring Port Royal; the plantation managers realized almost £280 that year from jobbing, a sum nearly equal to the amount brought in by the crop. As the going rate for jobbing in Upper St. David was 2 shillings 6 pence per day, Cherrington could have been realizing as much as £72 per month; in two months, a jobbing gang could thus return an amount about equal to the annual salary of a coffee plantation overseer. It is clear that Cherrington at least occasionally jobbed his laborers out as a gang; the Radnor plantation book contains several entries like this one from April 1825: "21 hands from Mt. Pleasant with great gang." Cherrington was also leasing out mule teams from Friendship's Retreat, further supplementing his income.

Fortunately for Cherrington, Mt. Pleasant was contiguous to Radnor, by far the largest of the Upper St. David coffee plantations. In the late 1810s and early 1820s, Cherrington served as the overseer at Radnor; he was apparently talented at coffee plantation management, for when Robert Morgan left St. David to become an absentee proprietor, he hired Cherrington as his attorney to manage Radnor in his absence. Cherrington used this position to his advantage; not only was he likely collecting a salary and commission on crop exports, but – as attorney – he was responsible for making arrangements to supply the plantation with foodstuffs, supplies, and tools. Although most of the manufactured and imported goods flowed to Radnor through a wharf owned by John Biggar in Kingston, Cherrington transformed Mount Pleasant into a provisioning estate, containing more than 200 acres, primarily for Radnor. He was thus able to sell the produce of his estate, including hogs, to Radnor, an estate he managed, to further supplement his income.

The multilayered financial arrangements constructed by Cherrington proved to be most profitable for him. By 1823, Cherrington was able to augment his enslaved workforce; the number of enslaved workers at Mount Pleasant increased from twenty-two in 1810, when Cherrington acquired the estate, to seventy-nine in 1823. By the mid-1820s, through a combination of (most likely) jobbing, leasing mules, provisioning Radnor, and collecting a salary and commission for crop sales from Radnor, Cherrington was able to comfortably emerge as a middling coffee planter.

John Barclay's career followed a similar trajectory to Cherrington's, although he may have been even more successful. In 1802, Barclay worked for a time as a bookkeeper at Whitfield Hall; by the end of the year, he had been promoted to overseer at Abbey Green, where he would later work with John Cherrington. Barclay remained the manager of Abbey Green until 1813. In 1806, he acquired twenty-five enslaved workers, which, like Cherrington, he likely jobbed out. Five years later, in 1811, Barclay was added to the quit-rent and land tax lists, indicating that he had purchased at least 500 acres of land in the parish. That run of land, which was purchased by a subdivision of part of the northern reaches of River Head estate, was improved and became known as Woburn Lawn. Barclay remained as proprietor of Woburn Lawn into the 1840s. By 1833, the last year slavery was legal in Jamaica, Barclay owned 109 slaves and 472 acres of land. In terms of the control over the means of production, in this case land and labor, Barclay had become one of the wealthiest planters in the district, and, by 1835, a parish philanthropist, as he donated land in that year to erect a chapel for the parish.

In the years leading up to the abolition of slavery, Barclay adjusted his economic strategies to the fiscal realities of the declining productivity of old and worn out coffee plantations. In 1822, Barclay purchased Mavis Bank Plantation, just across the parish boundary in Port Royal. By that time, several of the old coffee estates in Port Royal had seen calamitous declines in coffee production, likely brought on by poor land management and the overworking of the friable soils of the Blue Mountain highlands (Delle 1996). Mavis Bank was one of the oldest coffee plantations in the area, having produced a crop as early as 1788 (Delle 1996). By 1821, it had become one of the least productive plantations in the area. By that time, the estate was dependent on jobbing out the labor gangs to make a profit. Barclay took advantage of the decline of Mavis Bank by purchasing and subsequently subdividing the estate. Like Thistlewood before him, Barclay had used a variety of means to elevate himself within the planter class; by 1840, he was significant enough a person to be appointed a Justice of the Peace for St. David. The Blue Mountains were certainly a land of opportunity for ambitious overseers. Men who drew wages for a living had found ways to elevate themselves within the planter class.

The existence of the local parish vestries and a centralized representative government in the Jamaica Assembly provided planters with a political apparatus to further their collective interests, both locally and island-wide. In the Parish of St. David, overseers, small planters, and large proprietors served together in public office, collected and spent tax revenue to improve the infrastructure for the movement of plantation produce, and determined, as in the case of Mary Hately and her daughter Catherine Logan, who – among the people of color in the parish – would be accorded civil rights. They shared sumptuous entertainments during vestry meetings, and, by networking with fellow overseers and attorneys, men like Cherrington and Barclay were able to rise from the status of bookkeeper or overseer to become middling or even wealthy planters. As an enclave, these men acted to transform the landscapes of Upper St. David in such a way as to reinforce their social and economic networks, not only by supervising the construction of roads, but by creating visual perceptions that reified their social position.

The Archaeology of Class Consciousness in Upper St. David

The formation of the planter class in Jamaica, and the concomitant rise of class consciousness among the planters, was dependent on the construction of both social solidarity between planters and social distance between the planters and their plantation laborers. In the late eighteenth and early nineteenth centuries, planters clearly recognized themselves as a social class. Even if there was great diversity in accumulated wealth between the wealthiest and poorest in the class, salaried employees could rise to the status of proprietor, and in the case of Upper St. David, some could serve on the vestry even prior to their acquiring property of their own. Until 1834, the social distance between planter and worker was defined by the institution of chattel slavery. As we have seen, the acceptance of chattel slavery in Jamaica allowed the planters to consider the members of the agrarian working class as part of the means of production. A dehumanizing process, the planters recognized that the buying and selling – and, through jobbing, the leasing – of laborers was a means by which planters could accumulate wealth. This wealth was not only generated through the cooptation of surplus value (in Upper St. David through the sale of the coffee crop), but by the definition of people as objects of value. Many planters calculated their wealth largely by establishing the value of their enslaved population; the greater the number of slaves, the greater the wealth of the planter.

Perhaps more than any other form of labor organization under capitalism, slavery required the use of power to define and maintain the boundaries between the social classes (Orser 1988). As we have seen, the planter class networked among each other as a means of establishing class solidarity, and used the political apparatus of the colonial administration to actualize their interests. However, it was the daily expression of power over the enslaved workers that allowed the planter class to establish itself as it did, to accumulate the wealth that defined it, and that was the foundation of the racist social order that structured the whole system.

For the social structure to operate, the planters had to act collectively; the development of class consciousness led to the recognition of shared interest and cooperation among the planters. Such collective action was not isolated to the vestry room and court chambers, however. Part of the mechanism by which class consciousness developed and through which power was exerted over the enslaved class was the manipulation of regional landscapes. As we have seen, the plantation enclave of Upper St. David was primarily situated in three river valleys. By archaeologically examining the most populous of the three, the Negro River Valley, it is clear that the placement of plantation houses in the valley, and the physical and social networks that existed between the planters, was part of the process by which class solidarity between the planters was formed at the same time the social distance between the planters and the enslaved workers was reinforced (see Figure 4.3).

It has long been recognized that the location of sites within a region can be usefully analyzed to say something about how power was exerted through space. The study of settlement patterns, and how they relate to social complexity, has long been a mainstay of landscape archaeology (e.g., Adams 1965; Sanders 1956; Sanders et al. 1979; Willey 1953). Although settlement pattern analysis was pioneered by prehistorians, an increasing number of historical archaeologists have seen the power that the landscape archaeology of regional settlement systems could have in explaining colonial-era social dynamics (e.g., Delle 1994, 2002; Leone

Figure 4.3. The Negro River Valley as seen from Abbey Green. Photo by James A. Delle.

1984; Lewis 1984; Kelso 1989; Kelso and Most 1990; Paynter 1982, 1983; Yamin and Metheny 1996). Some regional landscapes are created intentionally and experienced variously and actively within class, race, and/or gender based webs of power (Delle et al. 1999; Kryder-Reid 1994; Leone 1984; Weber 1996). Jamaica's Negro River Valley is one such regional landscape.

Historically, there have been a number of coffee plantations located in the Negro River Valley, and some of the famous Blue Mountain coffee originates here (Benghiat 2008; Delle 1998). Although the land in the Blue Mountain region, and the Negro River Valley in particular, was patented as early as the 1770s, large-scale coffee production did not get started in the valley until the closing decades of the eighteenth century. The Jamaican coffee industry experienced a classic series of boom-bust cycles in the nineteenth century: initially profitable during the French Revolution and early in the Napoleonic Wars, the coffee economy suffered from the closing of European ports under Napoleon's Continental System in 1806 and the postwar depression of the late 1810s. Coffee production rebounded somewhat in the 1820s, contracted again in the late 1830s following the abolition of slavery, had a brief resurgence in the 1860s, declined again until another boom hit in the 1980s (Delle 1998), and is now once again suffering a decline.

Not surprisingly, the history of settlement in the Negro River Valley parallels the booms and busts of the coffee industry. In the early decades of the nineteenth century, coffee was an extremely profitable commodity for British colonials, primarily because the Haitian Revolution had cut off Europe's main supply of coffee which had originated in the French colony of St. Domingue. The Jamaican highlands, featuring an ecology similar to the highlands of nearby Haiti, became a locus of coffee production as colonial agents attempted to fill the European coffee vacuum. The political ecological landscape of the valley was imprinted at this time, as a number of coffee plantations were carved out of the tropical forest; to this day, the administrative divisions and locations of settlements in the valley are based on the location of these original plantations. Interviews with local informants and an analysis of the cartographic history of the valley indicate that, at the turn of the nineteenth century, eleven plantations operated in the Negro River Valley, including New Battle, Abbey Green, Brook Lodge, Eccleston, Epping Farm, Farm Hill, Friendship's Retreat, Mount Pleasant, Radnor, Sherwood Forest, and Whitfield Hall. Over the ensuing three decades, several new plantations were established, or subdivided out of older estates, including Minto, Carrick Hill, Woburn Lawn, and the division of New Battle into Upper New Battle and Lower New Battle.

One of the richest primary sources for reconstructing the economic history of Jamaica is a series of documents kept by the colonial government recording the amount of produce exported by individual estates, known alternately as the Accounts Produce or Crop Accounts. These records indicate that coffee was exported out of the Negro River Valley as early as the opening decade of the nineteenth century – Sherwood Forest exported coffee in 1801 and Radnor exported in 1806. It seems that some of the plantations never turned much of a profit, as for example, although both Brook Lodge and Eccleston are evident in the cartographic and archaeological records, neither ever appear in the Accounts Produce (although this may be an artifact of the owners processing or storing coffee elsewhere, or simply selling it as a raw product to another estate); by 1837, both Brook Lodge and Eccleston were referred to in the documents as being "appendages" to Sherwood Forest. Reflecting the post-emancipation collapse of plantation production in Jamaica, by the mid-1850s, all of the estates disappear from the documentary record; the Accounts Produce were suspended in 1866 when Jamaica was brought directly under the control of the British government as a crown colony. In these decades, many estates in the Jamaican highlands were subdivided and sold to small farmers – emancipated slaves and their descendants – even though the coffee works, great houses, and immediately surrounding land were largely kept in white hands (Satchell 1990). In the late nineteenth and early twentieth centuries, Jamaica went through a period of land consolidation. During this time, many of the Negro River Valley estates were acquired and coopted by a local land baron named Robert Stott who held title to thousands of acres of land until his death in the late 1950s, apparently making his money through rent extraction. After Stott's death, many of the estates passed again into numerous smaller holdings. Coffee cultivation began again in earnest in the early 1980s, although many of the estate houses and industrial works had fallen into ruin.

As a highland valley that produces an exportable commodity, the Negro River Valley is a contained ecological system connected to the outside world through a complex political economy. During the nineteenth century, this political economy relied on the expression of coercive power – both corporal and economic – to extract the amount and kind of labor power required by coffee planters to produce exportable crops. The various coffee planters, rather than being competitors, operated under a colonial economic system in which they constituted a class – defined by world systems theorists as a "regional elite" (Paynter 1985; Peregrine and Feinman 1996; Wallerstein 1979, 1980, 1989) – which shared many common interests. Among these were an interest in keeping the cost of labor low by maintaining the structures of slavery, dominating ownership of coffee works, land, and other means of production, and thus controlling both the objective and subjective forces of production.

But how was this materially expressed? In valley systems, one manner by which elites can express power is through the strategic placement of buildings on the landscape. It is well-known that in class-stratified societies from both prehistoric and historic contexts, temples, palaces, and other structures in which power is housed are often raised up on naturally occurring landforms, or failing their presence, on artificial landforms including platform mounds or stepped pyramids. Such placement reinforces the authority of the ruling class by symbolically raising the elites above the natural view of the commoners (Delle et al. 1999; Emerson and Pauketat 2002; Epperson 2000). In the case of the Negro River Valley coffee plantations, the most symbolic structures, those endowed with the most symbolic power, were the great houses in which the planters lived. During an archaeological survey of the Negro River Valley conducted in 1998, it became obvious that great houses were placed high in the valley to create a panoptic view for the elite inhabitants, not unlike that created by Jefferson at Monticello (Epperson 2000), and similar to the more microlevel management of plantation layout explored in Chapter 3.

One way to model the logic behind the placement of such seemingly important structures is by analyzing what has become known as viewshed; that is, modeling what can be seen by the human eye from particular points in the landscape. This type of analysis has gained a number of adherents, and has been usefully applied to archaeological studies in the Caribbean. For example, Torres and Rodriguez Ramos (2008) have used viewshed analysis to model the visual connectivity between individual islands in the Caribbean archipelago. To produce a viewshed analysis of the Negro River Valley, my students and I constructed a three-dimensional model of the Negro River Valley and we calculated the viewshed visible from the center points of the great house locations, determined through the survey of the valley conducted in 1998 (see Figure 4.4). At that time, we were able to locate the sites of seven great houses – three still standing and occupied (Abbey Green, Farm Hill, and Sherwood Forest), and four in ruins (Radnor, Eccleston, Upper New Battle, and Lower New Battle). We chose to calculate viewsheds from three meters above the surface of the ground from each of these points, providing a relatively conservative estimate of the entire viewshed visible from each great house (Burdick 2000).

The most striking result of the viewshed analysis is that each of the great houses whose locations could be reconstructed – with the sole exception of Sherwood Forest – was strategically placed so that its view would encompass the location of at least two other great houses. From the Eccleston Great House, one could simultaneously see the great houses at three other plantations; four from Farm Hill; five from Abbey Green; five from Upper New Battle; four from Lower New Battle; four from Eccleston; and four from Mt. Pleasant. Although Sherwood fell into the viewshed of only Lower New Battle, it is likely that, given the house's orientation to the south, Sherwood would have fallen into the viewshed of other plantations located down river in areas not covered by our 1998 survey.

Located at about 1,200 meters above sea level, the Farm Hill house was situated such that the viewshed from the great house encompassed a panoramic view of the eastern slope of the Negro River Valley. From the house, one had a clear view of the great houses at Abbey Green, Mt. Pleasant, Upper New Battle, and Eccleston (see Figure 4.5). Abbey Green, the northernmost of the seven houses located during the 1998 survey, also sits at about 1,200 meters above sea level. The viewshed from the house at Abbey Green encompasses five of the six remaining great houses; the only exception is the house at Sherwood Forest, which is located on the southern slope of a hill, and thus sits in a view shadow from the north. One has a commanding view of the entire Negro River Valley from the great house at Abbey Green (see Figure 4.6).

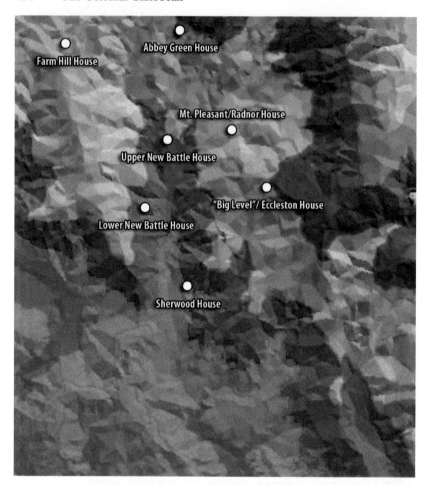

Figure 4.4. Digital elevation model showing the location of the seven great houses identified during the Negro River Valley Survey. Illustration courtesy of John Svatek.

Although situated at an elevation some 275 meters lower than either Abbey Green or Farm Hill, as was the case with Abbey Green, the great house at Upper New Battle commands a view of five of the six remaining houses; again with the exception of Sherwood Forest. One can see Abbey Green to the north, and the remaining four house sites to the south (see Figure 4.7). The house at Mt. Pleasant, located at about 1,000 meters above sea level, commands a view of the western slope of the Negro River Valley. The viewshed from the house encompasses the sites of the houses

Figure 4.5. Viewshed analysis from Farm Hill House. Illustration courtesy of John Svatek.

at Farm Hill, Abbey Green, Lower New Battle, and Upper New Battle (see Figure 4.8).

Lower New Battle, located at 850 meters above sea level, is situated on the western slope of the valley. The great house was located such that it commanded a view of the eastern valley slope, and incorporated views to the east and northeast. The viewshed from Lower New Battle encompassed Abbey Green, Upper New Battle, Mt. Pleasant, and Eccleston (see Figure 4.9). Eccleston, situated at approximately 1,200 meters above sea level, was the easternmost site located during the 1998 survey. The

Figure 4.6. Viewshed analysis from Abbey Green. Illustration courtesy of John Svatek.

viewscape from Eccleston encompasses Farm Hill, Abbey Green, Upper New Battle, and Lower New Battle, and commands a view of most of the western slope of the valley (see Figure 4.10).

Placing great houses in direct view of each other, and elevated above the valley floor, allowed for several things. This placement allowed the planters inhabiting these houses to be in visual, and possibly audible, contact with one another, literally creating a communication network between the houses located in the enclave. From these vantage points, messages could

Figure 4.7. Viewshed analysis from Upper New Battle. Illustration courtesy of John Svatek.

have traveled very quickly from one house to the other. Such a system of communication would have been an extremely powerful tool; one elderly informant reported in 1998 that his grandfather remembered sometime around the turn of the twentieth century, that the white inhabitants used to talk to each other from house to house using megaphones to warn each other of local labor unrest (Lewis Richards, personal communication, 1998). Establishing such a network in which messages could be passed up the valley very quickly allowed the planters to exert control over the

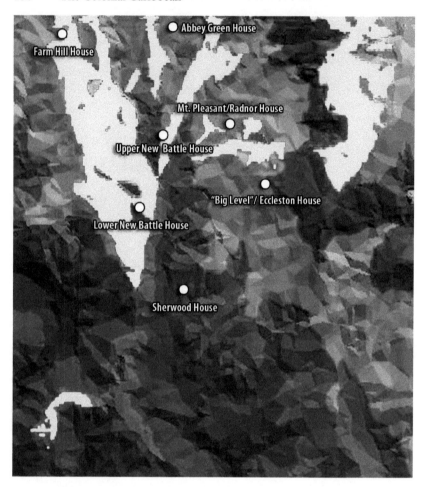

Figure 4.8. Viewshed analysis from Mt. Pleasant. Illustration courtesy of John Svatek.

entire length of the Negro River Valley. Equally important, the local laborers in the valley would have known, as Mr. Richards's grandfather apparently did, that the whites would be able to quickly mobilize should there be unrest in the valley; this knowledge could well have been a deterrent to collective action in the valley. In both events, the regional landscape of the Negro River Valley was designed and lived to promote relationships between the white planters, and thus served to materially reinforce a sense of collective belonging, a solidarity that emerged as class consciousness among the planters developed.

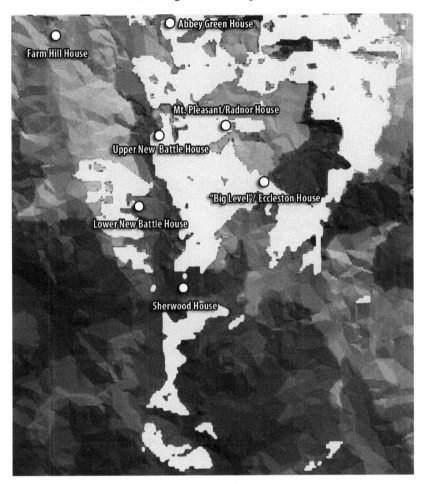

Figure 4.9. Viewshed analysis from Lower New Battle. Illustration courtesy of John Svatek.

Conclusion

The development of class consciousness in the enclave of Upper St. David was simultaneously a material and social phenomena. The small group of resident planters in the district met regularly to determine who among them would fill public offices, and how the revenue coming into the parish would be spent. They used the political apparatus of the parish vestry to organize the laying of roads that connected plantations to one another and to the outside world. The maintenance of these roads facilitated the

Figure 4.10. Viewshed analysis from Eccleston house. Illustration courtesy of John Svatek.

transportation of coffee out of the parish, and to the wharves in Kingston. As is seen in the case of Mary Hately, a free woman of color who ran a tavern popular with the vestrymen of St. David, the vestry could also use its authority to define who among the African-descent people in the parish would be granted "special privileges" and thus be afforded some greater measure of civil rights. By networking through the medium of the vestry, as well as through the social events like vestry and election dinners that were part of the quarterly meetings of the planters of St. David, the members of the plantation enclave defined their common identity and interests, and through their common access to the vestry, used the apparatus of the local government to materially express their class interests.

At the same time, the planters of Upper St. David created a regional landscape that materially supported their class interests. By locating plantation houses as they did, the planters created a visual, and possibly aural, network in the Negro River Valley. In so doing, the valley landscape became a medium of social interaction. Although they were isolated in a remote highland valley, the viewscapes from the plantation houses created a sense of shared place. In being able to see each other (and possibly talk to each other, if Mr. Richards's anecdote is based on actual events) from the relative comfort of the great houses, the small population of resident planters and their overseers not only provided some measure of comfort to each other, but reinforced each other's position in the social hierarchy. In this way, the landscapes that emerged in the Negro River Valley served both to create and reinforce the planters' understanding of their own positions within the social and physical geographies of Upper St. David, and thus worked as one way in which class consciousness was created and reinforced.

5   Contradictions and Dialectics: Village Landscapes of the Enslaved

Few archaeologists today would argue that archaeological data can be interpreted in the absence of an overarching theory explaining how and why societies form, operate, and change. Indeed, the modern history of archaeological thought has been characterized by the convincing use of many theoretical constructs to explain human cultures and histories: cultural ecology (e.g., Steward 1990), logical positivism (e.g., Binford 2002), behavioral ecology (e.g., Bird and O'Connell 2006), sociobiology (e.g., Shennan 2008), practice theory (e.g., Delle 2011), chaos theory (e.g., Beekman and Baden 2005), game theory (e.g., Neiman 2008), performance theory (e.g., Pearson and Shanks 2001), queer theory (e.g., Croucher 2005; Voss 2000), signaling theory (e.g., Bird and Smith 2005; Galle 2011), semiotics (e.g., Prucell 2006), hermeneutics (e.g., Johnsen and Olsen 1992), cultural materialism (e.g., Harris 2001; Price 1982), and Marxism (e.g., McGuire 1992). Each of these theoretical frameworks has at its base a distinct philosophical underpinning composed of an ontology defining the nature of human existence and an epistemology shaping the nature of archaeological inquiry.

An ontology, literally defined as a "study of being," is a philosophical framework that defines how material and social phenomena are categorized, and how these phenomena actively relate and link to each other to create human experience. An ontology thus defines both the boundaries of what is known to exist and what can be known; creates categories of existence; and proposes causal links between humans, objects, and events. Whether consciously or not, all archaeological theories emerge from ontological frameworks defining what can be known about the past, and how we can relate the artifacts we recover in the twenty-first century to the experiences of people who lived in the past.

The ontology shaping Marxist archaeological theory has emerged from an intellectual tradition known as dialectical materialism (see Rosenswig 2012 for a discussion of Marxist ontology). The philosophy of dialectical materialism is based on two primary concepts. The first of these, the concept of dialectics, explains how social and material phenomena relate to each other. The modern definition of dialectics is often credited to the German philosopher G. W. F. Hegel, who posited that reality was both ideational and dialectical; that is, human reality existed primarily as a set of ideas that exist only in the presence of their opposite; thus, the concept "all" could not exist without its contrary antithesis "none." As the human mind contemplated each contradictory set of ideas, characterized as a thesis and an antithesis, a mediated solution to the basic contradiction between the concepts would emerge, known as a synthesis; the synthesis of "all" and "none" being the concept "some." Human intellectual progress could thus be explained as a dialectical process of resolving ideational contradictions, a process that resulted in the formation of new ideas. Later theoreticians, particularly Frederick Engels, expanded the concept of dialectics to explain the nature of all being outside of the human mind. To Engels, reality consisted of matter and motion (or energy); all matter from the smallest microscopic particle to the largest galaxy was in constant motion. That motion was created by the constant working of oppositional forces; analogous to the thesis-antithesis-synthesis process, motion was the result of particles of oppositional matter coming into contact (thesis-antithesis), creating tension (contradiction), and resulting in motion (synthesis). Just as magnetic forces had oppositional poles that either repelled or attracted to create motion, and electrical forces had positive and negative charges that could also create motion, all matter was subject to the oppositional laws of motion. Human beings, being composed of matter, were subject to these forces; human societies, being composed of human beings, were likewise subject to such oppositional forces (Engels 1979).

The second primary concept that defines the ontology of dialectical materialism is the idea that human experience, including the structure and operation of social relationships, is shaped by material reality. Whereas fundamentalist Hegelians would argue that the physical world is given meaning only through ideational perception, Karl Marx famously asserted that he was standing Hegel on his head by arguing the opposite (Marx 1992). To Marx, the ideational world (including the ideas that define social relationships) emerged only through the interaction of human beings with the realities of the physical or material world. The concepts of "plow" and "field" could thus not exist without the material need to turn over soil to plant seeds in the ground to grow food. It was the need for food – the material reality – that generated the concept of "plow" and resulted in the formation of societies defined by the concepts of "landlord" and "serf."

Whereas an ontology defines the philosophical concepts underlying an archaeological theory, an epistemology defines the boundaries of its methodology. In its most common usage in the sciences, the term "epistemology" (literally "the study of knowledge") refers to a theory of knowledge defined by specific principles that explain how the world functions, and how we create knowledge about the world. An epistemology thus defines scientific principles, what is known about the world, and how knowledge about the world is constructed and reproduced. The epistemology of Marxist archaeology derives from the application of dialectical materialism to understanding the historical formation, functioning, and change of human societies, an epistemology known as historical materialism. As we have seen in our discussion of the plantation mode of production, a historical-materialist approach to understanding the human past contends that human societies are composed of coherent factions whose material interests exist in opposition to each other. Human action (referred to by some as "agency") can serve to create or expose contradictions within the organization of society. Structural change in social formations will emerge when these dialectically opposed interests collide to resolve the emerging contradictions in society. As a result of human action through revolution or reform, new class relations can emerge (e.g., through the abolition of slavery or the introduction of wage labor) or new technologies can be introduced that shift the nature of the relationships between humans, their fellows, and the environment. The epistemology of historical materialism thus contends that when social systems are comprised of social classes, contradictions can exist in the social relationships that bind classes together, conflict between classes can emerge when these contradictions lead to social instability, and new social and material realities can emerge through the dialectical reconciliation of those contradictions.

As we have seen in the preceding chapters, the human realities of colonial Jamaica were formed through the emergence of the plantation mode of production. In the eighteenth century, that mode of production resulted from the formation of social classes that had dialectically opposed interests and that were developing increasingly sophisticated class consciousnesses. As the nineteenth century dawned, the two great classes – the planters and the enslaved workers – were living under a mode of production whose contradictions were becoming increasingly clear to both. In the early 1830s, those contradictions resulted in the great uprising known as the Christmas Rebellion/Baptist War and the nearly immediate abolition of slavery, a social formation without which the plantation mode of production could not function.

It is the goal of this chapter to further examine the nature of one of the primary contradictions of the plantation mode of production. As we have seen, Jamaican planters claimed the surplus value resulting from the use of slave labor to produce export commodities, yet enslaved laborers owned the products of their labor resulting from the cultivation of their provision grounds. These parallel phenomena led to the development of a contradiction in the social relations of production. In exploring the nature of this contradiction, this chapter examines the origin of the provision ground system as the basis for this significant contradiction in the plantation mode of production, the rise of consumer behavior among the enslaved, the development of slave villages and households as landscapes controlled by the enslaved as the nexus of commodity production and consumption, and the landscapes of provision grounds as means of production crucial to the development of the plantation mode of production but simultaneously the source of its primary contradiction.

The Origins of the Contradiction

In any given mode of production, the most important economic activity is the production and/or procurement of food, for without adequate sustenance, human existence is not possible. But, as Sidney Mintz and Douglas Hall (1960) have pointed out, seventeenth-century Jamaican planters had to make a choice when developing their first plantations: purchase imported food to feed to the enslaved workforce; compel the enslaved to work to produce food as a term of their enslavement; or require the enslaved to feed themselves. By the middle of the eighteenth century, a provisioning system that incorporated elements of all three of these options was embedded in the plantation mode of production. As the provisioning system developed, the third of these three options – requiring the enslaved to feed themselves – became dominant, largely because the planters believed this system was conducive to extracting the greatest possible surplus value from the enslaved. Although required by this system to work for themselves after their sometimes dangerous, often exhausting, and always unpaid duties to the plantation were done, by the turn of the nineteenth century, enslaved Jamaicans had manipulated the provision ground system to their own benefit. By selling goods they produced on their own time in the provision grounds, including both food stuffs and craft items, enslaved people had access to cash as a thriving consumer market controlled by slaves existed throughout the island. Although the enslaved were prohibited from working for wages, they could sell the products of their labor – things like crafts, vegetables, charcoal, and meat – in these weekly Sunday markets (Berlin and Morgan 1995; Hauser 2001, 2008, 2011; Mintz and Hall 1960; Mullin 1995; Simmonds 2004). The Sunday markets were enabled by the provision ground system, a mutually understood arrangement through which enslaved workers could grow and sell food produced on plantation land.

Its earliest origins still somewhat obscure, the provision ground system may well have arisen in the earliest days of British colonial Jamaica and developed as it did out of a necessity born from the instability of the seventeenth-century colonial world. Mintz and Hall (1960) suggest that the provisioning system likely began as early as 1660; they cite a reference to provision grounds published by the early Jamaican historian Richard Blome in 1672 as evidence for the early introduction of the provisioning system. As the archaeologist James Deetz (1977) has suggested for contemporary British settlements in New England, mid-seventeenth-century colonies developed idiosyncratic cultural systems that, although based on British antecedents, diverged significantly from English culture. Similarly, Mintz and Hall (1960) suggest that the organization of plantation settlements can be traced in a way to feudal arrangements – the great house of the proprietor as analog to the manor house of the lord, surrounded by agricultural fields attended by laborers attached to the estate, and featuring a village of workers and artisans dependent on the landlord. And indeed, some of the earliest British planters may well have hoped to recreate little feudal seignories in the seventeenth-century Caribbean, manned by indentured servants from the British Isles (Beckles 1990; Dunn 2000). Provision grounds can thus be thought to have antecedents in the feudal rights of serfs to grow food and raise livestock on lands owned by a great landlord (Mintz and Hall 1960). Once established in Jamaica, the plantation system quickly diverged from this antecedent, particularly as the profitability of chattel slavery rapidly canceled any notion that the British colony of Jamaica would be populated by an agrarian working class of white settlers from the British European possessions.

The historical context of the early British period created conditions that allowed for the provision ground system to develop. Established in 1655, the British colony in Jamaica began to flourish only in the late 1660s, when an influx of experienced British planters arrived from Barbados and Surinam (Sheridan 1974). It did not take long for the African population to outnumber the European, as by 1673 there were some 7,700 whites and 9,500 enslaved Africans in Jamaica (Edwards 1798; Sheridan 1974). The economic and political vagaries of the late seventeenth century resulted in the fledgling colony having some difficulty in establishing itself. In the late seventeenth century, a blight destroyed the island's cacao trees, crippling an industry that was, in part, funding the initial investments required to start up a successful sugar colony. This ecological disaster was made worse by global events. The late 1680s saw renewed conflict in the British world, first in the Glorious Revolution (1688) between the supporters of King James II and those of his brother-in-law William of Orange. Subsequent warfare broke out between Protestant England and its Dutch allies against the Catholic France of Louis XIV. The Nine Years War (1688–1697) was a multi-fronted conflict, as hostilities broke out between the principle parties, their allies, and colonies, in Europe, North America, Asia, and the Caribbean. The peace concluded between the European powers in 1697 did not last long, as another conflict, the War of the Spanish Succession (1701–1714) soon broke out between rival Spanish factions, one side loyal to the reigning Hapsburg dynasty and their British and Dutch allies, and the other loyal to the Bourbon claimant to the Spanish throne and his French allies. Like the Nine Years War, this conflict was global in scale. In the New World, the conflict (sometimes known as Queen Anne's War in the colonies) was fought on the North American mainland and as a series of naval engagements in the Caribbean Sea (Dunn 1979; Konnert 2008).

In the Caribbean, the War of the Spanish Succession was largely fought through economic warfare, as privateers and men of war targeted enemy merchant shipping for plunder. For the plantation colonies of the Caribbean, the decades of conflict led to unpredictable disruptions in the flow of goods to and from their European mother countries; it was difficult at this time to rely on the regularity of trade from home. As a result, privateering and contraband trade (smuggling) between islands became an increasingly important part of the economy. It was in this climate of uncertainty and conflict in Europe and on the high seas that the plantation mode of production fully developed in Jamaica, and it developed with a social division of labor dependent on the enslavement of African people and their descendants. Not surprisingly, given the irregularity of trade during the nearly three decades of war between 1688 and 1714, the planters and the people they enslaved became dependent on their own agency to produce the necessities of life. The provisioning system thus was an integral component of the plantation mode of production from the start, arising perhaps as much from necessity as from choice.

Although the provisioning system was not the inevitable outcome of the establishment of the plantation economy in Jamaica, once established it provided the material basis for slavery on the island. The planters were more than willing to cede control over remote and, to them, economically marginal areas on their estates for the establishment of provision grounds. They were also quite willing to allow the internal marketing system to develop. Although there were occasional attempts to curtail the independent economy of the enslaved population by limiting the movements of itinerant peddlars (known as "higglers") and regulating the types of objects that could be sold in the Sunday markets (Hauser 2008), the planters were never able to establish any firm control over the internal economy of the enslaved; many small planters and overseers, and some large planters as well, were themselves dependent on the provisioning system for their food supply. Whereas slavery was clearly based on a racist social hierarchy and the often brutal mistreatment of people, under the circumstances the provision ground system resulted in the development of systems of labor and exchange that benefited both the enslaved, who could own and sell the products of their labor, and the planters, who were spared the expense of feeding the population and who also could purchase fresh provisions from the enslaved for use on their own tables.

We can thus see that two labor systems, each with its own internal logic, developed in plantation Jamaica. The first, and more famous, was the system of chattel slavery in which people were owned, bought, and sold as commodities and through which the products of labor were owned exclusively by the planters. The second was a system under which the enslaved had access to the means of subsistence production, including land, tools, and their own labor, and which allowed them to own and sell the products of that labor. Any surplus value produced under the second labor system was owned by the worker him- or herself, as the plantation proprietors were concerned solely with the accumulation of wealth through the export of staple crops. So long as the provisioning system worked to their benefit, the planters tolerated its existence.

Although social unrest about the existence of slavery was common throughout Jamaica, prior to 1760 (and perhaps for some time after that date), the two labor systems – while contradictory – coexisted with little disruption. The Jamaican historian Bryan Edwards characterized the situation quite eloquently:

The practice which prevails in Jamaica of giving the Negroes lands to cultivate ... is universally allowed to be judicious and beneficial; producing a happy coalition of interests between the master and the slave. The negro who has acquired by his own labor a property in his master's land, has much to lose, and is therefore less inclined to desert his work. He earns a little money, by which he is enabled to indulge himself in fine clothes on holidays, and gratify his palate with salted meats. ... [T]he proprietor is eased, in a great measure, of the expense of feeding him. (Edwards 1793: 131)

It can thus be seen, at least from the perspective of an eighteenth-century Jamaican planter, that the provisioning system worked to the benefit of both the enslaved and the proprietor, and, tellingly, would not have been tolerated it if the planters did not perceive the system as being beneficial to their economic interests. Not only did the proprietors mitigate the costs they would have to assume should they be required to either import the majority of food for their plantation workforce or to incorporate food production directly into their plantation labor regime, but the ascendant marketing system that arose from the provisioning system provided an inexpensive way to provide produce for their own households and the households of their overseers and bookkeepers. The Jamaican historian Edward Long allude do this when he stated that Jamaica was in need of more free flowing small coin to "enable the housekeepers and Negroes to carry on their marketing for butchers meat, poultry, hogs, fish, corn, eggs, plantains and the like" (Long 1774: 562). The "housekeepers" Long refers to include the head domestic servants of white households situated either in one of Jamaica's towns or close enough to one of the market towns that food could be purchased for the use of the planter families. Whereas some of the better organized plantations could afford to plant their own kitchen gardens, sometimes known as "plantain walks," smaller estates and those without resident proprietors or attorneys might have neither the resources nor the desire to limit profits by maintaining these for the overseers and bookkeepers, requiring these employees to find food for themselves. Of all the members of the planter class, it was thus the overseers and bookkeepers that were most dependent on the marketing system, and thus on the ability of the enslaved to grow and sell foodstuffs in the markets.

By the third quarter of the eighteenth century, enslaved Jamaicans had the ability to use their own resources to purchase necessities and, as Bryan Edwards suggests, consumer goods that included clothing and imported meat. However, the prevailing economic logic of 1690 that defined the genesis of the provisioning system, despite Bryan Edwards's late reference to the "happy coalition of interests" between planter and enslaved, was quite different from that of a century later. By the end of the eighteenth century, the contradictions in the plantation system were beginning to rend the mode of production apart, in part because of the changing nature of consumerism that developed in the late eighteenth century.

The 1760s saw the widespread introduction and proliferation of new techniques and technologies for the production of consumer goods, a set of historical events often collectively referred to as the Industrial Revolution (Hobsbawn 1999). Most historical archaeologists recognize that the mass production of consumer goods after 1760 changed consumer behavior, and that this shift is visible in the archaeological record (e.g., Cook et al. 1996; Klein 1991; Mullins 1999a, 1999b; Orser 1992). The ubiquitous presence of refined earthenwares in archaeological contexts – particularly cream-wares, pearlwares, and whitewares – is a reflection of these shifts in behavior (e.g., Deetz 1977; Leone 1999; Mrozowski 2006; Orser 1996).

Figure 5.1. Fragments of a yabba vessel (left) and a stoneware cognate, both recovered from Marshall's Pen. Photo by James A. Delle.

Enslaved Jamaicans were deeply embedded in the developing consumer markets of the late eighteenth century, and as mass produced goods began to flood the colonial markets after 1760, increased demand for these objects necessitated an increase in the volume of cash flow emanating from enslaved people to purchase the wider variety of imported goods available (Delle 2007; Hauser 2008; Wilkie 1999; Wilkie and Farnsworth 2005). Whereas planters had depended on the importation of manufactured goods since the earliest days of British settlement in the seventeenth century, prior to the 1760s, enslaved people were largely dependent on locally produced objects – including gourds, baskets, wooden objects, and locally made ceramics (see Figure 5.1). This material reality is revealed in the work conducted by Doug Armstrong in the enslaved village at Drax Hall, a sugar plantation on Jamaica's north coast. Because Drax Hall operated as a sugar estate from as early as 1690 into the early twentieth century, Armstrong was able to collect diachronic data documenting consumption patterns over time. Armstrong excavated six pre-emancipation house yards at Drax Hall. Based on his analysis of datable British ceramics recovered from each house yard (using a technique known as "mean ceramic dating"), Armstrong was able to assign relative dates to each of the six households: 1754 (House Area [HA] 15), 1759 (HA 48), 1784 (HA 91), 1787 (HA 1), 1790 (HA 37), and 1800 (HA 52). In his analysis, Armstrong calculated the ratios of locally produced and imported ceramics for each house area. Remarkably, the two houses with mean ceramic dates preceding 1760 produced much higher percentages of coarse pottery, of which the majority was locally produced yabbas (82.6 percent and 85.6 percent) than did the four households that post-dated 1760 (25.2 percent, 21.2 percent, 16.9 percent, and 3.8 percent). Even more remarkably, the percentages of imported refined ceramics recovered from these houses increased in direct relation to the mean ceramic date derived for the house (1754 = 14.4 percent, 1784 = 74.4 percent, 1787 = 78.8 percent, 1790 = 83.1 percent, and 1800 = 96.2 percent). As these data indicate, by the end of the eighteenth century, imported ceramics had nearly completely replaced locally produced ceramics at Drax Hall. In a similar study conducted at the enslaved village at a sugar plantation known as Montpelier, Barry Higman notes only negligible percentages of yabbas recovered from early-nineteenth-century house areas (HA 14, mean ceramic date of 1837= 0 percent yabba; HA 26, mean ceramic date of 1829 = 1.2 percent yabba; HA 37, mean ceramic date of 1818 = 2.6 percent yabba). Although the sample is small, the trend is clear; the later the house, the greater percentage – and overall number – of imported ceramics.

By the end of the eighteenth century, capitalism was developing a significant consumer sector, and the industrialists producing consumer goods like textiles and ceramics saw the enslaved communities of the West Indies as a potential market for their products. This relationship between producer and enslaved consumer was not lost on the Jamaica planters. One estate agent, Robert Fairweather, commented in an 1833 letter home that the abolition of slavery would "ruin all those connected with the West India Colonies ... and be also the Complete ruin of many of the manufacturing people at home" (CM 25/11/159). The changing consumer markets of the late eighteenth century required that people have access to cash, or some other instrument of exchange, to fully participate in the circulation and use of widely popular mass-produced objects. Because it was not in the best interest of the planters to provide the enslaved with expensive consumer goods beyond those mandated by law, the consumer markets were driven by the internal economy of the enslaved. The landscapes of the enslaved, both in their house yards and provision grounds, were thus productive spaces, not only producing food stuffs for subsistence, but providing the enslaved with a mechanism through which they could produce commodities to exchange in local markets, the value of which was then translated into consumer goods imported from Europe. As desire for consumer goods transformed into need, the contradiction between the two labor systems became increasingly tense, leading eventually to increased social unrest, as we have seen through the example of the Baptist War, and the eventual dissolution of slavery in the British West Indies.

The material manifestations of the contradictory labor systems can be read in the landscapes of plantation villages in Jamaica, like that of Marshall's Pen, a coffee plantation established in the opening decades of the nineteenth century.

Landscapes of Contradiction at Marshall's Pen

Like most people in pre-emancipation colonial Jamaica, the population of Marshall's Pen lived in a plantation village attached to an agricultural estate. Marshall's Pen was a coffee plantation located on what is now known as the Manchester Plateau in south-central Jamaica. Situated at about 600 meters above sea level, Marshall's Pen was one of three contiguous estates owned by an absentee planter and Scottish nobleman, Alexander Lindsay, the sixth Earl of Balcarres. Lord Balcarres, who served as governor of Jamaica from 1795–1801, was a career military man who served first as a major then a colonel in the British army during the American Revolution; by 1803, he had attained the rank of general. While serving as governor of Jamaica, Balcarres began to speculate on coffee production, acquiring multiple properties in the old parishes of St. Elizabeth (now Manchester) and St. George (now Portland). At the conclusion of his term as governor, he departed Jamaica to take up residence in Lancashire, England, and focused his attention on the Haigh Ironworks, which he had founded in 1790. Upon his return to Haigh, Balcarres oversaw the development of what became a very successful foundry, producing industrial equipment including locomotives and mine pumps. Although a successful industrialist, Balcarres maintained and expanded his coffee estates in Jamaica. By around 1810, he had acquired an undeveloped property known as "Douglas Run," which, when developed for coffee production in 1812, was rechristened Marshall's Pen. Upon his death in 1825, the Jamaica estates were bequeathed to Balcarres's heir, James Lindsay, the seventh Earl of Balcarres and twenty-third Earl of Crawford. As his father had done, the younger Earl managed the Jamaica estates as an absentee proprietor. In the early 1850s, the seventh Earl sold Marshall's Pen to the local Muirhead family (Arthur Sutton, personal communication, 1998).

In 1812, the first of two villages was built at Marshall's Pen; this first village would be occupied only for a single generation, as it was abandoned soon after slavery was fully abolished in Jamaica. At that time, the population removed to a newly formed township. The village was but one component of the plantation's built environment. Like other Jamaican coffee plantations of the early nineteenth century, the infrastructure at Marshall's Pen included an overseers house; pulping, grinding, and fanning mills; a range of barbecues; a coffee warehouse; a hospital for sick, injured, and pregnant workers; a graveyard; coffee fields; and provision grounds, where the enslaved workers raised food for their own use and for sale in local markets.

Marshall's Pen operated for several years without the presence of white supervision on the estate, being supervised by an overseer on Martins Hill, another of Balcarres's plantations located several miles away. It was not until 1819 that William Powell, the first white employee at Marshall's Pen, was hired to supervise coffee production there. Prior to this date, at least three separate groups of enslaved workers had been relocated to Marshall's Pen, creating the village and provisioning farms, simultaneously beginning the production of coffee on the estate. In 1814, the population of Marshall's Pen consisted of fifty-nine enslaved people, twenty-five of whom were younger than 14 years old; only two were older than 31. The population of the plantation grew primarily by the introduction of new people through the purchase of existing labor gangs and the transfer of people from the eponymous Balcarres plantation in the Parish of St. George. In 1816, there were 109 people in the village at Marshall's Pen; by 1829, the number of enslaved people had increased to 367, although many of these people resided in a new village that opened in 1821 (see Figure 5.2).

Archaeological investigations were conducted in the first village at Marshall's Pen between 1998 and 2002. The archaeological work included a controlled surface collection of the village site, a mapping project that recorded the surficial remains of ten house compounds, all of which consisted of multiple house platforms flanked by animal pens, the excavation of four house sites within the village, the controlled surface collection of a sheet midden associated with the overseer's house, and the excavation of a privy associated with the overseer's house.

An analysis of the results of that project reveals how the consumer revolution was experienced by enslaved people in Jamaica, and how the landscapes they lived can be considered to be landscapes of contraction in the plantation mode of production, reflected in the kinds of objects acquired and used by people on the plantation as well as the organization of their village, house yard, and provision ground landscapes.

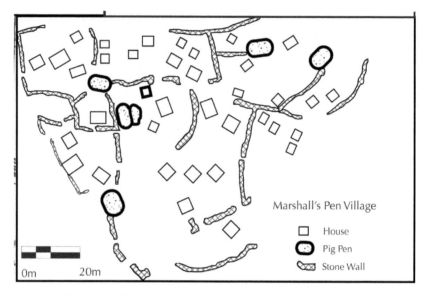

Figure 5.2. Reconstructed settlement pattern of the village at Marshall's Pen. Illustration by James A. Delle.

The "Consumer Revolution" at Marshall's Pen

It has been well-established by historical archaeologists and social historians that the mass production of consumer goods fostered a radical cultural transformation in England and its colonies, a transformation that has been referred to as the "consumer revolution" (e.g., Brown 2011; Carson 1994; Hauser 2008; Martin 1996; Pogue 2001). Although this revolution likely had its origins in the early sixteenth century, a strong case has been made that expressions of consumer behavior expanded exponentially in the second half of the eighteenth century, both in geographic scope and across social classes. The industrialization of the production of consumer goods like textiles and other items of clothing, iron products, and ceramics made mass-produced goods plentiful and inexpensive throughout the British Empire (e.g., Carson 1994; McKendrick 1982). Considerable evidence of consumer behavior was recovered at Marshall's Pen.

What we now refer to as consumer goods circulated into the village at Marshall's Pen in one of three ways: (1) documentary evidence clearly suggests that some kinds of material goods were provided to the enslaved community by the plantation – prevailing custom and local law required that at least once a year clothing (or at least the textiles and material required to make clothing) and certain other necessities were distributed to the enslaved population of Jamaican plantations; (2) contemporary observers have left a significant body of evidence detailing that objects, both locally produced and imported, were sold in weekly Sunday markets, providing an avenue for the purchase of consumer goods by the enslaved (Hauser 2008); and (3) itinerant peddlers known as higglers moved between plantations with consumer goods to sell.

That mass-produced goods were distributed by Marshall's Pen to the enslaved is documented in a series of letters sent from Jamaica to the Earl of Balcarres at Haigh House in Lancashire. As was the case with many absentee proprietors, both the elder and younger Earl retained a merchant house in Kingston to serve in the capacity of attorney for their Jamaican properties; much of the correspondence from the attorneys has been preserved by the Lindsay family and is currently housed in the National Library of Scotland. The name of the Jamaica firm retained by Balcarres changed several times, reflecting the death of partners: in 1811, it was known as Atkinson, Bogle, and Company; in 1813, simply Atkinson and Bogle; in 1814, the firm took on two partners to replace the deceased Mr. Bogle, becoming Atkinson, Adams, and Robertson. By 1815, the firm changed name to Adams, Robertson, and Company. By the early 1820s, Adams had returned to England; from this point forward the correspondence to Balcarres was signed by individual attorneys employed by Adams on the Earl's behalf.

In February 1813, the sixth Earl of Balcarres inquired of his attorneys about securing supplies for the newly formed plantation at Marshall's Pen. Atkinson, Bogle, and Company replied in May of that year:

On the subject of the British supplies; it is quite clear, that one part can be furnished cheaper from home, [Britain] than here [Jamaica], for example, all articles of iron-ware and clothing, such articles, therefore, should be imported from the cheapest British market, we would recommend Glasow, which we have always found lower in its price for such goods, than London. (CM 23/8/9)

Balcarres clearly took the advice of his attorneys. In February of 1814, a shipment of goods arrived at the Salt River wharf to be brought the forty or so miles overland for the use of the enslaved population at Marshall's Pen. Among the mass-produced goods landed were "1 crate earthenware"; "1 box pipes"; "30 iron pots"; "6 tierces, 3 bales, and 1 box clothing"; "2 dozen pots ex. John William"; and "4 dozen iron pots" (nb: a "tierce" is a medium-sized staved container, smaller than a hogshead but larger than a barrel; a tierce contained about forty-two gallons of volume). Other mass-produced goods that found their way into the village from the Salt River wharf later that year included nails, hoes, saws, and axes. A significant amount of food was also transported from Salt River to Marshall's Pen in 1814, including one tierce and two hogsheads of salt, three barrels of shads, one barrel each of beef and pork, twenty-five barrels of herrings, four "half barrels of provisions," one barrel of salmon, two hogsheads of fish, and two barrels of flour (CM 23/8/390).

The second way that consumer goods would find their way into the village at Marshall's Pen was through exchange in local markets. The town of Mandeville, only a few miles from Marshall's Pen, was laid out and established in 1816 as the seat of the newly established parish of Manchester. Although the exact date of its establishment is not yet known, it is likely that the Mandeville market was established at least by 1816 (Hauser 2008). The third vector of consumer goods was purchase from itinerant traders known in Jamaica as "higglers." As Mark Hauser describes, higglers would travel from plantation village to plantation village, selling consumer goods to the people in the villages.

It is hard to know which of these three exchange systems supplied the enslaved population of Marshall's Pen with their first set of mass-produced consumer goods. The long list of consumer products landed at Salt River suggests that some were distributed by the plantation. Furthermore, in 1815, when a group of enslaved people were transferred from another of the Balcarres estates to work at the newly developed Marshall's Pen, the estate distributed "presents to Negroes on removal ... to this property" to the tune of £43 6d 3p, and purchased 500 gallons of rum, presumably for the same purpose (CM 23/8/384). It seems likely that consumer goods would have been included among the presents.

In any event, a controlled surface collection of the site, coupled with the archaeological testing of four houses conducted in 1998–2002 revealed the kinds of consumer goods that circulated among the villagers of Marshall's Pen. The artifact assemblage is dominated by three classes of material: ceramics, glass, and iron. Of these three, ceramics are most closely related to consumer behavior.

Ceramics are commonly found on historic sites; by the turn of the nineteenth century, English potteries were turning out a dizzying variety of ceramic types, featuring a wide range of vessel forms, decorative styles and motifs, glaze treatments, and body paste. When analyzing these ceramics, historical archaeologists tend to distinguish between relatively high-fired stonewares and lower-fired earthenwares; each of these categories is usually further divided between coarse earthenwares and stonewares (generally thick-bodied vessels used for utilitarian purposes) and refined earthenwares and stonewares (usually thinner-bodied, well-glazed and/or decorated, used generally for serving food); these are

Table 5.1 Refined English earthenwares recovered at Marshall's Pen

Ceramic Type	Number of Pieces Recovered	Percent of overall ceramic assemblage
Tin-glazed	1	0.4%
Creamware	38	15.1%
Pearlware	104	41.3%
Mocha/Annular Ware	27	10.7%
Whiteware	32	12.7%

Table 5.2 Vessel forms and their functions recovered from Marshall's Pen

Vessel Form	Vessel Function	Percent of Overall Assemblage
Plate	Food Service	20.8%
Saucer	Food/Drink Service	4.9%
Bowl	Food Service	15.8%
Cup	Food/Drink Service	5.6%
Coffee Pot	Food/Drink Service	0.6%
Cream Pot	Food/Drink Service	0.3%
Mug	Food/Drink Service	0.8%
Jar	Utilitarian: Storage	9.4%
Bottle	Utilitarian: Storage	0.9%
Jug	Utilitarian: Storage	3.8%
Milk Pan	Utilitarian: Food Preparation	0.8%
Chamber Pot	Utilitarian: Hygiene	1.8%
Unidentifiable		34.5%

generally subdivided by glaze and decorative type (see Table 5.1). In Jamaica, as we discussed earlier, a locally made coarse earthenware, referred to as yabba, was very commonly used before the first half of the eighteenth century, and was made and used by some Jamaicans into the twentieth century.

Archaeologists are also interested in establishing the form of ceramics recovered as a way to better understand the lifeways of the people who used and deposited the artifacts we analyze. At Marshall's Pen, thirteen ceramic forms were identified, most of which are related either to food preparation or food consumption (see Table 5.2).

Three classes of utilitarian ceramics were recovered at Marshall's Pen: a buff-bodied refined earthenware known as yellowware, coarse salt-glazed brown stoneware, and only three sherds of locally produced yabba.

Table 5.3 Coarse ceramics recovered from Marshall's Pen surface collection

Ceramic Type	Number of Pieces Recovered	Percent of overall ceramic assemblage
Brown Stoneware	42	16.7%
Yellowware	5	2.0%
Yabba	3	1.2%

Together, the coarse ceramics comprise just less than 20 percent of the entire ceramic assemblage; most of this was imported brown stoneware (see Table 5.3).

Refined earthenwares can serve as a metaphor for the expanding variety of objects available beginning in the late eighteenth century. Although there had been a burgeoning ceramic industry in England in the early eighteenth century, the innovations in style and production techniques introduced by Josiah Wedgwood in the late 1750s and early 1760s led to a rapid industrialization of ceramic production in England. His introduction and subsequent marketing of cream-colored earthenware, known in its day as "Queens Ware" and generally referred to today as "creamware," was particularly important. Creamware was among the first mass-marketed consumer goods to be distributed globally; its appearance in contexts like enslaved villages demonstrates the success that Wedgwood had in marketing this particular kind of ceramic. Ceramics are also particularly interesting because they demonstrate how quickly innovations of the late eighteenth century led to quick turnovers in fashion; in rapid order, a wide range of new glazes and decorative techniques were introduced and were purchased and consumed throughout the British colonial world (see Table 5.4).

The archaeological record clearly indicates that mass-produced ceramics were being consumed by the enslaved workers in the village of Marshall's Pen. The documentary record of the estate preserved in the correspondence between Balcarres and his Jamaican attorneys indicates that some mass-produced items, particularly iron cooking pots, were frequently being purchased to supply newly arrived laborers and to replace broken and worn out pots; between 1814 and 1825, the plantation purchased no fewer than nine dozen iron cooking pots for use in the slave village (see Figure 5.3). Another fifty-six "jars and jugs" were purchased in 1818; these may actually be the brown stoneware vessels recovered from Marshall's Pen (see Figure 5.4). Similarly, entries in the annual accounts sent to Balcarres indicate that food staples (particularly rice and fish) were

Table 5.4 Ceramic varieties recovered from Marshall's Pen

Ceramic Type	Ceramic Variety	Number of Pieces Recovered	Percent of overall ceramic assemblage
Creamware	Plain	37	14.7%
	Edge Decorated	1	0.4%
Pearlware	Undecorated	38	15.1%
	Blue Edge Decorated	8	3.2%
	Green Edge Decorated	1	0.4%
	Debased Shell Edge	2	0.8%
	Embossed Edge	1	0.4%
	Hand Painted	1	0.4%
	Blue Transfer Print	52	20.6%
	Red Transfer Print	1	0.4%
Whiteware	Undecorated	20	7.9%
	Debased Shell Edge	1	0.4%
	Blue Transfer Print	4	1.6%
	Green Transfer Print	7	2.8%
Mocha	Annular	16	6.3%
	Dendritic	8	3.2%
	Engine-turned	2	0.8%
	Finger Painted	1	0.4%

bought for use in the village; the same can be said for bundles and barrels of "negro clothing." However, beyond the first instance of a "crate of earthenware" being unloaded at Salt River in 1814, no further mention of earthenware is made in the accounts. Presuming that the single crate unloaded in 1814 did not provide the population with their ceramics for the next twenty years, it is reasonable to conclude that some, if not most, of the ceramics recovered from Marshall's Pen were purchased by enslaved people for their own use, either in the Mandeville market or from itinerant higglers (see Figure 5.5).

A question remains, however: How did the enslaved people of Marshall's Pen get the money to purchase these ceramics?

The Contradiction of Planter and Enslaved

The answer to this question can be at least partially found in the accounting records sent to Balcarres by his attorneys. Although it is probable that some of the villagers at Marshall's Pen participated in marketing activities, selling produce and craft items in the Mandeville market, no records exist

Figure 5.3. Fragments of iron cooking pots recovered from Marshall's Pen. Photos by James A. Delle.

to document this activity. On the other hand, clear evidence does exist to suggest that the plantation itself purchased supplies from the people enslaved on it, a clear reflection of the growing contradiction developing in Jamaica's mode of production.

Figure 5.4. Imported stoneware in situ at Marshall's Pen; this is likely one of the "jars and jugs" unloaded at the Salt River Wharf in 1818. Photo by James A. Delle.

This economic relationship was not unique to Marshall's Pen. For example, on Radnor Plantation, a coffee estate contemporary to Marshall's Pen, although located on another part of the island, women were actively involved in the production of castor oil, which they sold back to the estate managers at the rate of 3 shillings 4 pence per bottle (Delle 2002).

According to the accounts sent to Balcarres, which followed a July 1–June 30 fiscal year, Adam White, the overseer at both Martins Hill and Marshall's Pen, approved frequent purchases of food stuffs from the enslaved for several years. In 1818–1819, the plantation purchased fresh pork from "the Negroes" at least once every month, except November. Pork sales amounted to just more than £55 that year, just less than the £60 paid in salary to the bookkeeper Richard Jackson. In addition to the pork sales, enslaved people at Marshall's Pen also sold "corn to plant" to the estate in February, March, April, and June; additional corn was purchased

Figure 5.5. Refined Earthenware recovered from Marshall's Pen; these annular wares were imported from England. Photo by James A. Delle.

from "Mr. Denton's Negroes." In 1820–1821, this trend continued; and even though purchases were made less frequently (none in June, July, September, or March), the plantation still purchased a bit more that £58 worth of pork from the enslaved workers. In that same fiscal year the plantation also "paid negroes for poultry had at sundry times" (£20..7..10), again purchased some corn to plant, and paid George Powell, an enslaved carpenter at Marshall's Pen £15..8..15 for "sundries for the use of the property." Additional sales from enslaved people were recorded for 1825–1826 including £34..9..7 for pork, £6 for hens, £1..10 for "nut oil" (likely castor oil), and £2..12..6 for six bushels of seed corn. In 1830–1831, the estate paid the enslaved £33..6..2 for pork, £6..13..4 for two barrows (castrated male pigs), 6 shillings 8 pence for seed corn, and 3 shillings 4 pence for a pigs head.

In two of the years during which provisions were purchased from the enslaved (1825–1826 and 1830–1831), the estate kept track of the individuals from whom they were purchased. In 1825–1826, the plantation purchased provisions from fourteen enslaved people, including nine men and five women. The sellers held a variety of occupations in the work force, including eight fieldworkers, two artisans, a watchman, a driver, and a doctress. Single purchases were made from each of them, except two: Jonathan Robertson sold pork on two occasions, and nut oil and seed corn on separate occasions. Jonathan Logan sold pork on one occasion, and a breeding sow on a separate occasion. With the exception of James Adams (age 22) and Ann Davis (age 53), the sellers were aged between 33 and 50. The purchases made in 1830–1831 follow a similar pattern; ten men and six women sold provisions to the estate, with only Ophelia Nelson (pork and a pigs head) and Francis White (pork on two occasions) appearing more than once. A variety of occupations was again represented, including six field workers, three artisans, and one doctor; two invalids and one woman "hired out" also appear on the list. Of note, one of the sellers, Jonathan Hall, was listed in the slave register as "minding hogs." The age range is also similar: nine of the fourteen identifiable ages fall between 33 and 50, with two younger than 33 and three older than 50; one of the two younger people was 32 and the other 27. The only immediately obvious demographic difference between 1825 and 1830 is that, in the latter year, several invalids sold pork to the estate, including 74-year-old Francis Waugh and 59-year-old Jonathan Hall, who was one of only two people to appear on the lists from both years, the other being James Adams (see Table 5.5).

Table 5.5 Identified individuals selling produce to Marshall's Pen, 1825–1826

Name	Gender	Age	Occupation	Purchased	Amount
Jonathan Robertson	Male	34	Field	217 lbs pork 6 bottles oil 6 bushels seed corn	£14..0..10
J. Archibald	Male	36	Watchman	70 lbs pork	£2..4..4
Jane Edwards	Female	33	Field	90 lbs pork	£2..16..3
Anora Francis	Female	35	Field	157 lbs pork	£3..5..5
Jonathan Hall	Male	47	Field	64 lbs pork	£1..6..8
Jonathan Logan	Male	41	Field	Breeding sow, 90 lbs pork	£4..12..1
William Atkinson	Male	50	Field	55 lbs pork	£1..4..4
James Adams	Male	22	Cooper	22 lbs pork	£0..13..9
Kitty Lindsay	Female	37	Doctress	124 lbs pork	£2..12..6
Ann Davis	Female	53	Field	50 lbs pork	£1..15..0
James Morrison	Male	37	Field	79 lbs pork	£1..12..11
George Powell	Male	42	Carpenter	52 lbs pork	£1..12..6
Smart Hall	Male	36	Driver	72 lbs pork	£2..5..0
Saline**				95 lbs pork	£1..19..7

**Does not appear on slave list

Table 5.6 Identified individuals selling produce to Marshall's Pen, 1830–1831

Name	Gender	Age	Occupation	Purchased	Amount
Susanna Smith	Female	48	Invalid	Pork	£2..3..9
Elizabeth Adams	Female	39	Field	Pork	£1..17..9
Henry Archibald**	Male			Pork	£1..9..7
Joseph Morrison	Male	56	Field	Pork	£2..0..5
Francis White	Female	32	Hired out	106 lbs pork	£2..16..3
William Bogle	Male	47	Field	Pork	£2..0..0
Eleanor Thomson	Female	25	Field	64 lbs pork	£2..0..0
George Lewis	Male	34	Doctor	115 lbs pork	£3..11..10
Francis Waugh	Female	74	Invalid	85 lbs pork	£2..13..1
Charles Gourley	Male	33	Mason	Seed corn	£0..6..8
Jonathan Hall	Male	59	"Minds hogs"	27 lbs pork	£0..16..10
Joseph Robertson	Male	41	Carpenter	56 lbs pork	£1..15..0
Jonathan Richards	Male	27	Mason	70 lbs pork	£2..3..9
Robert Logan	Male	42	Field	100 lbs pork	£3..2..6
James Adams	Male	35	Field	85 lbs pork	£2..13..1
Ophelia Nelson**	Female			68 lbs pork	£2..2..6

**Does not appear on slave list

Figure 5.6. House Area 1 at Marshall's Pen under excavation. The stone feature in the background is a double bay pigpen. Photo by James A. Delle.

Landscapes of Contradiction

Whereas the landscapes of the plantation proprietors, overseers, and bookkeepers were constructed around the needs of export production, the landscapes of the enslaved were designed and lived to facilitate this kind of small-scale production for subsistence and local exchange. Most plantations contained at least two spatially segregated landscapes controlled by the enslaved and intertwined with the subsistence economy that emerged from the provisioning system: what were generally referred to as "negro villages" and what were referred to as "provision grounds."

Although some members of the community, particularly domestic servants, were quartered in the houses of the proprietors, overseers, and bookkeepers, the majority of the enslaved community lived in concentrated settlements generally known as villages. Jamaican plantation villages tended to follow one of two general layouts; some villages were composed of clusters of house compounds sharing some common space, others consisted of linear rows of houses flanking a road. Which layout structured the village appears to be directly related to the management strategy imposed by planters. Where the planters attempted to exert the most control over the landscape, the villages tended to be linearly organized; where the planters attempted to exert less control, the villages tended to be clustered rather than linear (Armstrong and Kelly 2000; Delle 2008).

This difference in settlement pattern was discerned by Doug Armstrong in his work at Seville Plantation. According to his analysis, the earlier of two plantation villages at Seville, dating from the opening decades of the eighteenth century, consisted of houses symmetrically placed in linear rows flanking a road connecting the village to the great house; this village was in full view of the plantation house. Armstrong concluded that the plantation suffered storm damage in the later part of the eighteenth century; as a result, both the original great house and the village were reconfigured. The village was moved to a location out of the immediate viewshed of the great house, and was organized as a series of house compounds surrounding a central common. Armstrong concluded that the plantation management was so occupied with the reconstruction of the destroyed great house, that they let the enslaved community rebuild their own village with little interference. In this moment of relaxed spatial control, the workers built a village that suited their economic and social needs (Armstrong 2011; Armstrong and Kelly 2000).

That this configuration was not simply a factor of temporal change is reflected in the fact that a similar, though inverted, shift in village settlement pattern occurred at Marshall's Pen. As we have seen, when the plantation was first developed, the clearing of forest land and the construction of the village and works was completed without the supervision of a resident plantation management staff; indeed, no staff was actually employed to oversee the first phases of plantation development at Marshall's Pen. The village, which was first occupied in the 1810s, was organized as a series of clustered house compounds, most of which featured several houses sharing a common yard and pigpen. A second village, first occupied in 1821 when the plantation was in full production and supervised by a resident white staff, was organized much as the first village at Seville had been, in symmetrically ordered rows flanking a central road (Delle 2009). As had been the case at Seville, when left to their own devices, the enslaved people at Marshall's Pen designed and built a landscape that suited the needs of small-scale, local production.

That built environment consisted of yards, animal pens, and houses. Whereas many houses in Jamaican plantation villages were constructed of wattle and daub, the debris patterns at Marshall's Pen suggest that houses in the first village there were constructed differently. Several of the houses in the village were constructed using a technique known locally as "Spanish Wall." Similar to what is known as "nog" construction, the Spanish Wall technique involves constructing a light timber frame, and filling the spaces between studs with rubble. The rubble is held together with lime mortar, and the wall is covered with plaster (see Figures 5.7 and 5.8).

Prior to their development for coffee plantation and cattle husbandry, the Jamaican highlands featured old-growth, tropical hardwood forests. Lumber was thus a plentiful building material when plantations like Marshall's Pen were developed, and as a result, wood was commonly used for construction. Some of the houses at Marshall's Pen were what are locally called "board houses." As the name implies, board houses, like the Spanish Wall houses, were constructed with a light timber frame, which was then covered with weather boards. The weather boards were then either sheathed with clapboards or shingles. It is likely that both types of houses featured shingle roofs, and given the number of pulled nails recovered from house areas at Marshall's Pen, it also seems likely that board houses, at least, featured raised plank flooring, which was curated and moved when the village was abandoned. The standing overseer's house at Marshall's Pen, made with the Spanish Wall technique, features floorboards made out of locally harvested mahogany. As the carpenters who built this house were the same men who built the houses in the village, it is likely that this same hardwood was used to floor the houses in the village (see Figures 5.9, 5.10 and 5.11).

Figure 5.7. (a): A nineteenth-century Spanish Wall house still standing in the town of Porus, just a few miles from Marshall's Pen. Segments of the shingle roof are visible on the far left and right. (b): Detail of the house showing the Spanish Wall construction technique. Photo by James A. Delle.

Figure 5.8. (a): The remnants of a Spanish Wall House at Marshall's Pen, designated House 1 in House Area 1. (b): A fragment of Spanish Wall with pieces of wood still adhered to the plaster. Photo by James A. Delle.

Figure 5.9. A nineteenth-century board house in Porus. Photo by James A. Delle.

Figure 5.10. The remnants of a board house in the village of Marshall's Pen. The construction of this house, designated House Area 6, was very similar to the surviving board house in Porus. Photo by James A. Delle.

Figure 5.11. Hand-wrought iron nails recovered from House Area 6 at Marshall's Pen. These nails were likely pulled from the floorboards when the village was abandoned. Photo by James A. Delle.

The two contradictory village settlement patterns were a reflection of the dialectical differences existing between planters' understanding and use of the land and that of the enslaved. To the enslaved, the house yard and garden were crucially important space. It was in this space that the villagers of Marshall's Pen were able to raise livestock for their own use, and for sale in the markets and to the estate management. To management, the villages were necessary for housing, and little else. Indeed, the plantation theorist P. J. Laborie recommended that coffee plantations house their workers in large tenements, with little free access to the space required to raise poultry and hogs. It was this conflicting sense of space, which emerged from the contradictions inherent in the plantation mode of production, that produced this visible variation in the settlement pattern of plantation villages in Jamaica.

As we have seen, Jamaican planters usually required the enslaved population to produce their own food. Heads of enslaved households were granted access to land known as provision grounds; the food grown in provision ground gardens provided most of the nutritional requirements for the population, as well as the surplus exchanged in local markets and sold to the estates. Prior to emancipation, it was recognized by both the

planters and the enslaved that the enslaved controlled the sale and distribution of produce grown in these provision grounds. The actual size of the
allotted plots probably varied depending on the individual planter and the
quality of land designated for provisions (Mintz 1960). For example, in
1790 the Jamaican plantation observer William Beckford commented that a
provision ground equaling a "quarter acre . . . will be fully sufficient for the
supply of a moderate family, and may enable [them] to carry some to
market besides" (Beckford 1790: 257). John Stewart elaborated on this
phenomenon:

Each slave has . . . a piece of ground (about half an acre) allotted to him as a
provision ground. This is the principal means of his support; and so productive
is the soil, where it is good and the seasons regular, that this spot will not only
furnish him with sufficient food for his own consumption, but an oversurplus to
carry to market. . . . If he has a family, an additional proportion of ground is allowed
him, and all his children from five years upward assist him in his labors. (Stewart
1969[1823]: 267).

Although provision grounds were transient spaces, some observations can
be made about how they were organized on Jamaican coffee plantations.
For example, a pre-emancipation estate map of Mavis Bank identifies 79
of the estate's 302 acres, approximately 26 percent of the estate's acreage,
as "Negro Grounds and Provisions." Whereas the boundaries of the
"Negro Grounds" are clearly demarcated on the map, no internal subdivision is rendered. However, as the enslaved population of Mavis Bank
in 1817 numbered 106, it can be estimated that approximately one acre
was allocated per capita; it remains impossible to say, however, just how
much of the land was under cultivation at any given time.

   An 1806 depiction of Radnor Plantation gives some further indication
of how provision grounds fit into the internal division of material space
on coffee plantations (Higman 1986, 1988). Of the estate's 689 acres,
133 acres were in "Negro grounds and provisions," and an additional
222 acres were in "woodland and Negro grounds." There were four
separate areas of the plantation designated as "Negro grounds," and a
fifth identified as "woodland." As was the case on Mavis Bank, most of
this land was located along the periphery of the estate. On Radnor, just
less than one acre of provision ground and woodlot was allocated per
capita in 1806 (Higman 1986).

   A bit more information about the organization of provision grounds can
be gleaned from the immediate post-emancipation record of coffee plantations. For example, an estate plan of Green Valley rendered in 1837,
during the period of the apprenticeship, was drawn specifically to measure
the extent of the provision grounds cultivated by the laborers attached to

the estate. According to this plan, the section of the estate utilized for provisions was divided into eighteen pieces, ranging in size from 3.5 to 13.5 acres, and each piece – with the exception of one six-acre grass piece that was cultivated by a single individual – was cultivated by between six and twenty people. The average amount of land per capita within each provision piece, again excepting the one grass piece, ranged between one-third acre and 1.5 acres per person. Provisions grown on the plots included congo and pigeon peas, yams, cassava, sweet potatoes, bananas, plantains, and fruit (Delle 1998; STA 366).

The testimony given by Alexander Geddes to the Parliamentary committees on Jamaican cultivation provides some insight as to the extent and nature of provision cultivation that occurred in such grounds following emancipation, and thus likely describes the pre-emancipation antecedents. According to Geddes, who managed several coffee estates throughout the island, African Jamaicans would generally cultivate a provision ground of between one-half and two acres as well as a garden attached to their house. Geddes described the extent of these house gardens as being between one-eighth and one-quarter acre. Whereas people would grow tubers and other staples crops in their provision grounds, Geddes testified that cash crops, particularly coconuts, were grown in the house gardens. According to Geddes, a small garden plot could support a dozen coconut trees, which in turn could provide an income of between £10 and £30 sterling per annum; in later testimony, he admitted that this high sum may have been an exaggeration (PP 1842/13/741).

Geddes further reported that the provision grounds were cultivated on a short rotational basis; perhaps on a swidden system. When asked whether half an acre was sufficient to provide a laborer with all he needed, Geddes replied that it had "never been the custom to restrict the negroes; they culled the richest spots, and having taken one half acre, and used that for two or three years, they then take another; a half acre thus used is competent to subsist [sic] a man, his wife and three or four children a whole year" (PP 1842/13/467).

Whereas we can determine the size and extent of provision grounds on coffee estates rather easily, it is more difficult to interpret just how these landscapes were experienced by the enslaved. One line of evidence is an estate plan drawn up as part of a boundary dispute between Balcarres and one of his neighbors. The plan depicts in some detail the disputed area, which includes some of the provision grounds on Marshall's Pen. This cartographic evidence indicates that several houses were dispersed among the provision grounds and coffee fields of this estate. This arrangement would have allowed people the opportunity to live nearer to their fields. Alternatively, these may represent smaller houses that were occupied periodically by people who lived in the villages, but maintained smaller shelters near their provision grounds, using them for shelter during sudden storms, or as a private retreat. This settlement pattern can still be observed among Jamaican farmers today, who may reside in a village or other settlement, but maintain a small house on lands they cultivate, which sometimes can be several miles away from their main home.

The existence of what are known in West Africa as "field houses" in Jamaican provision grounds may explain the curious phenomena of "petit maroonage." Maroonage was a process, common throughout the slave-holding colonies of the New World, by which enslaved laborers left the estates of their own free will and either joined existing indigenous communities or else formed sovereign communities of their own. Petit maroonage can be considered a variant of this phenomenon, and may be a dialectical synthesis existing between Maroon and enslaved. Petit maroonage was a process by which enslaved laborers left their bondage temporarily, returning of their own free will to their estates after a brief period of escape.

The process of petit maroonage is well-documented in the surviving daybook of Radnor Plantation. At Radnor, the estate management commonly listed people as absconding, being absent, or running away; all synonyms to describe movements off of the estate unauthorized by the planters. The Radnor Plantation Book covers the period from January 1822 through February of 1826, except the period January 4 through July 5, 1823 which is missing from the book. The plantation staff recorded the names of workers who escaped from the plantation, the dates they left, and the dates they returned; in some cases, the plantation book records short remarks about the circumstances of their return.

In all, twenty-five people – about 11 percent of the total population or 16 percent of the adult population – absconded from the plantation a total of thirty-three times; eight escaped twice, seventeen escaped once. The dates of escape and return for all but eight of these incidents were recorded. Of the twenty-five people who managed to escape, eleven were women and fourteen were men. Of these, all but one, Phoebe, eventually returned to the plantation. Of the incidents with recorded dates of escape and return, the average time away from the plantation was eighteen days. Besides Phoebe, only Trim (seventy-nine days), Flora (twenty-one days), Little Quomin (fifty-five days), Murray (thirty-six days), and Matthew (forty-three days) were gone for a longer period than the

Box 3: The Maroons of Jamaica

One manifestation of resistance against slavery was the self-emancipation of those who fled the system and created communities beyond the control of the plantation elites. Such sovereign people have historically been known as the Maroons. Maroon groups have been known to exist in slave-holding areas near remote hinterlands where those escaping slavery could create their communities safely away from the plantations, often settling with or near Native American communities similarly attempting to keep their distance from the incursions of the Europeans. Large Maroon communities existed in Brazil, Virginia (in the Great Dismal Swamp), Florida, Surinam, Mexico, Columbia, Cuba, Hispaniola, and – of course – Jamaica.

The Jamaican Maroons established two separate communities, one in the Blue Mountains in eastern Jamaica, usually referred to as the Windward Maroons, and the other in the cockpit country of west-central Jamaica, known as the Leeward Maroons. Concerned about autonomous people of African descent in their hinterlands, the British waged several wars against the Maroons in Jamaica. What is generally referred to as the First Maroon War was in fact a long series of clashes between frontier planters and raiding parties of Maroons, dating from the late 1670s through 1739. In March of 1739, a peace treaty was signed between the Maroons and the colonial government, which promised personal freedom and economic sovereignty for the Maroons if they agreed to cease hostilities against the planters, to return any newly escaped slaves trying to join them, and to be available to defend the island against rebellion or invasion. The ensuing peace lasted until the outbreak of the Second Maroon War in 1795. This latter conflict erupted when Maroon groups believed that the British colonists were not respecting the treaty terms agreed on in 1739. After what amounted to a nine-month stalemate between the guerilla forces of the Maroons and a combined force of British regulars and island volunteers, the Maroons agreed to a second peace treaty. However, when the Maroons surrendered their arms in accord with the treaty, the Earl of Balcarres, who was then governor of the island (and who later owned Marshall's Pen), broke the terms of the treaty, imprisoning hundreds of Maroons in prison ships, and eventually deported 600 people to Nova Scotia, effectively breaking the military power of the Maroons.

The Maroons of Jamaica remain proudly sovereign, and maintain villages in both the eastern and western parishes of Jamaica.

mean. The journal records several additional instances of unsanctioned movement that cannot be quantified, as the date the people returned and/or the number of days they were absent from the plantation does not appear in the journal.

Although this is still somewhat a matter of conjecture, it is quite possible that these incidents of absconding were in fact expressions of petit maroonage, during which the enslaved people left the employ of the estate, not necessarily with the intention of permanently running away, but to tend their provision grounds to maximize their ability to participate in the local economy. The cartographic reference to "negro houses and huts" on the estate plan of Marshall's Pen clearly indicates that houses existed in the provision grounds, giving members of the enslaved community the ability to live on their remote farms outside of the view of the planters. It is also possible that enslaved people were squatting on undeveloped land outside of the estate as well.

Conclusion

As Hauser demonstrates, by the turn of the nineteenth century, the planter class attempted to more stringently regulate the weekly Sunday markets in which commodities and cash changed hands as they began to perceive that the independent economy controlled by the enslaved threatened their ability to maximize control over surplus value (Hauser 2008). At the same time, efforts were made by some planters to more closely regulate the landscapes of the enslaved, at least in their villages. By this time, the provision ground system, through which the enslaved had been able to organize and control a local economy, was fully developed. These efforts were manifestations of the conflicts emerging as the fully mature industrial mode of production began taking hold in Great Britain, and its social and material effects felt in its remote colonies like Jamaica.

As the parallel economies of the planter and the enslaved developed, dialectical conflict emerged in the plantation mode of production. Different understandings and uses of landscapes emerged; in plantation villages, both the enslaved and the planters imagined the spaces as loci to fulfill their own needs. The same holds true for the provision grounds. Whereas the planters saw these spaces as part of the means of production necessary for the maintenance of their working population, the enslaved saw them as spaces necessary for the production of commodities for exchange in local markets.

The ontology of dialectical materialism indicates that such dialectical conflict will need to be resolved one way or another, and that resolution will result in some sort of material change. The epistemology of historical materialism suggests that the contradictions inherent in the plantation mode of production will result in synthetic changes to the forces and relations of production. When applied to anthropological archaeology, this means that the contradiction between the enslaved and the planter classes would result in a new, synthetic mode of production in which elements of both the planter's vision of the mode of production, and the enslaved vision of the mode of production will result in an emergent social structure that, while related to its antecedents, was an entirely new organization of society. Archaeologically, this means that new landscapes forms should develop and new social relations should emerge.

The great uprising of 1831 can thus been seen as both the outcome of the contradiction emerging within the plantation mode of production, and the catalyst for dialectical change. How culture change emerged from this contradiction is the question to which we next turn.

6   Dialectics and Social Change: Plantation
Landscapes after Slavery

Archaeologists have long been fascinated by what is generally referred to as the collapse of complex society. There is archaeological evidence scattered around the world – from the deserts of Mesopotamia to the jungles of Mesoamerica – of highly ordered, stratified civilizations whose societies fell apart and whose cities were abandoned and have since fallen into ruin. Much of the imaginative portrayal of archaeologists in the popular media depicts dashing heroes and heroines prying through the forgotten tombs and abandoned cities of such "lost" civilizations, seeking to discover the mysteries of why and how such grandeur could have fallen so thoroughly into ruin, and indeed, many real archaeologists seek to answer these very same questions.

Marxist archaeologists are rarely puzzled by the presumed collapse of complex societies. When one travels to Central America or the Indus Valley and sees the ruins of long abandoned cities, one will meet with the descendants of the people who built and lived in those ancient places. To Marxist archaeologists, the concept of "collapse" is in fact misleading; societies change over the course of their history, change that sometimes leads to a restructuring of the social order defining how people relate to each other, how they make their living, and how they design and live within their social and physical landscapes. In short, modes of production sometimes change as a result of dialectical conflict, and that change can result in the abandonment or redefinition of those elements of the forces of production no longer required for the newly emerged social relations of production to work and be reproduced. This phenomenon is clearly visible in the many abandoned landscapes dotting our world, not only in ancient contexts like the abandoned cities of Tikal and Harrappa, but in the more recently abandoned industrial landscapes of Britain, New England, and the American Midwest, and in the abandoned and redefined plantation landscapes of Jamaica.

When the plantation mode of production experienced its great dialectical crisis in the early nineteenth century, the social and physical landscapes of Jamaica were transformed. When slavery was abolished, the social relations of production in Jamaica changed dramatically. The proprietors and their

177

attorneys were no longer at liberty to buy and sell people as elements of the means of production; they were required by law to establish wage relationships with the people employed on their plantations. Members of the emancipated workforce were now theoretically free to sell their labor power on the open market for a wage, or else to find a way to acquire the land, tools, and supplies necessary to maintain what is sometimes referred to as peasant production; that is, the kind of small-scale agricultural production that had driven the development of the provisioning system and local economy that had emerged under the plantation mode of production. Simultaneously, the old plantation landscapes were reconstructed; many plantations were abandoned and, like the fallen cities of the ancient world, descended into ruin. The once-enslaved population dispersed into the abandoned lands, sometimes buying small farms, sometimes squatting in remote places far from the gaze of the declining planter class. As a post-plantation economy struggled to emerge, the forces of production, particularly land use patterns, transformed (see Figure 6.1).

Although this culture change resulted from the resolution of the primary contradiction that beleaguered the plantation mode of production, resolutions like this did not happen immediately at the wave of some historical magic wand. Negotiating the terms of newly emerging social

Figure 6.1. The ruin of the Great House at Upper New Battle, one of the plantations in Upper St. David that failed and was abandoned after the collapse of the plantation mode of production. Photo by James A. Delle.

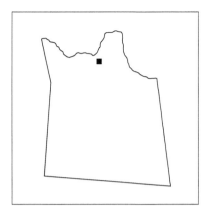 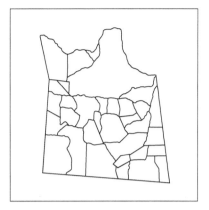

Figure 6.2. The subdivision of Mt. Charles. The image on the left depicts the original shape of the 300-acre plantation as it was patented and first settled in the late eighteenth century. The image on the right depicts the post-emancipation subdivision of the estate when it was conveyed in small lots to formerly enslaved workers. Redrawn illustration courtesy of Nick Stover. *Source*: National Library of Jamaica Manuscript Maps STA 56 and STA 68.

relations of production can take decades; the resulting changes in the means of production can also be a contested and drawn-out process. In some cases, as was so in nineteenth-century Jamaica, conflicting class interests can lead to extended periods of uncertainty as to how newly defined social relations will shape daily experience. Nevertheless, the dialectical resolutions of contradictions can lead to the reformation of modes of production with new sets of relations of production and newly defined forces of production, a process, as was the case with plantation Jamaica, that can lead to the eventual abandonment and redefinition of landscapes no longer relevant to the operation of the newly emergent mode of production (see Figure 6.2). As the forces and relations of production change, new modes of production emerge, new class interests form, new landscapes are created, and the dialectical process begins anew.

This chapter considers how dialectical change, resulting in the restructuring of the forces and relations of production, was manifested in the post-emancipation era in the coffee producing region of Upper St. David. Like many of their peers and counterparts in Jamaica and the rest of the British West Indies, the planters and workers faced epochal changes as the plantation mode of production rended apart. As new class relationships were negotiated and new strategies for creating wealth emerged, the landscape of Upper St. David similarly changed. Some of the planters subdivided their old estates, others simply abandoned them, and yet others tried to hold on and continue coffee production with wage labor under the newly emerging mode of production. In the end, new relationships between people and the means of production emerged, and new landscapes were formed.

Redefining the Relations of Production

For new modes of production to emerge, dialectical conflict must result in the redefinition of the existing relations of production. This is rarely an easy or direct process, even in cases in which specific forms of labor relations are legislated out of existence. For more than a century, the relations of production within the plantation mode of production in Jamaica had been based on chattel slavery. In 1834, slavery was abolished by statute in the British West Indies. The British, anticipating that this transition in the relations of production would be difficult, implemented a new labor system known as the apprenticeship. British elites designed the apprenticeship system as a form of gradual emancipation serving as a transitional step toward the proletarianization of agricultural labor that they hoped, in both the short and long term, would maximize their accumulation of surplus value in the absence of slavery (Brass and Bernstein 1992). Employed on land belonging to their former owners, able-bodied agricultural workers remained attached to the estates on which they had been enslaved as "praedial" apprentices; children younger than the age of six were emancipated unconditionally (Butler 1995: 30; Green 1976: 134). Praedial apprentices were to provide unpaid labor for six years before they were fully emancipated. Under the terms of the apprenticeship law, the former slaves were required to work for forty-five hours each week for the planters. Beyond this weekly period, the apprentices were free to use their labor power as they saw fit, either working in provision grounds to grow food for sale in local markets, or else selling their labor power to the planters for wages. It was hoped by the British who concocted this scheme that the apprenticeship would acclimatize the former agricultural slaves to the discipline of wage labor, smoothing the transition away from the plantation mode of production into a more formalized version of agrarian capitalism (Holt 1992: 56–57). In large measure, owing to the widespread resistance to the apprenticeship system exerted by both Jamaican workers and the antislavery lobby in Britain, the apprenticeship system was terminated two years ahead of schedule, on August 1, 1838 (Green 1976: 129–130; Wilmot 1984).

Box 4: An Act for the Abolition of Slavery throughout the British Colonies

In 1833, the British Parliament enacted legislation to abolish slavery in most of its colonies, including the plantation islands of the West Indies. The legislation was a compromise between factions in England, one of which had advocated for immediate emancipation, the other of which had sought a more gradual process for emancipation.

According to the act, on August 1, 1834, slavery was abolished as an institution throughout the British Empire, with the exception of Ceylon, St. Helena, and the possessions of the British East India Company. Emancipation was conditional, however, as all able-bodied people older than the age of six were to become "apprenticed labourers," who, for a period of years not to extend beyond 1840, were still required to work for their former masters for forty-five hours per week without compensation. The law distinguished between agricultural laborers who worked directly for their masters, agricultural laborers who worked in jobbing gangs or otherwise not directly for their owners, and non-agricultural laborers, including domestic servants.

Slave holders throughout the colonies were compensated £20,000,000 for the value of the emancipated slaves, but those who had been enslaved received no compensation for the years of unpaid work they had been forced to complete. The apprenticeship system was fraught with tension, and was ended in Jamaica on August 1, 1838, the day that all people on Jamaica gained "full freedom."

Discontent with the system of apprenticeship had appeared nearly from its inception. This discontent was manifested in Upper St. David as elsewhere in Jamaica. In 1835, the first year of the apprenticeship, Frederick French, overseer of Green Valley, reported to a committee of the Jamaica Assembly on the labor problems he was experiencing. When asked whether the apprentices were working "as cheerfully and as well as they did previous to the 1st of August" (i.e., the beginning of the apprenticeship system), French replied:

Most unquestionably not. While slaves, they were contented and industrious, and, in this neighborhood, remarkable for their good conduct; but now, with the same allowances as formerly, and additional time allowed them by law, they are lazy, insubordinate and extremely insolent; the most civil question put to any of them is invariably answered impertinently, and generally accompanied with threat that they will go to the magistrate. (PP1835/50:100)

Although the apprenticeship was overtly designed to facilitate transition in the relations of production, it did not work out quite as planned. The class of emancipated workers set out to establish what can be referred to as a peasant economy of local production for local exchange, while the planters sought to transform the work force into a wage-earning, and easily controlled, agrarian proletariat producing commodities for exchange in global markets. A contested process thus emerged between "peasantization" and "proletarianization" (Brass and Bernstein 1992). The British social engineers had expected the formerly enslaved workers to quickly conform to the demands of wage labor, a social condition that few Jamaican people eagerly accepted. The concept of free time had been built into the apprenticeship system, and it was assumed that the formerly enslaved people would be eager to earn wages in their free time by performing the same tasks on the plantations that they had done while enslaved, and which they were still required to perform for forty-five hours per week without compensation. Green Valley's French reported that few people were willing to work on the estate during their "free" time, testifying that "I have several times begged them to pick coffee in their own time ... but could not get one to do so this year" (PP1835/50:100).

The relations of production changed dramatically when slavery was abolished in Jamaica. The island's economy remained primarily agricultural, but the planter class had a difficult time adjusting to the new social realities. The coffee industry was particularly vulnerable during this period of dialectical change, as the small planters who dominated the coffee industry could not control labor, and had a much more difficult time securing the means to pay for labor than they had when enslaved workers were purchased on credit as a capital asset. The labor issue was primarily based on the resolution of the old local consumption versus export dialectic. When made apprentices, and then following full emancipation, many Jamaican people preferred to work toward creating self-sufficient small farms for themselves. Manifestations of this change in the relationship between the planter class and the formerly enslaved class can be read in the testimony given by Jamaican planters to both the local legislature and to Parliamentary committees concerned with the decline in the productivity of Jamaican plantations. For example, in a sworn statement before a special committee of the Jamaica Assembly appointed in 1847, William George Lowe, who owned coffee properties in three parishes contiguous to St. David (Port Royal, St. George, and St. Andrew), reported that he had been forced to abandon one of his estates for "want of labour" (PP 1848 23/3:163). Another St. David coffee planter, David McLean, the owner of Middleton Plantation and manager of Sheffield and Manheim, all coffee estates in St. David, provided corroborating testimony, stating that "I do not receive half of a fair day's work for the money paid; the people work only four days in the week, even when the coffee is ripe in the fields, and at Christmas time, when the coffee is falling from the tress, they will not work on any terms" (PP 1848 23/3:164).

The Emancipation Act that created the apprenticeship system did anticipate that the transition away from slavery would create tension within the social relations of production. In the attempt to mitigate the conflict between labor and the planter class, the Emancipation Act called for the empowering of a number of "stipendiary magistrates." These magistrates, envisioned as a counterbalance to the local Justices of the Peace, most of whom were members of the slave-holding class, were primarily responsible for adjudicating conflicts between laborers and planters. Recruited from England, from the formerly "free people of color," and from white Creoles, the stipendiary magistrates mediated the transition in the relations of production during the period of the apprenticeship (Watts 1990: 57–58).

The initial reports sent to Parliament from stipendiary magistrates Patrick Dunne and Henry Kent, assigned to the environs of Upper St. David, noted that the apprenticeship began with little conflict between labor and management. In June of 1835, Dunne reported that he considered "the negroes in my district as well disposed, from their having on every occasion of my applying to them entered into arrangements to work during crop seven hours per day beyond the time fixed by law" (PP 1835 50: 254). Kent confirmed that a similar condition existed on the estates in his district: "the negroes in general throughout this district seem well disposed, and I think perform their labor willingly" (PP 1835 50: 258–259).

The contradictions between the reports made by estate agents, who bemoaned the difficulties of finding affordable labor and getting people to work, and those made by the stipendiary magistrates, who described a well-disposed and willing labor force, may indicate that the African Jamaican population actively attempted to recruit the magistrates as allies against the planters (Holt 1992: 64).

They would have done so with good reason. In the attempt to reshape the conditions of labor under the new social relations of production, Parliament empowered the stipendiary magistrates to administer disciplinary punishments on the apprentices; it was the understanding that the overseers and drivers who had controlled corporal punishment during slavery would transfer their power and authority to these government officials. That the magistrates were willing to use their power to punish the apprentices is documented in a table appearing in the British Parliamentary Papers in 1836 (PP 1836/48: 219). During the first year of the apprenticeship system, Parliament required the special magistrates to quantify the "offenses" perpetrated by the apprenticed laborers in their respective districts, and to report on the kind and quantity of punishments they had meted out. In the region around Upper St. David, between August 1834 and July 1835, Patrick Dunne inflicted punishments on 562 people – 357 men and 205 women. The most common offenses can be categorized as expressions of resistance to the new labor regime: 279 people were found guilty of "neglect of duty," 144 for "disobedience," 52 for "indolence," 21 for running away, 60 for theft, and 6 for cutting or maiming cattle. In the three months between May and July of 1835, Henry Kent reported that he had punished sixty-three males and thirty-two females: thirty-nine for neglect of duty, twenty-seven for disobedience, six for indolence, three for running away, and twenty for theft. Punishments for these expressions of refusal to conform to the demands of apprenticed labor ranged from floggings to labor fines and imprisonment. Dunne and Kent frequently compelled laborers to make up missed time that they owed an estate (Delle 1998).

Many laborers chose to expedite their emancipation by purchasing their freedom early. Stipendiary magistrates were empowered to establish a value on the time remaining for an apprentice. If a person could provide the valuated sum, they were to be immediately released from their bondage. In Upper St. David, thirty people acquired their freedom this way; twenty-four women and six men. The average valuation of the women was £29..11s..0d; and the men paid £57..18s..2d. Three of the six men who purchased their freedom were artisans; the average price paid by the non-skilled male laborers was £36..12s..6d, still better than £7 – or 25 percent – more than the women paid on average.

The magistrates monitoring the transition to wage labor were not always warmly embraced by the planters. For example, Henry Kent was denied access to Sherwood Forest and Radnor, which were both managed by Andrew Murray. Kent reported that he was denied "any information respecting these properties by Mr. Andrew Murray ... the information [was] obtained from the Head people, which I believe to be correct." By "head people" Kent meant the African Jamaican labor supervisors, who were known as drivers under slavery, and were generally referred to as "rangers" following emancipation. Kent faced the same kind of difficulty with Alexander Bizzet, the resident proprietor of Chesterfield, who reportedly "decline[d] to give any information and demand[ed] to know what the Government ha[d] to do with his private affairs" (PP 137/242/241).

The apprenticeship system did not create a disciplined and submissive agricultural working class as its designers had hoped. Across Jamaica, many laborers left plantation employ as soon as they could. The situation in Upper St. David was no different. As early as February 1839, only six months after the end of the apprenticeship system, magistrate Henry Kent complained that "few people are employed on the estates as compared with the number of apprentices they had on the 31st of July ... there is a clear falling off in labor and I regret to say it is now eight o'clock before they get to the fields" (CO 137/242/238). Kent further reported that in the Upper St. David district "few people are at work on the estates" (CO 137/242/240). Kent compiled labor statistics comparing the number or laborers at work on the various estates in 1839 with the number of apprentices attached to the estates in 1838, clearly documenting a dramatic decrease in the number of people employed on the estate. These are reproduced in Table 6.1.

The labor difficulties reported by both the planters and the stipendiary magistrates were the product of the transition away from the relations of production that had characterized the plantation mode of production.

Table 6.1 Comparison of number of laborers in 1839 to number of apprentices in 1838 (Source CO 137/242/238–41)

Estate	Apprentices, July 31, 1838	Average Number of Workers, January–February 1839
Sherwood Forest	103	51
Radnor	165	50
Minto	69	16
New Battle	63	34
Mt. Pleasant	52	13
Abbey Green	108	71
Whitfield Hall	54	42
Farm Hill	127	70
Penlyne Castle	65	21
Woburn Lawn	81	20
Epping Farm	104	50
Mt. Charles	93	nd
Flamstead	22	nd
Chesterfield	nd	nd
Chester Vale	179	60
Clydesdale	114	56
Industry	54	11
Strawberry Hill	83	31
Westphalia	99	31
Orchard	222	65

Many formerly enslaved people had no desire to continue to work for the benefit of the planters and sought ways to implement a more fully self-sufficient local economy. The planters faced the dilemma of needing to have ready cash on hand to pay those laborers who were willing to work for them, and also to acclimatize themselves to the reality that they could no longer force people to work against their will. Henry Kent reported that the larger estates had more "hands than they can afford to pay at the present rate of wages," whereas on the smaller properties, "great difficulty is found in procuring labor, as the Negroes are certainly more intent in working their own grounds than cultivating the estate, finding it more profitable than any wages that could be offered them" (CO 137/242/241).

The coffee planter Alexander Geddes was quite poignant in his analysis of why the plantation mode of production could not survive once slavery was abolished in Jamaica. In his testimony to Parliament, Geddes noted that "in a state of slavery, the planter may go on from day to day and from year to year upon credit, working the estate by the labor of his slaves; but in the present state of society he cannot move an inch unless his pocket is full of money. In a state of slavery there was no money outlay; in a state of freedom there is a constant drain upon the planter" (PP 1847 48/23). Geddes statement clearly articulates a shift in the relationship between labor and capital, as well as a shift in the strategies in the ways in which wealth was created and distributed in post-emancipation Jamaica. Unable to tabulate the value of workers as a capital asset, the planters were unable to draw on credit as they had once done, using the enslaved population as collateral. Under the emerging relations of production, the planters needed to have ready cash to pay their workers, many of whom, at least temporarily, were expressing their role in the "state of freedom" as independent settlers, working toward fulfilling their own interests, and no longer willing to sacrifice those interests for the good of the planters.

Redefining the Forces of Production

As the relations of production changed in the years following the end of slavery, so too did the class interests of the planters and the emancipated laborers. The planters felt that the African Jamaican population should remain a subordinate laboring class, whereas they themselves, the planters, should remain the supervising, dominant class. The redefinition of the plantation mode of production, and its apparent failure to restructure given the newly emerging social relations of production, resulted in what may well have been an unresolvable contradiction between the class interests of the planters (who wanted to create a dependent working class) and the interest of the laborers (who wanted to create a state of social and economic independence in which they controlled access to the surplus value they themselves created). The material nature of this new manifestation of contradiction in class interests can be seen through the examination of how the forces of production changed following 1834, and how both the planters and the laborers struggled to redefine the forces of production to suit their emerging class interests.

One significant change in the forces of production was the reevaluation of the intrinsic value of agricultural land. The overall agricultural output of an estate was always a key to determining the amount of wealth that a planter could derive from plantation production. However, during the florescence of the plantation mode of production, ascension into the planter class required the possession of property (both real estate and human capital), regardless of the overall quality of the land one purchased. In Marxist terms, the exchange value of the land and the attached enslaved workers – that is, the value a plantation had as an exchangeable commodity – was the key factor used in relating the means of production to the social status of the planter. The quality of the land and its internal improvements were important factors in determining this value, but the productive value of the land was a secondary concern; the key to establishing and maintaining class status was the acquisition of land and slaves. When the relations of production were redefined such that slavery was no longer a legal means by which to define relationships between people, the productive output of agricultural land became the far more important characteristic of the plantation. Following emancipation, rather than have a gang fell old growth forests on demand, planters would need to pay dearly to clear forest land for the establishment of new coffee fields. Maintaining adequate levels of production in existing coffee fields, and acquiring existing fields from neighboring plantations, became a new focus of plantation management. This shift is clearly evident in the changing nature of estate maps in Upper St. David and its environs drawn following emancipation.

Changes in the conventions for mapping coffee estates provide evidence for this post-emancipation change. The few estate plans that exist for the pre-emancipation period for Upper St. David tend to focus on the boundaries of the estates, with some gross estimates of the amount of land allocated for coffee fields, provision grounds, woodland, and what was called "ruinate"; some of these maps also indicate the locations of estate buildings and slave villages, but generally lack detail. In contrast to the pre-emancipation plans and plats, post-emancipation plans do not necessarily focus on the boundaries or even the extent of the various estates, but provide great detail on the internal layout of the plantations, particularly the shape, dimensions, and size of the coffee fields. This reflects a shift in the value that land held in the post-plantation mode of production; land was now being valued for its ability to produce commodities for sale, a value that could only be determined by establishing the relationship between acreage, the number of coffee-bearing trees, and the overall production of the various coffee fields.

The domestic material spaces of the elites further reflect changes to the material world of the planters following emancipation. Modifications made to the overseer's house at Sherwood Forest provide an example of such change. As we saw in Chapter 3, the original overseer's house was constructed of field stone covered with lime plaster; the exterior walls of this building were twenty-one inches thick. The small building contained two rooms. One room was the domestic space for the overseer. A veranda provided the overseer with a southern view which encompassed the coffee drying platforms, or barbecues. An eighteen-inch thick interior wall separated the overseer's room from the pulping mill, which obviously was contained in the same building as the overseer's domestic space. As long as he was in his room or on his veranda, the overseer on this plantation could survey the production of coffee. From his veranda he could monitor the coffee crop as it dried. From his room, he could watch the coffee as it was pulped and channeled to the drying platforms. This spatial arrangement created an intensive capacity for the surveillance of production (Delle 1998, 1999).

The second phase of construction at the overseer's house, which was likely completed in the 1840s (Delle 1998) was much more gracile and served to remove the overseer from the direct surveillance of production. The second house was constructed on top of the first, with the older stone house serving as the foundation for the newer wood-framed structure. The pulping and grinding mills remained in place, in what was now the basement of a larger house. The veranda of the second building is oriented to the east, providing a scenic view of the valley and surrounding hills; it takes a conscious effort to supervise production from this vantage point (Delle 1998, 1999).

This new spatial arrangement reflects one strategy employed by planters in the post-emancipation period. Beginning in the late 1840s, Sherwood Forest began acquiring the estates that bounded it to the east and south; the previously independent estates of Arntully and Eccleston were defined in the crop accounts of the 1850s as appendages to Sherwood Forest. The evidence suggests that the owners of Sherwood Forest were, at this time, acquiring contiguous estates in an attempt to increase production by absorbing previously developed coffee fields, thus saving the expense of clearing new patches of forest. The renovated overseer's house was transformed into a post-emancipation great house from which the affairs of the several plantations were managed. The African

Jamaican village that had been the focus of surveillance from the original overseer's house had been removed (Delle 1998, 1999).

The abolition of slavery redefined the relationship that the laboring class had to land as part of the forces of production. Now legally able to purchase land and use it as they saw fit, many formerly enslaved people sought material independence from the export economy controlled by the planters. Controlling the ability of African Jamaican people to gain access to productive land was the best, and perhaps only, way to ensure that the Europeans could exercise control over the labor power of the population and thus ensure the reproduction of the plantation mode of production to which they still clung, and which they hoped to somehow reestablish. For this mode of production to continue, Jamaican land had to produce commodities for export. To the laborer, ownership of land ensured access to provision farms for local consumption, a right that many planters tried to curtail.

In 1843, resident proprietor Robert Paterson succinctly described the nature of the contradiction emerging between capital and labor:

It delights the eye of the traveler to see patches of land cleared, houses erected, and their occupants living in seeming contentment; but alas! these appearances are not solid – the staple productions of the soil are neglected–and unless this evil be immediately remedied, the country ... will ultimately become a colony of small settlers, without capital, without enterprise, without circulation of any kind to stimulate them to improvement. (Paterson 1843: 4)

Paterson's observations both describe the basic contradiction in land tenure and reveal the nature of the conflicting class interests and how the two classes sought to best use land. The elites saw land as a means for producing export commodities and thus stimulating the circulation of capital, and wished to proletarianize the emancipated workers into an agrarian, wage-earning working class. The African Jamaican settlers saw land as a means of creating self-sufficient farms producing goods for local consumption, independent of the Eurocentric political economy, and thus sought the independence of peasant production for local exchange.

Alexander Geddes provided great insight on how the provisioning system, once the backbone of the plantation mode of production, had proved to be deleterious to the accumulation of capital in the era of free labor. In 1842, he testified that Jamaica's emancipated workers "betake ... to the cultivation of waste lands, which can be purchased at nominal prices. One great source of our misfortune in Jamaica is, that the negroes were taught to place their sole reliance for subsistence upon the cultivation of the roots common to the country; and it is impossible to eradicate that habit; it is now our great bane" (PP1842/13/469). Geddes's comments reflect a sophisticated understanding of the dialectical irony that doomed the plantation mode of production. The planters had believed it cheap and expedient to force the working population to produce its own food under slavery, and – as we have seen – some planters themselves were dependent on this source of food for their own subsistence. The enslaved laborers had created a sense of ownership over the means of production required to produce surplus value in the provision grounds; once emancipated, they were certainly not willing to abandon this system in favor of wage labor for the planters.

In the absence of slavery, the planters used rent exaction as a mechanism to retain control over the forces of production by alienating local producers from the means of production. It was their hope to reshape the relations of production under a free labor system to suit their own class interests. In 1839, the stipendiary magistrate Henry Kent commented on how the coffee estates of St. David collected rent by compelling laborers to work one day per week in return for the use of the houses and grounds they occupied (CO 137/242/240–41) as well as on how well the mitigation of the contradictions in the mode of production were going for the planters. For example, on Mt. Charles, located on the boundary between St. David and Port Royal, Kent reported "great discontent on this property in consequence of Mr. George Wright, the attorney, making the heavy charges [for rent] against the people and which the overseer Mr. Anderson stated in court was for their making so many complaints to the magistrates" (CO 137/242/241). Both Wright and Anderson, on Anderson's own admission, apparently hoped to teach the working class a lesson by raising their rents as a consequence of their attempting to exercise their right to seek redress over labor grievances from the stipendiary magistrates. There may have been a similar strategy employed at Flamstead; although no motive is expressed, Kent reported "great excitement on this property in consequence of the Receiver, Mr. Fyfe, doubling their rent." On Pleasant Hill, rent was also used as a means to attempt to coerce the population to conform to the planter's labor demands. Kent reported "their daily task used to be hoeing from 5000 to 4000 perches [nb: between 25 and 32 acres] and as they will not do it since the death of their master Mr. Simon Taylor, the present proprietor Mr. George Taylor is raising the rent."

Several of the proprietors used even more coercive spatial negotiations in their attempt to control the means of production. For example, Kent reported that with his arrival to Green Valley, the proprietor James Law Stewart had "served [the people] with notice to give up their provision grounds in 3 months from 7 January which has produced great consternation among the negroes." According to Kent's account, the manager of Minto utilized a similar coercive strategy: "a great many people [have] left and been ejected – and are denied the right to take out their provisions – I regret that upon the opinion of the Attorney General I can render them no assistance" (CO 137/242/241). Incidents such as these indicate that the post-emancipation transition in the mode of production was rent by class conflict over access to the means of production necessary to maintain the subsistence economy embraced by the laboring class, a form of conflict seemingly endemic to agrarian capitalism (Byres 2009).

Although no explicit motives are given for these actions on the part of the planters, they can be interpreted as attempts to exert greater control over the means of production in the hope of limiting the economic independence of the agrarian working class. Such efforts may have been enacted in the hope of compelling African Jamaicans to provide more labor on better terms for the estates. Such motivation may be revealed in Kent's comment about Mt. Faraway. The management of that estate was experiencing great difficulty controlling the labor force, as management could not "get them to work on the term offered; [they] will only work to pay their rent and then go off to other properties" (CO 137/242/241).

The newly emerging relations of production, mediated by wages and the inability of the planters to exert absolute control over the conditions of labor, provided the formerly enslaved population with some power to negotiate the terms of employment. In February of 1839, George Willis, one of the special magistrates assigned to St. David, reported that the management of Arntully plantation was engaged in a negotiation over wages with the estate employees. According to his report, the people had worked only one week between August 1838 and February 1839, and were currently engaged in a strike against the estate for better wages. Willis stated that the laborers were demanding 1s 8d, approximately one day's wages, for the weeding of 100 trees. On nearby Woburn Lawn, John Barclay had paid his laborers 1s 8d for weeding 125 trees. Unfortunately, there is no indication as to what the managers of Arntully were demanding or how the dispute ended (CO 137/241/29). Nevertheless, such job actions surely reminded the planters about the depth of their dependence on the labor force.

The strategies employed by the planters seem to have backfired on them, as increasing numbers of people sought to abandon plantation labor in favor of acquiring new houses and grounds that they could operate independently of the whims of the planter class. According to Geddes, the rent system was not serving the planters' interests, and instead was driving more laborers into purchasing their own lands. This is revealed in the following exchange between the select committee on West India estates and Geddes, in 1842 (PP1842/13):

QUESTION: From what you have said as to the dislike of the laborers to pay rent, it appears that it is not your opinion that the system of paying rents has at all tended to inspire them with feelings of local attachment and unwillingness to leave their localities?

GEDDES: I consider that the exaction of rent, which was quite unavoidable under the circumstances, has been the means of inducing them to purchase lands.

QUESTION: Rather than pay rent?

GEDDES: Rather than pay rent.

The contest between the planters and the workers to define new terms for the relations of production, mediated by wages and rent payments, resulted in a synthesis by which an increasing number of African Jamaican people abandoned estate production in favor of creating their own farms. The conveyance of land to the emerging peasant class became a matter of concern for Jamaica's government, as indicated in a dispatch by Governor Charles Metcalfe to the Colonial Office in which he states that between August 1838 and June 1840, some 2,074 small lots of less than twenty acres had been conveyed in Jamaica. Of these new land owners, at least 934 had purchased enough to register as electors (i.e., were enfranchised to vote). Metcalfe remarked that prior to these conveyances, the number of electors throughout the island was 2,199 "to which even 934 would be a large relative addition." Metcalfe did not believe that by 1840 the newly enfranchised voters had yet fully exercised their rights. However, the acquisition of legal titles to land threatened the political hegemony so long enjoyed by the planter class (CO137/249).

As we have seen, some planters and their agents were both deeply concerned about how the post-emancipation economy would form and agitated against the unrestricted acquisition of land by the emancipated workers. However, the solidarity of the planter class quickly eroded, as many planters in Jamaica, faced with economic decline, began subdividing their estates and selling the parcels to the African Jamaican population. For example, Henry Lowndes, a sugar planter who resided in Jamaica for twenty-seven years, had been the proprietor, trustee, attorney, and/ or lessee of eight sugar estates in the central parish of St. Thomas in the Vale. Lowndes reported to the Select Committee on West India Plantations that he himself had sold "a great quantity of land ... in small lots." Lowndes was able to get £3 sterling per acre, but charged an additional £3 to £4 sterling to cover the expense of surveying and transferring the land. Even at this price, the lots bought by the African

Jamaican people from Lowndes were usually from five to ten acres in extent (PP 1842/13/369).

Several plantations in the Upper St. David region were similarly subdivided and sold in lots to small settlers. In a report to the Colonial Office in June of 1855, Henry Kent reported that "small settlements" were forming throughout the Blue Mountains "on coffee properties which have been sold and cut up into lots to suit the laboring class, at prices varying from £4 to £6 per acre." In acquiring such lots, the laboring population was actively defining a new mode of production. As Kent put it, the people were "satisfied to sit down on their acquired freeholds and just cultivate sufficient to supply their own wants, with a little coffee to purchase clothing and necessaries, which in its rude cured state they sell in Kingston for 5 or 6 dollars [sic] per 100 pounds" (CO 137/327/97). Although Holt reports that at least two estates, Belle Claire and Middleton, were purchased in their entirety by "peasant proprietors" (1992: 145), it seems that the more common strategy employed by African Jamaicans in the Blue Mountains was to purchase smaller subdivided lots carved out of old coffee plantations.

Evidence for this process exists for Mt. Charles and Mavis Bank, two Port Royal estates that border Upper St. David to the west. Both plantations were subdivided and sold off in the post-emancipation period, and have since become villages in the modern parish of St. Andrew. An undated plan of Mount Charles indicates that the estate was subdivided into nineteen lots ranging in size from one to twenty acres; this plan probably post-dates 1838, when the estate was mortgaged. Although the plan is lacking in some detail, it does provide the acreage for each of the subdivided plots; the average plot size was 5.65 acres (see Figure 6.3 for the redrawn map of Mt. Charles).

The cartographic record of Mavis Bank is more informative on this issue than it is for Mt. Charles. John Barclay first subdivided Mavis Bank in 1840 into a few larger plots, including a sixty-acre estate purchased by Dr. William Thomson, and seventy-five acres retained as a reduced Mavis Bank Plantation by Robert Sylvester, like Barclay, a former overseer. In 1850, Sylvester's parcel was further divided; by this date, the former plantation had been transformed into a village containing approximately forty-five homesteads of between one and fifteen acres (see Figure 6.4 for the redrawn map of Mavis Bank).

Although not identified by name in the dispatch by Henry Kent, it is possible that the estate he was referring to in his letter to the Colonial Office was either Mavis Bank or Mt. Charles. If so, the African Jamaicans who purchased lots on these estates were paying between £4 and £6 sterling per acre. The space of these former plantations had been

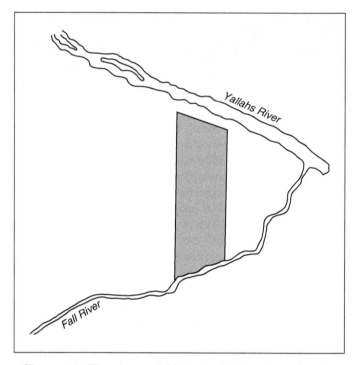

Figure 6.3. The shape of Mavis Bank plantation when it was first patented in the late eighteenth century. Redrawn illustration courtesy of Nick Stover. *Source*: National Library of Jamaica, Manuscript Map STA 66.

redefined as expressions of spatial independence by a population that had formerly been attached to such estates as slaves. The spatial meanings of some coffee plantations, like Mount Charles and Mavis Bank were completely redefined, as coffee estates were subdivided in the 1840s, and developed into village communities. Just as the relations of production shifted after the dialectical crisis of the early nineteenth century, so too did the landscapes of production. By the middle of the nineteenth century, it was increasingly clear that a new mode of production had emerged, and that the old way of doing things would likely never return.

Conclusion: Social Change and the Collapse of the Enclave of Upper St. David

In 1865, growing tensions emerging from the negotiation of the post-emancipation relations of production exploded in an uprising in the town

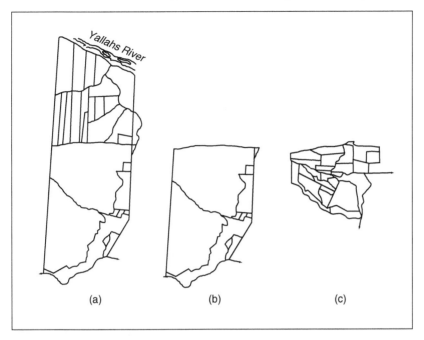

Figure 6.4. The subdivision of Mavis Bank Plantation, conducted between 1841 and 1851. Redrawn illustration courtesy of Nick Stover. *Source*: National Library of Jamaica Manuscript Maps STA 35, 45, and 60.

of Morant Bay, an event that saw a well-organized group of Jamaica agriculturalists take up arms against the vestry of the parish of St. Thomas in the East. The incident was serious enough that a member of the Jamaica Assembly, who was a man of color, was hanged, as were several hundred other people rounded up under martial law. The ensuing crisis led the British government to suspend the Jamaica Assembly and bring the colony under direct rule as a crown colony.

The Morant Bay incident was precipitated by the arrest of a man who had established a small provision farm and pasturage on a long-abandoned estate; he was arrested and held for trespassing. Throughout the 1850s, the planter class attempted to curtail the independence of the laboring class through a number of strategies such as this. Many of the plantations that had been divided into plots for small settlers were being reconsolidated by new investors interested in reestablishing a revised version of the plantation mode of production using imported contract labor and increasingly mechanized processes for the reduction of coffee and sugar into exportable forms. In these decades, local vestries were increasingly focused on limiting access to crown and abandoned plantation lands, prosecuting small settlers who could not produce titles for the lands they were cultivating. High taxes on small farmers were forcing some small settlers into default. Plantation wages were extraordinarily low, and a worker could expect to receive no more that about £8 in a year (Holt 1992: 265). Import duties on consumer goods primarily purchased by the laboring class, including the raw materials for craft production, increased dramatically and resulted in high rates of inflation. Infrastructure repairs on the island were focused on estate roads, and those main roads that served local producers were subject to tolls. Unrest was spreading across the island, as the reforming planter class reestablished its class consciousness and used the political apparatus of the colony to subvert the interests of the agricultural laborers.

The tensions between the classes did not emerge from nowhere and were closely linked to the decline of the plantation mode of production. Coffee production had been on the decline in Jamaica generally – and in St. David particularly – since the beginning of the apprenticeship period. According to the records kept by Parliament, coffee production fell dramatically in 1835 and 1836, and never fully recovered. The average annual crop exported from Jamaica in the five years immediately previous to the implementation of the apprenticeship system (1830–1834) was 16.7 million pounds (by weight); whereas in the five years following apprenticeship (1835–1839), the annual average crop dropped to 11.1 million pounds, a decrease of nearly 34 percent. The Upper St. David plantations for which records exist reflect this trend. The average crop reported by the management of Green Valley, which reported a crop of more than 106,000 pounds in 1830, dropped 48.1 percent between the two half-decades. The average coffee crop on Radnor, another estate that reported a crop of greater than 100,000 pounds in 1830, dropped an astounding 52.9 percent during this period. Small estates, like Mt. Charles, Whitfield Hall, and Chester Vale, each demonstrated a significant drop in production, but the averages were more on par with the island-wide decrease (Delle 1998). By 1845, only 5 million pounds of coffee was exported from the island; the largest coffee crop reported, in 1814, was more than 34 million pounds. Production continued to fall throughout the post-emancipation period. By the late 1850s, many Jamaican coffee plantations had ceased production and were abandoned. In an anonymous dispatch dated February 1857, a Jamaican magistrate reported that in the parish of St. David, there were only "three out of eleven estates remaining" (CO 137/334/24). In 1852, it was reported to Parliament that only seven coffee plantations were operating in St. David (PP 1854/43/55), down from the twenty-one plantations that had been reported to have produced a crop in 1836 (PP 1836/48/242). In the 1850s, only Sherwood Forest, Arntully, Chester Vale, and Green Valley reported production; by the late 1860s, only Green Valley remained.

By the 1860s, the once flourishing Jamaican coffee industry had all but disappeared. Most of the coffee plantations in Upper St. David had ceased production. Although many of the estates were abandoned, the landscape remained filled with people making a living from the surrounding mountain land. Despite the best efforts of the Jamaican planter class, the dialectical conflict that had emerged from the clashing interests of the planters and workers, so deeply imbedded in the plantation mode of production that had developed in the eighteenth century, had resulted in culture change, and an emerging society in which the great estates of the plantation mode of production were no longer relevant. As with the great temples of the Maya, and the Ziggurats of Sumer, the plantations in the enclave of Upper St. David were abandoned to fall to ruin and become part of the archaeological record.

7   Plantation Landscapes in Comparative Perspective

The goal of this book has been to evaluate how well a Marxian theoretical framework can be used to interpret the plantation landscapes of colonial Jamaica. In so doing, we have examined a number of material and social realities experienced by those who lived and labored in that colonial context. One danger anyone faces when applying a theoretical framework to a specific case, however, is falling into the trap of tautology. To test the strength of applying Marxist theory to an archaeological study of Jamaica's plantation landscapes, we must see if the concepts explored in this book can be effectively applied in other plantation contexts. Although many such contexts could be considered, I have chosen here to test the strength of this approach by applying it to what would prove to be England's most valuable mainland plantation colony, and the locus of much historical archaeology, seventeenth-century Tidewater Virginia.

The Old Dominion: The Colonial World of Plantation Virginia, 1607–1622

Virginia was, of course, England's first successful colony on mainland North America, and its early history somewhat reflects that of its two most important Caribbean possessions, Barbados and Jamaica. Like Barbados, Virginia was colonized in the opening decades of the seventeenth century with the hope that the poor of the English realms could be transported to a New World to provide a suitable class of servants for those who would make great wealth; like Jamaica by the end of that century, a small oligarchy controlling vast stretches of land held as private property would rule the social world of the colony through the exploitation of enslaved African people. However, the social formations in the Jamaica and Virginia colonies followed different trajectories, both of which can be analyzed through the lens of Marxist landscape archaeology.

Unlike the Caribbean colonies of the later seventeenth century, Virginia was established by what was, in effect, a private corporation. In the late sixteenth and early seventeenth centuries, the forerunners of today's venture capitalists, known in their day as "adventurers," experimented with a new type of social organization known as the joint-stock company. Like today's modern, publically traded corporations, a joint-stock company would raise capital by selling shares in the company, but, at least in England, required a royal charter to legally do business. The "adventurers" – that is the investors who ventured their capital – would share in the profits of the joint-stock company based on the number of shares they had purchased. In the belief that quick profits could be made by the exploitation of metallic wealth to be gained through both mining operations on the North American mainland and plundering raids on Spanish treasure fleets, Jamestown was established in 1607 as the New World headquarters of such a privately financed joint stock company, the Virginia Company of London, usually referred to as the London Company (Bailyn 2012; Craven 1957). Unlike its Caribbean counterparts, Virginia was thus established with its entire land base capitalized even before a single English settler landed on its shores (Bailyn 2012; Horn 2006; Kupperman 2007).

In the opening years of its business, the London Company was very successful in attracting investors, including many who chose to pay their own passage to Virginia as part of their investment. As has been well-understood by historians for generations, this arrangement was fateful for the fledgling colony, as these self-styled "gentlemen" did not expect to be engaged in manual labor in the new colony, but instead to live a high life surrounded by retainers and servants, financed by the profits their investment in the London Company would surely return (Craven 1957; Kupperman 2007; Morgan 1975).

The investors and settlers who founded Jamestown did not expect to establish a plantation mode of production in Virginia. The intent was to emulate the Spanish model by creating wealth through the exploitation of the New World's mineral deposits, and the company was better equipped to mine gold than to establish any practical form of agriculture. Not producing or even procuring their own food, the first settlers of Jamestown were dependent on the largesse of the native population to provide them with food, whether purchased, begged, borrowed, or stolen. As the investors in the London Company soon came to learn, the Virginia Tidewater was not made of gold and wealth did not fall from the sky. The form of mercantile capitalism they hoped to establish did not take root, no surplus value was generated, and the opening years of the Jamestown settlement were characterized by a tenuous life of privation (Billings 1968; Kelso 2008).

In its early days, the social organization of Jamestown reflected its corporate nature. Under the charter granted by King James I in 1606, the settlement was to be ruled by a seven-man council appointed by the crown and responsible to the company. All assets, including land, would be the property of the company; the surplus value produced in Virginia would be distributed to the investors based on the number of shares they held. Those who had come to work would be treated either as employees of the company or the private servants of particular investors, and the products of their labor would be the basis for the production of surplus value (Craven 1957; Morgan 1975). Given this structure, it was perhaps inevitable that the first concern of the council was to determine how best to make a profit for the company, and agriculture was not on top of their list. Although it was assumed that an appropriate working class would be transported to the settlement, the products of their labor, including food, were to be the property of the company, whose officers in the council would be responsible for its redistribution. Given that settlers were not required to work to feed themselves, did not have access to private land to establish farms even if they had wanted to, and were not accumulating any surplus value, this division of labor quickly led to chronic food shortages. It did not take long before the council was beset with the difficulty of feeding a growing population of idle gentlemen investors and their servants. In the attempt to stabilize the critical shortage of food, John Smith, serving as president of the council in late 1608, required all of the settlers, regardless of their presumed station, to work. But poorly provided settlers continued to appear at Jamestown; some 600 arriving between 1608 and 1609. Despite the best efforts put forth by Smith and his fellow council members, many of Jamestown's first wave of settlers died of starvation or nutritional diseases brought on by the company's inability to produce, procure, or purchase food sufficient for the needs of the settlement (Bernhard 1992; Billings 1968; Kelso 2008; Kupperman 2007).

It quickly became clear that the emergent capitalist mode of production was not functioning well in Tidewater Virginia. The failure of the Jamestown settlers to generate surplus value for the Virginia Company of London, not to speak of keeping themselves alive, led to a rapid succession of new royal charters, each of which was designed to improve the fortunes of the company and its investors through a reorganization of the company (Kupperman 2007). In 1609, the company's second charter ceded the king's right to appoint a ruling council for the colony, empowering the company to select a governor from among themselves to manage the company's affairs. The second charter also allowed the company to grant small land allotments to settlers for growing their own food; the company would collect a levy from each of the newly landed settlers in a type of quitrent arrangement (Morgan 1975: 81–82). As settlers dispersed onto private farmsteads, they came into increasingly violent conflict with the indigenous peoples of the tidewater, who the early governors of Virginia wished to push back rather than incorporate into their colonial social world (Morgan 1975: 81–82).

Despite its lifting of the restrictions on private possession of land, the fortunes of the London Company did not turn with the granting of its second charter, and Virginia's colonists continued to face significant hardships. As news of the "deplored condition" (Billings 1968) of the enterprise trickled back to England, worried investors began to sue the company, which was found to be in significant debt with little hope of profit. In the attempt to ward off bankruptcy, the company once again reorganized under a third charter granted by James I in 1612. Several key provisions of this third charter established the conditions under which Virginia's incipient plantation mode of production would develop, and under which it would begin to transform Virginia from a corporately owned possession of a joint-stock company into a governable colony of privately owned plantations. The 1612 charter allowed the company to establish a legislative body to enact and enforce laws for Virginia. This would lead to the establishment of Virginia's colonial government, including an elected House of Burgesses and a Council of State appointed by the governor, creating the structure through which a local ruling class could develop. Governor George Yeardley called the first assembly of the burgesses and councilors together in 1619 (Bailyn 2012; Kupperman 2007).

Equally important for the development of Virginia's plantation mode of production, the third charter called for the privatization of land in the colony. In part to settle the debts of the company, in part to attract new and wealthier investors, and likely in part because mercantile capitalism had been failing so badly in this context, the third charter allowed for the patenting of land to individual owners. In 1616–1617, the company granted land in fifty-acre lots to settle its debts with its investors (Billings 1968). After 1619, 100 acres was given to each settler who had served a seven-year term of labor for the company, or who had paid their own passage to Virginia; those coming after 1619 were granted 50 acres each under the same conditions. Those settlers who had invested in the company were given an additional 100 acres for each share that they had bought. At the same time, the system known as "headright" was established, granting any investor the right to patent fifty acres for each person they brought to the colony, whether family member, servant, or slave (Morgan 1975: 92). Those settlers without means but sent to Virginia at company expense would be assigned land to work as sharecropping tenants under the direction of a company overseer, with most surplus value being returned to the company. During their seven-year tenancy, these farmers would turn half of their earnings over to the company; at the end of their service, each would be granted fifty acres and elevated to the status of freeman, theoretically free to control any surplus value they generated (Kupperman 2007; Walsh 2010).

What emerged from this restructuring of land tenure was a new class structure composed of: (1) wealthy landholders who consolidated and capitalized large private holdings through a variety of means; (2) a class of independent freeholders who held legal rights to small 50-, 100-, or 150-acre plots granted to them at the end of their indenture (or who had enough capital to pay for their own transportation to Virginia without being indentured); (3) landless freemen (who may have served their indenture but lost or sold their rights to their allotments); (4) a servant class still on indentures who aspired to acquire property when their term of service was complete; and (5) a small but growing number of enslaved laborers of African descent, bound to work for life (Bailyn 2012: 168ff). This class structure would come to define the social relations of production in colonial Virginia for the subsequent two centuries, based as it was on the coercive extraction of surplus value from laborers, both indentured and enslaved, who during the term of their servitude had no right to the products of their labor.

The transformation of Virginia into a land of privately held plantation estates began in earnest when the London Company expanded this system to allow investors to establish sub-corporations or associations to establish "particular plantations" to be peopled by tenants brought over on terms by these investors; in other words, peopled by indentured tenants who would work for the owners of the "particular plantation" for a term of some seven years. The investors would be given 100 acres for every share of stock they purchased in the company, and 50 acres for each tenant brought over to work. Investors thus simultaneously collected profits (which were few) and acres (which were many). The relationship between privatization and colonial government was also established at this point, as government officers were well-compensated in land and tenants. The governor was granted 3,000 acres and 100 tenants; the treasurer and marshal of the colony were each granted 1,500 acres and 50 tenants; lesser officers received smaller land and tenant grants (Billings 1968; Kupperman 2007; Walsh 2010).

Tenancy and indentured servitude differed in that tenants were allowed to keep a percentage of the products of their labor, whereas indentured servants and enslaved workers were not. Those settled as tenants on land controlled by the London Company, a particular plantation, or a government official were allowed to keep half the product of their labor, with the other half going to the said company, investors, or official (Outlaw 1990).

The restructured mode of production got off to a fair start, as some 44 individuals and groups received patents for particular plantations, and some 3,500 new settlers, mostly tenants, arrived in Virginia between 1619 and 1622 (Morgan 1975: 98). By 1622, Virginia was composed of an amalgam of private settlements ("particular plantations"), quasi-private lands in the possession of government and company officials (who had the right to exploit the land, tenants, and servants allowed them for personal gain), and company plantations, all worked by a combination of tenants, servants, and slaves (Walsh 2010).

The inpouring of voluntary settlers – whether investor, tenant, or servant – was made feasible by the introduction of tobacco production. Although famous in popular culture as the husband of the Indian "princess" Pocahontas, John Rolfe's greatest contribution to the history of the Virginia colony was his experiment in cultivating West Indian tobacco in Virginia (Breen 1988). After 1617, tobacco became the life-blood of Virginia, eventually becoming the accepted medium of exchange among colonists. For most of the rest of the colonial history of Virginia, the social relations of production, access to the means of production through rules defining land tenure, and the definition of the value of labor were tied into the production of this commodity; in sum, as the 1610s drew to a close, a plantation mode of production developed in Virginia as tobacco emerged as the staple export product of the colony.

As the lure of tobacco profits attracted large investors and small set-tlers, it soon became clear that it was one thing to arrive in Virginia; it was something all-together different to survive there. Not only were the swampy lowlands of Tidewater Virginia infested with disease-bearing insects, but the expansion of tobacco settlements led to direct conflict with the Algonquin peoples of eastern Virginia, loosely allied into a tributary organization known as the Powhatan Confederacy (Gleach 1997). In the late 1610s and early 1620s, access to the waterfront was a crucial element of the means of production; particular plantations, hop-ing to develop into large corporate tobacco producing enterprises, were dispersed along the banks of the James River, often claiming up to ten miles of waterfront (Noël Hume 2001). The patenting of such large particular plantations inevitably led to the establishment of settlements further upriver, deeper into indigenous territory. In 1622, the Powhatan Confederacy, likely quite fed up with their newly arriving English neigh-bors and hoping to rid themselves of them once and for all, attacked the Virginia settlements, killing nearly 350 English men, women, and children, nearly a quarter of the surviving population (Billings 1968;

Fausz 1977). A cycle of violence ensued, with revenge killings taking place on both sides. Virginia thus plunged into spasms of murder and mayhem, collectively known as the Second Powhatan War. Alarmed by the violence, the investors back in London opened the books of the company, and what they saw was not pretty. Of the 4,270 people that had been sent to Virginia, only 1,240 were alive in 1622 before the out-break of violence, meaning that two thirds of the embarked settlers had died before the Powhatan attacked (Morgan 1975: 101). Appalled by what was revealed to him, James I appointed a commission to look into the affairs of the Virginia Company of London. The commission reported that despite their reform efforts, the company was bankrupt, people had been sent to Virginia with inadequate supplies to establish themselves, and many would-be settlers arrived in Virginia too weak to do much other than die, as ship captains preferred to fill their holds with fare-paying passengers than the supplies needed to keep said passengers alive and well during the trans-Atlantic crossing (Craven 1957; Morgan 1975: 101). In 1624, James I suspended the charter of the Virginia Company of London, bringing to an end the experiment in privately financed colonialism in the Virginia Tidewater. From this point forward, Virginia was run as a crown colony, with a governor appointed by the king. The Assembly, however, including both the elected House of Burgesses and the appointed Council of State, remained in place (Kupperman 2007).

Several archaeological projects conducted in Tidewater Virginia have revealed the nature of the early-seventeenth-century settlement pattern that emerged from this chaotic colonial genesis. Up until the time of the Second Powhatan War, and the subsequent revocation of the London Company's charter, the colonial landscape was one that featured a single concentrated settlement, at Jamestown, that might be considered a town, flanked at intervals of about five miles both up and downstream by a combination of particular plantations and the fortified homesteads of tenant farmers (Kelso 2008; Noël Hume 2001). Tidewater Virginia would come to be defined by four major river systems (including, from north to south, the Potomac, the Rappahanock, the York, and the James) from the estuaries of the Chesapeake Bay to the point upriver known as the fall line, where the coastal plain rises into the rolling foothills of the Appalachians. In essence, Virginia would be comprised of three penin-sulas jutting into the Chesapeake Bay, the lands south of the James River (known as the Southside), and the Eastern Shore of the Chesapeake. The particular plantations were distributed, primarily at this time, along the James, resulting in a dispersed settlement pattern of English settle-ment, lacking any concentration of population outside of Jamestown (Fausz 1971).

The best documented of the pre-1622 particular plantations was an establishment known as Martin's Hundred. Located on a tract of land now called Carter's Grove and owned by the Colonial Williamsburg Foundation, Martin's Hundred has been the subject of numerous archaeological projects dating from the early 1970s through the early twenty-first century (e.g., Malios 2000; Muraca 1993; Noël Hume 1982, 2001).

Martin's Hundred was among the earliest of the particular plantations to be chartered and settled by a joint stock company. Established by a group of investors known as the Society of Martin's Hundred, likely directed by one Sir Richard Martin of London, the company sent some 220 settlers from England in the late winter of 1619 (Noël Hume 1982, 2001). Arriving in Jamestown in April, apparently without a recognized leader, the settlers were put to work for the Governor of the London Company, Samuel Argall. After a year's service working for Governor Argall, the survivors removed some five miles downstream, establishing their particular plantation, likely sometime in 1620. Noël Hume (2001) suggests that one of the leading settlers, John Boyse, established a fortified homestead at Martin's Hundred while the settlers were impressed to work the Governor's Land. Boyse was soon joined by William Harwood, newly sent from England by the Society of Martin's Hundred to be the "governor" of the particular plantation, and some seventy or so of the settlers who survived their time working for the governor (Noël Hume 2001).

The cultural landscape of the particular plantation at Martin's Hundred was centered around a waterfront settlement known as Wolstenholme Town (see Figure 7.1). The "town" was a small cluster of earthfast (post-in-ground) buildings, including the palisaded residence of Governor Harwood, at least one smaller residence (others may have since eroded into the James River), a large barn, and a palisaded "company compound" that consisted of a two- or three-unit domestic "long house," which may have housed recently arriving settlers, officers of the company, or, alternatively, indentured servants working directly for the particular plantation. A small cow shed or byre was attached to one end of this structure. The compound also included the company store, in which goods and supplies for the settlement would have been kept, a shed, and what has been interpreted as a pottery drying shed (Noël Hume 2001). The majority of the settlers would have lived in small earthfast houses fanning out from the central compound. The corporate settlement pattern reflected at Wolstonholme Town would not survive the Second Powhatan War, as this particular plantation, like the corporate model for colonial settlement of which it was a part, was destroyed in the violence.

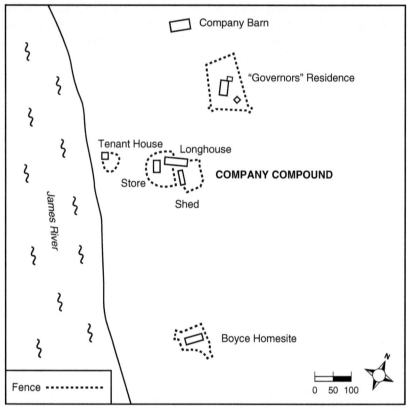

Figure 7.1. Martin's Hundred, c. 1622. One of Virginia's "particular plantations." Illustration courtesy of Nick Stover. *Source*: Noël Hume (1982).

The Rise of Virginia's Plantation Mode of Production, 1624–1652

Virginia's plantation mode of production was restructured, in the absence of corporately capitalized land, following the 1624 suspension of the London Company's charter. Virginia's emergent mode of production had its own idiosyncrasies based on labor relations, rules of land tenure, and – above all – the material and social forces required to produce and export tobacco, which were significantly different from those required in Jamaica for sugar or coffee. As we have discussed, a mode of production is defined by the interrelationship between the forces of production, including the tools, knowledge, land, and labor required to make goods for sale, and the relations of production, composed of the social structures and rules defining how people interact with each other.

As was the case in Jamaica, the most important elements of the forces of production for tobacco were land and a labor system that allowed planters to accrue as much surplus value as possible. By the time the Virginia Company of London lost its charter, tobacco production was already beginning to boom. For most of the ensuing seventeenth century, although slavery was not absent, the relations of production for tobacco agriculture in Virginia emerged from a system of coerced labor known as indentured servitude. As we have already seen, by the late 1610s, the "headright" system, in which settlers were granted fifty-acre allotments for each servant brought to Virginia, encouraged a boom in settlement for tobacco production. Theoretically, at least, these servants would be given fifty acres of their own at the end of their period of indenture, which was typically set at seven years.

As we have also seen, the demographic realities of the seventeenth-century tidewater created what one noted historian has called a "charnel house" in the colony (Morgan 1975: 110). Many servants brought over to Virginia did not survive the terms of their indenture; even by mid-century as many as 30 percent of children in some Virginia counties were orphaned before their eighteenth birthday (Bailyn 2012: 170). Enterprising planters used the legal system in place to expand their holdings by claiming the lands that would have gone to their deceased servants or their children, and by claiming rights to the labor power of servants and tenants whose master had died. After the violence of 1622, many freeholders who had tried to establish small farms were obliged to work for a large landholder; according to Edmund Morgan, large planters were finding ways to gather such men to themselves, either by claiming rights to servants after the death of their previous master, or by providing shelter to those who could not claim nor keep their fifty acres as they did not have the means to meet the requirement to improve their land grant through the construction of houses and outbuildings (Morgan 1975: 116–117).

By the middle of the 1620s, business-minded settlers recognized that the economy of scale for tobacco was directly related to the number of servants employed; the greater the number of servants working, the greater the amount of tobacco produced, and thus the greater the profit (Breen 1988; Kupperman 2007; Morgan 1975). During their terms of service, these workers were considered a form of chattel that could be exchanged between planters. So valuable was their labor to the rising planter class that the emerging ruling class of Virginia used the legislative power of the Assembly to enact a variety of pieces of legislation to extend the terms of service for indentures. Servants who attempted to run away, who killed cattle or swine roaming free in the bush, or who were impudent when addressing their "superiors," could have their terms of service extended by years. Women who became pregnant during the period of their indenture had their terms of service extended by two years (Brown 1996; Morgan 1975). Given the high mortality rates, it seemed a better investment to extend the terms of those who were already proven capable of surviving the harsh conditions of Virginia's plantations than to invest in new laborers, who might very well die quickly.

In contrast to the tropical products of the Caribbean, the means of production for tobacco required a relatively simple set of tools, buildings, and techniques. The primary techniques used to produce exportable tobacco were generally similar throughout the Chesapeake tidewater. As was the case with Jamaican coffee production, the first step for Virginia tobacco farmers was the acquisition and clearance of land suitable for agricultural production. Once a tract of land was patented, the best agricultural land was cleared of trees and scrub. Seedbeds would then be established in which the tobacco seeds were planted. After about two months of growth, the seedlings would be transplanted from the seedbeds into small hills, about eighteen inches high, spaced about three feet apart. During the next few weeks of growth, the tobacco fields would be constantly hoed, to prevent the young plants from being choked by weeds or attacked by cutworms (caterpillars that hide in the soil by day and attack the stems of tobacco plants by night). After about two months of additional growth, the tobacco plants would be primed and topped; these processes involved harvesting the bottom leaves of the stem, which are the first to mature, and trimming the top of the plant to prevent it from flowering and going to seed. In mid-summer, the plants needed constant care to prune unproductive suckers growing from the top of the stem, and to remove potentially harmful pests from the leaves, particularly the tobacco hornworm (a moth caterpillar that can grow to seven centimeters in length and devours tobacco plants). In late summer, harvest would begin. This process involved cutting the stems of the plants with a sharp tool, and transporting the leaves for curing. In the early days, the plants would be allowed to sit on the ground to cure; by the 1620s, the leaves were hung either from posts or on lines in tobacco barns or sheds to cure for four to six weeks (Breen 1988; Kulikof 1986).

Once cured, the tobacco leaves would be struck (removed from the posts or lines in which they were hung) and prepared for market. This usually involved laying the tobacco leaves on the ground or on the floor of a barn to sweat – that is, absorb moisture from the humid tidewater air. Once sweated, the tobacco leaves would be pliant enough to be twisted together and rolled into ropes. The ropes of tobacco would be wound into balls weighing about 100 pounds, then placed into large barrels known as hogsheads that would be rolled to riverside wharves to await shipment. Like coffee, properly packed tobacco was relatively stable, and could be stored in the hogsheads for weeks until sold or consigned for shipment to England. In the first half of the seventeenth century, as Tidewater Virginia had nothing that resembled a port, merchant ships would sail up the primary rivers, collecting hogsheads of tobacco from individual wharves scattered along the banks of the navigable rivers. Riverfront wharves were thus a crucial element of the means of production (Breen 1988; Kulikof 1986).

The tools required for tobacco production were thus very simple, even though they needed to be imported: felling axes, saws, chains, and ox teams to clear forest land; hoes and knives to cultivate and harvest crops; drawknives and chisels to make hogsheads. In contrast to the mills, aqueducts, cisterns, barbecues, and boiling houses required to produce sugar and coffee in the Caribbean, very little in the way of permanent plantation infrastructure was required for tobacco beyond housing for the workers and sheds to dry tobacco and store hand tools. Seventeenth-century Virginia plantation buildings – whether houses, barns, or sheds – tended to be inexpensively built, with posts sunk directly into the ground, with walls made of wattle and daub, and with roofs made of thatch or locally made redware tile and earthen floors. Such structures have been typically characterized as "impermanent" and "earthfast" buildings by historical archaeologists (e.g., Carson et al. 1981). But for a few notable examples, such as Governor William Berkeley's mansion at Green Spring Plantation, even the houses of the planter elites were constructed this way (Neiman 1978, 1980). Requiring little permanent infrastructure, suffering from the impermanence of labor brought on by high mortality rates and the finite indentures of those who managed to survive, and taking a terrible toll on the fertility of the soil, the plantation mode of production of seventeenth-century Virginia created a near nomadic settlement pattern, with houses and farmsteads frequently being abandoned every five years or so (Morgan 1975). Such a system required plenty of suitable agricultural land, and those with the means to acquire vast estates eagerly did so.

Virginia's plantation mode of production thus encouraged the private capitalization of large tracts of land. Tobacco production was notoriously hard on the soil; yields could begin declining after a single crop. Virginia planters thus preferred to plant tobacco in virgin soil, making the acquisition of land a central concern for those involved in this mode of production. By the middle of the 1630s, the seeds of class conflict, tied directly to the acquisition and improvement of tobacco lands, were already beginning to sprout. Even those servants who managed to survive to claim their fifty acres had a very limited patrimony. Within a few short years, the soils on these small farms would be stressed to the point at which yields would be in significant decline. As the wealthier planter class continued to aggrandize their landholdings in the tidewater, it became extremely difficult for small freeholders to acquire new tobacco lands, forcing many former servants back into tenancy on lands owned by the grandees. For those unwilling to resume such a dependent social relationship, the only option was to move upriver, to try to claim and plant as yet unpatented lands. Although at first blush the seventeenth-century planters saw a virtually unlimited supply of land stretching before them, it did not take much further inspection to realize that the vast interior of North America was not an unoccupied wilderness at their immediate disposal. The first requirement for expanding tobacco production was thus the removal of the Indian population from the tidewater (Fausz 1987; Gleach 1997).

Much of the history of early Virginia revolved around negotiation and warfare with the various Algonquian-speaking nations that inhabited the tidewater. After the violence of 1622, it became clear to many settlers that the native population of Virginia needed to be pushed back, eliminated, or enslaved. Virginians showed few scruples in dealing with the Indians. One favorite strategy was to settle a treaty with a group of Indians, and once they were settled peaceable down, to mount a surprise attack on unarmed men, women, and children. One particularly notorious event occurred in 1623 when Dr. John Pott allegedly served poisoned wine to a number of Native Americans with whom the Virginians had just concluded a peace treaty. As many as 200 people died as a result of this infamous poisoning (Billings 2004: 43; Morgan 1975: 100). Pott went on to become acting governor of the colony, the patentee of land in what would be known as Middle Plantation (today's Williamsburg), and the primary beneficiary of the raising, at public expense, of a defensive palisade between tributaries of the James and York Rivers. A second uprising of the native peoples in 1644 resulted in the remnants of Powhatan's confederacy having their territory further reduced. The 1646 treaty, ending what is sometimes referred to as the Third Powhatan War, created a legal boundary between Indian territory and the English colony defined on the north by the York River to its falls, southwesterly from there to the Falls of the James River near modern-day Richmond, and then southeasterly to the Blackwater River, which flows southerly to Albemarle Sound in modern North Carolina. The treaty required the leaders of each of the remaining tribal groups to accept tributary status as vassals of the King of England, and crucial for the development of the plantation mode of production, opened hundreds of thousands of acres of land on the Virginia Peninsula, and what would become known as the Southside (land south of the James River), for tobacco production and settlement (Bailyn 2012; Gleach 1997; Morgan 1975).

The native population was thus removed from the Virginia Peninsula, the narrow stretch of land between the James and York Rivers, the southernmost of the tidewater's three peninsulas. In a fortuitous turn of events, the disbanding of the London Company had opened the way for the Virginia planters to distribute the newly acquired land among themselves. After 1636, most land grants were made by county courts, pending approval of the Council of State and the governor, who had appointed the officials to the county courts in the first place (Billings 1968, 2004a).

Land tenure was somewhat complicated by the questionable status of both privately held and corporately owned land originally distributed by the defunct Virginia Company of London. Although their charter was suspended by James I in 1624, there was no indication if and when the Company might be reestablished. For some twenty years there were occasional hints about, and active lobbying in Parliament for, the establishment of a successor to the London Company, which could potentially reclaim all of Virginia's developed land as corporate property, or at least to channel its profits back into a joint-stock company. The question was not settled until 1641 when Sir William Berkeley was dispatched by James I's successor, King Charles I, to serve as the royal governor of Virginia. After this point, the formation of a new company was all but out of the question, and Virginia remained a dominion of privatized land, dominated by the plantation production of tobacco (Billings 2004b).

Between 1624 and 1651, the plantation landscape of Virginia emerged, although alternate visions of how the means of production would be organized persisted. One of these visions, favored by those wealthier settlers hoping to create large estates in the wake of the Second Powhatan War, resulted in the establishment of fortified plantation compounds inhabited by plantation proprietors and their servants. These fortified settlements could be flanked by a series of smaller homesteads inhabited by tenants on their land. Several archaeological projects have been conducted on such fortified plantation sites dating to the post-company era of Plantation Virginia, including a component at Martin's Hundred that post-dates the Second Powhatan War, and one at a site on the Southside of the James known as Jordan's Journey.

In both cases, a palisade surrounded the domestic quarters of a planter's family and those of their indentured servants. Notably, the houses of both master and servant in both contexts were of earthfast construction, and there appears to be little physical or material distance between the proprietors and the servants. In the late 1620s, Jordan's Journey contained four earthfast longhouses, each of which contained two or three rooms. Three of the longhouses measured sixteen feet wide by about fifty-five feet long, with the fourth measuring sixteen feet by thirty-six feet. At Jordan's Journey, it is difficult to distinguish which of the several longhouses served as the planter's home, although it is likely the central Structure 10, given that Structure 4 was thought to have been dismantled before 1635, Structure 5 is the smallest of the dwellings on the site, and Structure 1 is attached to what was likely a farm yard. No more than twenty feet separate any of the houses (see Figure 7.2). The clustered settlement suggests that

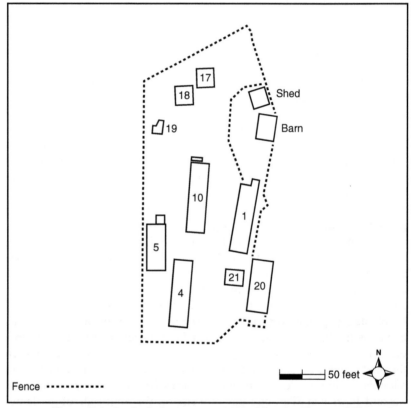

Figure 7.2. Jordan's Journey, c. 1630. Like the Harwood Plantation, Jordan's Journey contained the planter's house (probably Structure 10), several houses for indentured servants (Structures 1, 4, and 5), and a number of agricultural outbuildings. The servants' houses were of a form known as longhouses, each one room deep by two or three rooms long, and each of which likely housed a number of servants. Illustration courtesy of Nick Stover. *Source*: Morgan et al. (1995)

masters and servants were living in quite close contact, in houses of about equal size and quality, though it is probable that each of the servants' dwellings were divided into a series of two or three rooms, and each was likely occupied by more people than would have lived in the main house (McCartney 2011; Morgan et al. 1995).

A similar settlement structure developed when Martin's Hundred was re-inhabited after the Second Powhatan War, when what Ivor Noël Hume called "Site A" at the abandoned "particular plantation" was claimed by William Harwood as a privately owned property. After taking possession of the plantation, Harwood constructed a fortified domestic settlement at "Site A" (see Figures 7.3 and 7.4). Like Jordan's Journey, "Site A" was surrounded by a palisade, and both the master's family and their indentured servants lived inside the walls. All of the houses were, again, of similar dimension and of earthfast construction, and placed quite near each other. The main house consisted of two ground-floor rooms, each measuring approximately 16 feet square, whereas the two servants' quarters were 16 feet square. As was the case at Jordan's Journey, the compound included a buttery/kitchen and several outbuildings, which were likely used for curing and storing tobacco. "Site A" was flanked by at least four tenant houses, each of which stood outside the palisade walls of the fortified compound of the Harwood Plantation (Noël Hume 1982, 2001).

The plantation landscape in the second quarter of the seventeenth century was characterized not only by fortified private plantations like these, but by scattered tenant and freeholder farmsteads. Because the land records for most of Virginia's counties were destroyed during the Civil War of 1861–1865, it is difficult at times to distinguish whether a specific small homestead was located on land leased through tenancy or freely held by a former servant who had claimed his headright. Nevertheless, it is likely that most of the small homesteads, whether of a tenant or freeman, were similarly constructed.

Three presumed tenant houses, dating between 1625 and 1650, have been excavated at Martin's Hundred. Each of these homesteads consisted of a single, small earthfast building. Excavations at one of these ("Site E") revealed no additional features, whereas the other two (44JC647 and "Site B") featured what was known as a slot fence. Such a fence was constructed by excavating a narrow ditch, standing hewn or split boards vertically in the ditch, and then backfilling the ditch; this would create a solid fence that could be used to keep animals penned in a yard, or to prevent roaming animals from getting into a yard (Edwards 2004; Noël Hume 1982).

Another tenant/freeman homesite was excavated near Martin's Hundred. Dating between 1630 and 1650, this homesite may represent

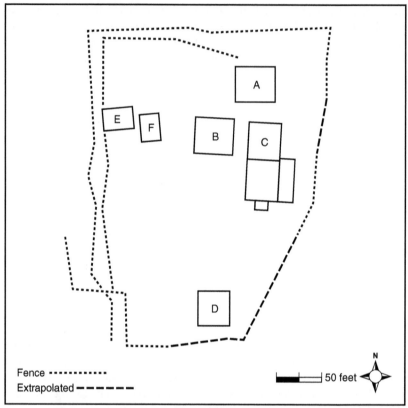

Figure 7.3. The fortified homestead within the Harwood Plantation, c. 1630. Structure C is the earthfast house of the planter; Structures A and B are quarters for indentured servants; Structures D, E, and F are agricultural outbuildings. The entire complex was surrounded by a defensive fence. Illustration courtesy of Nick Stover. *Source*: Noël Hume (2001, 1982).

an early freeman's house in the post-London Company era. Like the tenant houses at Martin's Hundred (or more specifically, at the William Harwood Plantation), this site likely featured a small earthfast house (see Figure 7.5). Although the location of the house has been obscured by a modern intrusive feature, the presence of two wells and a fence line indicate the location of the house. This site, known as the Buck Site (44JC568), was surrounded by a slot fence, creating an enclosed house yard. Within that yard were the house and three wells, four small sheds likely used for curing tobacco and storing agricultural implements, and a small graveyard containing nine burials (Mallios 1999).

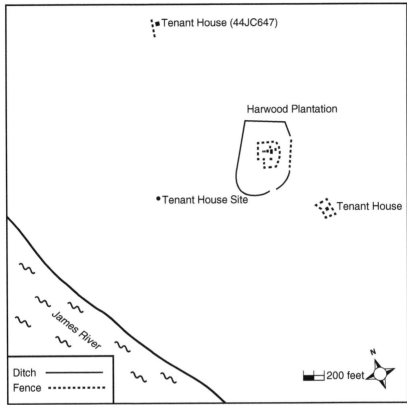

Figure 7.4. The Harwood Plantation, c. 1630. A privately owned plantation that post-dates the destruction of Wolstoneholme Town. Illustration
courtesy of Nick Stover. *Source*: Noël Hume (2001, 1982).

The Rise of the Planter Class, 1652–1676

The late 1640s were a time of great conflict and civil war in Britain,
culminating in the 1649 execution of King Charles I, and the subsequent
establishment of a Puritan-controlled Republican government known as
the Commonwealth. In 1652, nearly three years after the beheading of
his patron Charles I, Governor William Berkeley was met by an armed
deputation from the Commonwealth government, which politely asked
him to vacate his office. Having politely met the deputation with an
armed force of his own, Berkeley agreed to retire to private life, under a
series of conditions that would ensure that the freedoms and privileges
enjoyed by the people of Virginia would not be challenged, and that no

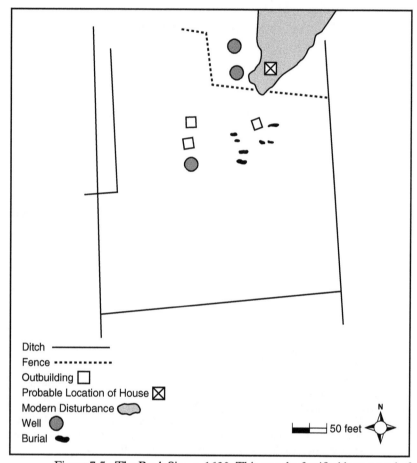

Figure 7.5. The Buck Site, c. 1630. This was the fortified homestead of an independent freeman or tenant. Unlike the larger plantation settlements at places like Jordan's Journey or the Harwood Plantation, small settlers would establish modest homesteads like this, with a single house, small agricultural sheds, and, inevitably, the graves of the many victims of the demographic crisis of the early seventeenth century. Illustration courtesy of Nick Stover. *Source*: Malios (1999).

Virginian would be prosecuted for having taken the (losing) Royalist side in the late Civil War. Although the Commonwealth delegation did see to it that Governor Berkeley was replaced with Richard Bennett, one of the few prominent Puritans in Virginia, the negotiated settlement ensured that the trajectory of Virginia's social and political developments would not be disturbed by any unfortunate change of government at home (Billings 2004: 110–111; Morgan 1975: 147).

As Virginia's elites consolidated their control over the means of production during the ensuing two decades, the social relations of production that would define the emergent plantation mode of production congealed. In the years following the 1646 capitulation of the remnants of the Powhatan confederacy, the rising elite of Virginia had rewarded themselves with massive land grants in the newly opening territories to the south and west of Jamestown, and – in the succeeding decades – they sought to profit from their good fortune. It had been clear for some time that the tobacco road to great fortune required control over land and labor, both of which were quickly exhausted by the rigors of the mode of production in use. The headright system, which had been initiated to attract settlers to Virginia, remained it place, and was an active component of land and wealth consolidation by mid-century. Not only could wealthy investors who could afford to import servants gain claim to thousands of acres of land, but headrights became valuable commodities, exchangeable for land at one of the colony's county courts. Given the governing structure of the colony, it was up to the officers of the colonial government to decide how these headrights would be translated into land patents. Perhaps not surprisingly, it was often the officers and their immediate circles that wound up in possession of the land best suited for tobacco production (Morgan 1975).

The 1650s and 1660s witnessed both a rapid increase in the number of people emigrating to Virginia and the amount of land claimed as private property through the instrument of the land patent, two phenomena that were directly related through the custom of headright. Between 1650 and 1675, more than 2,350,000 acres were patented in Virginia, much of it in large parcels concentrated in the hands of a few men, many of whom were new arrivals in Virginia and allied with the still resident Sir William Berkeley (Bailyn 2012). For example, Morgan reports that the clerk of the court for Charles City County purchased headrights amounting to 38,500 acres, which he subsequently sold to land speculators who used the rights to patent land along the Potomac River on the Northern Neck (the northernmost of Virginia's three peninsulas). By 1660, some 100,000 acres along the Potomac were owned by only thirty men (Bailyn 2012; Morgan 1975: 219). Thus the colonial officers of Virginia were profiting by land transactions, tied directly to labor importation, while simultaneously ensuring that the freshest tobacco lands were consolidated into great land holdings that could be kept out of the hands of small settlers and their petty 50-acre farms.

Despite this continuous consolidation and aggrandizement of land, thousands of new settlers arrived in Virginia, some indentured servants, others small investors who came with their families and a few servants, and who hoped to rise in prominence by working their 150- or 200-acre headrights into profitable operations. Some came against their will; by 1660, headrights for enslaved Africans had reached nearly 700 claims (Coombs 2011), and Governor Berkeley had estimated that, by 1671, the population of Virginia included some 2,000 "black slaves" (Coombs 2011). It was not only Africans who were brought to Virginia against their will. Beggars, vagrants, and convicts were routinely rounded up from the English countryside and towns and transported to Virginia where they were sold as servants; orphans were sold out by parish officials, and the kidnapping of children to be sold into servitude was common enough to invoke government action (Bailyn 2012: 166–167). Of the approximately 100,000 Britons known to have immigrated to the tobacco coast of the Virginia and Maryland tidewater, as many as 85 percent were bonded servants; as late as 1668, 45 percent of the population of Virginia's Middlesex County consisted of indentured servants (Bailyn 2012: 165). The strategies employed to coerce children, the indigent, and other powerless members of English society to Virginia underscores the point that entry into labor relations was not voluntary for many, perhaps even for most (Brass and Bernstein 1992).

These processes resulted in the reinforcement of a sharply hierarchical class structure, dominated by a small land and office-holding class, under whom sat the so-called middling farmers and freemen with small land claims and perhaps one or two servants, the servant class itself, and enslaved Africans. Class consciousness had developed among the great planters of Virginia by mid-century. As was true in Jamaica, those who rose to economic prominence through the exploitation of land and labor used the power of the colonial government to secure and extend their collective interest. Those who had emerged out of the tumultuous opening decades as "grandees," that is the heads of those families who had exchanged headrights, consolidated land holdings, and controlled the labor of large numbers of servants, created and then used the mechanisms of government to forward their interests. Chief among these was the perpetual control of labor. It was recognized by mid-century that servants were "more advantageous ... than any other commodityes" for importation from England (quoted in Morgan 1975: 175), and that the best way to make a profit from tobacco production was to control the labor of those servants for as long as they were productive.

By statute and custom, indentured servants could only be bound for a fixed term of years; the colonial government, however, took it on itself to fix and extend those terms. Although people who had voluntarily agreed to indentures were typically bound for between five and seven years, those without clear indenture (including those kidnapped or transported to Virginia) arrived with ambiguous status. By the end of the 1640s, the Assembly had resolved this issue by determining that conscripts and others would be bound for four years if older than the age of 20 (later reduced to 19); five years between the ages of 12 and 20, and seven if younger than the age of 12. It was the county courts that would determine the age of the servants in a time where dates of birth were not always known. There is reason to believe that the court officials intentionally underestimated the age of servants to ensure they would be bound for the longest possible term. For example, between 1662 and 1680, the Lancaster County Court judged only 32 of 296 newly arrived servants to be older than 19; in Norfolk, only 1 of 72 was older than 19 in those same years (Morgan 1975: 217).

As we have seen, the social relations of production are defined by the social and legal rules that define how people relate to each other, and how they relate to both the forces of production and the products of labor. It is clear that class relations between land owners and their workers were materially based on the former's ability to extract surplus value from their indentured servants, tenants, and slaves; this was largely done by their directly assuming the product of labor in the form of tobacco. Relationships between the planter class and the freeholders were similarly based on the former's ability to extract value expressed as tobacco, but in a less direct manner.

One of the primary mechanisms used by the planter class in Virginia to accumulate tobacco capital from independent farmers was the use of public office to levy taxes and collect fees. Every government post, from county clerk to governor, came attached with a means to collect revenue, paid in pounds of tobacco, as a privilege of office. Office holders used their positions for private profit as governors, collectors, auditors, sheriffs, and secretaries began collecting and keeping fees for marriage licenses, departures from the colony, liquor licenses, naturalization of foreigners, issuing and recording of documents, writs of elections, warrants served, arrests made, hearing civil suits. Just about any official action carried a fee that was paid directly to the colonial official responsible for the office (Morgan 1975: 206–208). Burgesses and councilors were paid handsomely for the time they spent in Jamestown; hundreds of pounds of tobacco were added to the county levies for each day the Assembly met in session, increasing the already heavy tax burden of the small farmers.

By mid-century, Virginia was divided into a series of counties, which became the primary political division for the colony. Between 1636 and 1642, the Assembly had empowered each county to organize and hold monthly court sessions, eventually devolving all local governance to the county courts; this new system replaced the "haphazard system of particular plantations which had previously served as the units of local government" (Billings 1968: 39–40). By 1660, the county courts had become the most powerful units in the colony's government and a mechanism through which local elites were able to extract wealth from smaller planters in their counties (Billings 1968: 41).

Each county court consisted of a number of Justices of the Peace, a sheriff, constables, a clerk, and a variety of lesser officers, each of which enriched the office holder through the collection of fees. Having wide-ranging powers, county courts decided local judicial matters, dealt with a wide variety of administrative and ecclesiastical functions, and served as the court of record for the recording of wills, probate inventories, and property transactions. Among the most important of its duties, the county court levied county poll taxes, and then supervised the collection of these levies. As officers of the court, individual justices took depositions and settled petty cases, even when they were parties to these cases, and met monthly to collectively act on more important criminal and civil matters (Billings 1968: 43), collecting tobacco from their constituents at every opportunity.

The governor had great power in manning the social hierarchy of Virginia. Not only did the governor appoint the members of the Council, but he also appointed the commissioners (justices) of the county courts, who in turn appointed the lower officers. By the time that Berkeley politely left the governorship in 1652, appointments to county government and the Council of State, and election to the House of Burgesses, were reserved for the wealthy and powerful; no servant arriving after 1640 rose to serve in the House of Burgesses. In 1691, Thomas Milner, speaker of the House of Burgesses, was denied a position on the Council because he did not have "[e]state enough to be a Counsellor" (quoted in Morgan 1975: 209). Power was increasingly consolidated into an ever-tightening circle of families, as individuals were commonly appointed to multiple offices simultaneously, and the long-standing custom of consolidating the wealth of families by the marriage of widows continued (Morgan 1975: 210).

Although, as was the case in Jamaica, factionalism and dissent developed among the members of Virginia's elite class (Bailyn 2012: 87), the local and colonial governments served as arenas in which members of the planter class defined and consolidated their common interests, and thus established class consciousness. Among these common interests were mechanisms by which burgesses, county commissioners, and other officials maximized their incomes by increasing the tax burden imposed on freeholders. Sessions of the Assembly, which met in Jamestown, were particularly expensive for the freeholders, as their burgesses would rack up expenses in a few weeks' time that outpaced the annual income of an ordinary freeholder. For example, on top of their usual allowance, the Norfolk County burgesses charged their constituents 150 pounds of tobacco for a fiddler in 1653 and 500 pounds for a trumpeter in 1660 (Morgan 1975: 148–149). Certain members of the Council were empowered to collect duties on cargos entering and leaving one of the rivers, receiving a 10 percent commission on the value of the duties collected. When a planter named Benjamin Harrison brought abuses of this system to the attention of the colonial government, he noted that "takeing it to be their Common Interest to agree among themselves, do generally let such things sleep" (quoted in Morgan 1975: 202).

The year 1660 saw the restoration of both Charles II as King of England and William Berkeley as Governor of Virginia, a post the latter would hold for another seventeen years. During his second term in office, tensions between the classes mounted, and Berkeley, although he recognized the rising class conflict, did little to stem it. Describing Virginia's ruling class to the king, Berkeley suggested that they were a people "press'd at our backes with Indians, in our Bowills with servants ... and invaded from without by the Dutch" (quoted in Webb 1984: 6). In the years following his restoration, Berkeley championed a series of reforms that sought to diversify Virginia's economy. A generous evaluation of his motives would contend that the old governor envisioned a Virginia that was not dependent solely on tobacco production, and that provided more avenues of opportunity for the poorer classes; a more cynical view would hold that his intention was to further concentrate wealth into the hands of a small oligarchy of planters. Although his plans met with only a tepid response by the Crown and his contemporaries in Virginia, both of whom were profiting by the tobacco trade, Berkeley proposed a series of comprehensive reforms that would have dramatically changed the plantation mode of production, by cutting the freemen out of plantation production. His plan would have required European settlers to gather in towns rather than live on dispersed small farms. He envisioned a situation in which artisans, surrounded by customers, would not abandon their trades to plant tobacco; ships would be built; iron would be mined and smelted; wool would be harvested, spun, and woven; and corn and wheat would be produced for export to the West Indies (Billings 2004b; Morgan 1975).

The key element of his plan, and the only way to truly "encourage" the small farmers to abandon tobacco cultivation, was his controversial attempt to prohibit tobacco planting throughout Virginia, Maryland, and Carolina for a year from February 1667. His plan may have succeeded had not the proprietor of the Maryland colony, Lord Baltimore, balked at the plan, revealing a concern for the freemen and small planters who would not have had a means of livelihood during the intervening time it would take to establish a diversified economy (Morgan 1975). Apparently this was of lesser concern to Berkeley, who likely saw that the primary tensions emerging in his colony were between that very class of small farmers who needed land but could not get it and the great planters who owned more and more land and would not let it go. One of the not too subtle goals of the diversification policy would have been a great, if temporary reduction in the supply of tobacco to the English market, which likely would have considerably driven up the price of the addictive leaf. The suspension of production would have meant a great increase in profit for the great planters, but likely the ruin of many small freeholders and tenants, who would have been unable to pay their annual levy in tobacco, and were dependent on the meager income their small farms provided.

By the 1670s, the accumulation of wealth was ultimately tied to the mass production of tobacco. For most of the seventeenth century, Virginia's economy was based on the ownership of the products of labor, measured in hundred-weights of tobacco, based in a semi-feudal labor system in which individuals were bound as servants to a master for a number of years, but with few rights. The lot of the indentured servant was particularly difficult; during the years of their indenture, the masters of land controlled both the labor of the servant and the products of that labor. Following their set term, the servants theoretically ascended to the status of freeman, and were no longer bound to a master. Unfortunately for many, by the early 1670s, there remained little arable tobacco land available along the drainages of the great tidewater rivers, and an increasing number of former servants merged into a growing class of landless tenants, dependent on the great landowners for access to land, who in return would claim increasing proportions of the products of their labor. Recognizing their contradictory class interests, the political elite of Virginia passed laws blocking the landless from voting for their burgesses, one of the few avenues the ordinary people of Virginia had to participate in the governance of the colony. Such a move was clearly designed to protect the class interests of the planters (Bailyn 2012: 522 ff.).

The material manifestation of the impending crisis can be seen in the layout of Clifts Plantation. Established in about 1670 on the Potomac River in the Northern Neck, Clifts Plantation was the home of an unidentified well-to-do planter. Reflecting the growing land shortages of the third quarter of the century, like many settlers in what would have been Virginia's frontier, the resident planter of Clifts was a tenant, leasing land and a manor house from the wealthy Pope family (Neiman 1980). When established for tobacco production, Clifts included a sizeable earthfast house and a detached servants' quarter; both were flanked to the west by a series of smaller structures, likely tobacco sheds and other agricultural outbuildings (Figure 7.6). A few years after the construction of the house, a defensive palisade, featuring bastions on two corners, was built around the manor house. This latter feature was likely constructed as tensions on the frontiers were mounting, and newly arrived planters felt it necessary to defend their homes against the native population. Unlike the fortified settlements

Slot Fence ───────
Fence ············
Extrapolated ── ── ──

50 feet

N

Figure 7.6. The Clifts Plantation, c. 1675. Occupied immediately before Bacon's Rebellion, the Clifts house was a high-status domicile, yet was inhabited by a wealthy tenant who likely could not gain access to his own plantation land. When a defensive palisade was constructed at the site, it encircled only the manor house (A), and not the servants' quarters or the agricultural outbuildings. Illustration courtesy of Nick Stover. *Source*: Neiman (1980).

of earlier years, the defensive works at Clifts did not surround the servants' quarters, but it is possible that the servants would have been brought into the main house should there have been any sign of trouble.

Dialectical class conflict was developing in Virginia, and Berkeley clearly knew it. When gathering a force to defend Virginia against a possible landing by the enemy Dutch in the late 1660s, Berkeley noted that "at least one third are Single freemen (whose Labor will hardly maintaine them) or men much in debt, both which wee may reasonably expect ... wold revolt to [the enemy] in hopes of bettering their Condicion" (quoted in Morgan 1975: 241–242). More poignantly perhaps, Berkeley understood that the long-standing requirement that freemen hold and maintain firearms was potentially dangerous to the planter class. In July 1676, he commented on his own position in the rising crisis in a letter to William Ludwell: "[h]ow miserable that man is that Governes a People where six parts of seaven at least are Poore Endebted Discontented and Armed" (quoted in Washburn 1957: vi). The resolution to this emerging crisis, in the minds of wealthy planters like Berkeley, would be the replacement of servants, tenants, and small freeholders with the labor of enslaved Africans, a process already well underway by the 1660s (Bailyn 2012; Coombs 2011). The ultimate shift in the relations of production, through which slavery replaced tenancy and servitude throughout Virginia, would only be realized, however, in the wake of a violent dialectical crisis.

Contradictions and Dialectics: The Revolution of 1676

In 1676, the tensions that had been mounting between the ascendant planter class and the increasingly disenfranchised freemen and servants exploded into civil war. By the time the smoke had cleared from the tidewater, Jamestown lay as a smoldering ruin, the once popular William Berkeley was ignominiously recalled by the king, dozens of plantation houses had been sacked, and an untold number of settlers had been hanged, shot, or otherwise brought to an untimely end. The origins of this conflict, generally now known as Bacon's Rebellion, have been debated nearly since the first shot was fired in anger. Some have argued that the rebellion was a precursor to the American Revolution in its attempt to overthrow royal authority and replace it with local representative government (e.g., Wertenbaker 1940), others blame it on factionalism between wealthy newcomers and the old Virginia elite (e.g., Bailyn 2012), some suggest it was a conflict between two ambitious and headstrong men (e.g., Washburn 1957), others have thought that unmarried frontiersmen needed an outlet to relieve their pent-up frustration and so turned to war (e.g., Rice 2012), and still others see the rebellion as part of a more wide-spread though failed political and social revolution (e.g., Webb 1984). Despite the range of interpretations, most agree that the spark that began the fire was a dispute over how to deal with the native population on Virginia's northern and western frontiers.

A Marxist analysis would hold that each of these seemingly distinct explanations for the rebellion do not explain the situation fully, and that to develop a deeper understanding of why so many Virginians were willing to make war on each other, despite the real and threatening presence of angry native neighbors and Dutch adversaries, we must examine the conflict dialectically.

Seventeenth-century Virginia was characterized by labor conflict. Value was created and even measured by the production of tobacco. It thus followed that the creation of wealth in the colony was dependent on controlling the means of production for tobacco, particularly land and labor. To control both, the planters had used the headright system to their advantage, both in importing and then exchanging as many servants as could be found, and in patenting and otherwise acquiring as much river-side tobacco land as could be had. However, the system required that once free of their indentures, the former servants had the right to claim fifty acres for themselves, which they would own freely once they had improved the land by erecting a house, clearing forest, and establishing tobacco production. After 1660, it became increasingly difficult to find suitable land in the tidewater region, and more and more freemen, and even newly arrived wealthy planters who were not well-enough connected to receive land with good river frontage, had little choice but to work interior lands, and to take out patents near the fall line of the tidewater rivers. Herein lay a dialectical contradiction within the mode of production. The freemen had a legal right to receive tobacco lands at the end of their indentures, but it was not in the interest of the large planters to allow them to have free access to that land. More and more of the former servants and their adult children were among the "Poor Endebted Discontented" residents of Virginia that so troubled William Berkeley (Rice 2012; Tarter 2011).

That the rebellion began as a conflict between Virginians living near the fall line and the native population of Virginia is not surprising. The continual capitalization of the tidewater through the consolidation of large estates by the old elite pushed new settlers, both those newly freed from indenture and those well-to-do settlers, like Nathaniel Bacon, newly arrived in Virginia, to the borderlands of the colony. Their ambitions were checked by the alliances that the old elite, under Berkeley's leadership, had made with what were referred to as the tributary nations, those native groups who had pledged subservience to the English king, and who contributed to the accumulation of wealth by Berkeley and the old elite through their control of the fur trade. Virginia's official Indian policy reveals another aspect of the dialectical conflict emerging in Virginia. It was in the best interests of the ruling class to trade with the Indians – often exchanging guns for furs. The Indians then used those guns to defend themselves against the new settlers, who hoped to capture Indian land for their own use. When the Assembly resolved to settle the Indian question by increasing taxes to pay for the construction of what were said to be defensive works (but everyone knew really to be trading forts), class interest was once again exposed. The new forts were to be constructed on lands belonging to members of the old Virginia elite and their newly arriving friends and garrisoned by men from their downriver plantations, but would be paid for by a tax levied on the settlers in the frontier districts, who thought the forts would only attract the Indians rather than remove them (Rice 2012; Tartar 2011).

Bacon's Rebellion is often said to have begun when one of the wealthy young newcomers to Virginia, Nathaniel Bacon, incensed by a recent Indian attack at his plantation near the Falls of the James, organized an army of volunteers to make war against the Indians. Berkeley, favoring the trade solution at the soon to be constructed forts, and thus not having sanctioned such action, labeled Bacon a mutinous rebel. The governor led a force to the Falls of the James to arrest Bacon and stamp out the mutiny, but to no immediate avail, as Bacon and his forces remained in the field and did not give the governor the satisfaction of an arrest. Instead, on his return from the expedition, Bacon was elected as a burgess and proceeded to Jamestown accompanied by an armed guard of some forty men. At first allowing Bacon to take his seat in the Assembly, Berkeley bided his time and soon signed an arrest warrant, by which time Bacon had discerned the governor's intentions and had fled Jamestown. Within two weeks, Bacon had returned to the capital at the head of a rebel army of 500 men, demanding that the governor sign a commission elevating him to the rank of general. Refusing to bend, Berkeley stormed into his private quarters, at which point Bacon's men aimed their weapons at the burgesses assembled in the state house. Without much of a delay, the frightened burgesses acceded to Bacon's demands. The final step in this coup came when Bacon, echoing the actions of Oliver Cromwell a generation earlier, entered the state house at the head of an armed bodyguard. The captive Assembly had little choice but to prevail upon Berkeley to grant Bacon his commission, which he did. The Revolution had begun.

The basic military history of the subsequent conflict is well-known. Within a few months of Bacon's coup, Berkeley attempted to raise an army of his own against Bacon, but failing to attract enough men to face Bacon's force, the governor fled Jamestown for the safety of the Eastern Shore. A botched rebel effort to arrest Berkeley there led to the capture of the few ships that Bacon's men had hoped to use to control the Chesapeake Bay (Webb 1984). Once in control of the waterways, Berkeley returned to Jamestown in the attempt to regain control over the colonial government, only to face a siege by the Baconians. After a failed attempt to break the rebel siege line, the loyalists slipped out at night by boat; Bacon's force proceeded to enter the town and burn it to prevent a similar retaking of the colonial capital. Pitched battles between the loyalists and rebels continued for several months, as both sides waited for the arrival of regular troops from England.

The rebel general did not live to see the end of the contest. Plagued by lice, Nathaniel Bacon contracted typhus and died in October 1676. Despite the death of their leader, the Baconians carried on their revolution until December, when the last sizeable rebel force surrendered to the loyalists at a place in Virginia called West Point. Notably, of the last 100 men to surrender, 80 were black slaves, and 20 white indentured servants (Rice 2012; Webb 1984).

Dialectics and Social Change: The Rise of Slavery, 1677–1700

The mode of production that had prevailed before 1676 fomented a constant demand for labor. From its beginnings in the aftermath of the 1622 violence, that mode of production had been based primarily on extractive relationships between the planter class and those who worked on their land. As the demand for labor increased after mid-century, many landless wanderers were apprehended in England and transported to the colonies as indentured servants. Whether transported voluntarily or against their will, the system in place promised a new beginning for these men; if they were lucky enough to survive their indenture, they were supposed to become free men of property.

Yet at the end of their indenture, the freemen could be kept landless, be barred from participation in government, pilloried for libeling court officials, and burdened with taxes that could amount to as much as half of their annual production. The local tax rate was astronomical; annual levies were collected by the local elites, which included expenses accrued, often fraudulently, by the wealthy families who controlled the county courts. The local justices and their fellow county officers, including elected burgesses, found more ways to tax the freemen, collecting in tobacco or promissory notes to be exchanged for future production. These men were economically pressed; little productive land could be had even by the wealthy, except in the far frontier, and the numbers of disenfranchised, landless men, continued to grow. As Morgan described them, "frustrated by the engrossers of land, by the collectors of customs, by their elected representatives, by the council, and, above all, by the king himself" (Morgan 1975: 292), they were a constant worry to the local and imperial government, pressing at the bowels of Virginia's gentry (in the colorful language of Governor William Berkeley). And yet bound laborers were still the most valuable form of property for the wealthy planters of Virginia; and indentured servants kept pouring in.

In the years leading up to Bacon's Rebellion, the political and economic elite of Virginia did all they could, as Morgan portrays it, to hold laborers still for the fleecing, whether through taxation, tenancy, or indenture. Although the local and imperial ruling classes were developing increasingly intricate and burdensome ways to separate the freemen from their tobacco, a new social order was already emerging, in which servants need not be freed after an indenture, and which made it possible for the Virginians to have "unlimited exploitation of labor" (Morgan 1975: 292). Bacon's Rebellion made it clear that, under the right circumstances, the working class, both black and white, could be incited to rise up against Virginia's elite. In the aftermath of the Rebellion, the planter class took steps to ensure that there would be no repetition of such an uprising. To prevent any new rising of frustrated freemen, the social relations of production needed to change. The planters needed to free themselves of the cycle of indenture through the development of a new system of labor. The proliferation of slavery as the primary relation of labor can thus be seen as emerging from the dialectical conflict that had emerged between the once symbiotically linked freeman and planter.

Slavery was not unknown before Bacon's Rebellion. Recent scholarship on late-seventeenth-century Virginia has suggested that the wealthiest planter families were already deeply invested in slavery by 1670 (e.g., Coombs 2011); as early as 1669, an act of the Assembly had decriminalized the killing of a slave if lethal force had been exerted during punishment (Morgan 1975: 312). Nevertheless, the decades following the Rebellion witnessed an unprecedented increase in the number of enslaved Africans working the tobacco fields. By 1700, the number of slaves reached the number of white servants employed, and the House of Burgesses noted that white servants were mostly employed by poorer planters who could not buy African slaves (Morgan 1975: 305). By 1708, Edmund Jennings could write that virtually no white indentured servants had been imported into Virginia for years, in contrast to the thousands of Africans that were brought to the tidewater (Morgan 1975: 308).

Plantation landscapes in Virginia changed as slavery replaced indentured servitude. In much of Virginia, some numbers of indentured servants lived in the main house with their master's family; after 1680, however, the number of large houses decrease in number, reflecting removal of servants from the main house (Deetz 1977; Upton 1982). White and black servants were spatially segregated, and planters began to designate "a Separate House for the Christian Slaves, One for the Negro Slaves" (Epperson 2001). In time, on most large plantations, enslaved Africans and their descendants, bound for life in servitude, replaced white indentured servants altogether.

Several Virginia plantations dating to the last quarter of the seventeenth century demonstrate how landscapes were transformed when the mode of production shifted as the new social relations of production engendered by slavery emerged (see Figure 7.7). A telling example is Rich Neck Plantation. Rich Neck was established in the 1640s, at which time the plantation consisted of two brick buildings. The first of these was a two-room house with a central chimney inhabited by the planter family. The second building served as a kitchen and the residence of indentured servants. By 1665, the main house had been expanded to include four rooms on the first floor, and end chimneys replaced the central chimney. The kitchen was expanded to three rooms at this time, likely to accommodate an increased number of servants working on the plantation and living in the kitchen quarter. In the wake of Bacon's Rebellion, the plantation landscape was restructured again. The main house was further expanded, and although it is likely that some servants remained quartered in the kitchen, a small complex of earthfast buildings was constructed to house the enslaved workers on the plantation. Notably, the fencelines that defined spaces changed during these three phases. In the 1640s, the house and kitchen shared a bounded yard space, which was expanded in the 1660s. After the introduction of slavery to the plantation, the fence lines were changed, placing the exterior spaces of the kitchen outside the yard space of the main house. The new slave quarters were also spatially segregated by fence lines. This increased fragmentation of spaces, of black and white landscapes (Upton 1984), would prevail for the remainder of Virginia's colonial history (Vlach 1993).

Conclusion

As we have seen in this chapter, the Marxian framework used to explore plantation landscapes in this book is applicable in a variety of contexts. As was the case in Jamaica, the Virginia plantation landscape was simultaneously a product of the plantation mode of production, and an active

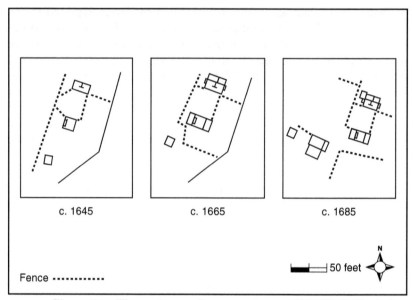

Figure 7.7. Three phases of construction at Rich Neck Plantation, showing the development of plantation settlement forms as the mode of production developed and changed. In its first phase, c. 1645 (left), there was little social or physical space separating the main house from the servants' quarters, and it is possible that some servants lived in the main house. By 1665 (center), both structures had expanded, likely reflecting the accumulation of servants to increase tobacco production. In the third phase, c. 1685 (right), fencing had been erected to separate the main house from the kitchen, and quarters for field workers had been built. By this time, enslaved Africans had replaced the indentured servants on this plantation. Illustration courtesy of Nick Stover. *Source*: McFadden et al. (1999).

agent in the spatial negotiation of the social relations of production. Like nineteenth-century Jamaica, seventeenth-century Virginia experienced a dialectical crisis in its mode of production. The product of that crisis was the transformation of the social relations of production, as systems of temporary indentured servitude were replaced with life-long bondage, reified, as in the Caribbean, by race. By the close of the seventeenth century, the aspirations of the working class to emerge as propertied freemen descended into a world dominated by slavery, racism, and the quotidian violence that set of social relations engendered.

8 Conclusion

On the morning of October 23, 1865, George William Gordon was hanged in the Jamaican town of Morant Bay. Gordon, who was born the son of a white planter and an enslaved woman, had spent his youth as a free person of color. By early adulthood, he had amassed significant wealth as a merchant and rose to political prominence, being several times elected as a member of the Jamaica Assembly. In the 1840s and 1850s, seeing that the end of the plantation mode of production had not brought economic prosperity or social justice to the vast majority of Jamaica's population, Gordon began to purchase abandoned sugar estates, subdividing and subsequently leasing them to small farmers. In the Assembly, he served as a lonely voice against the work of the planter class who still dominated the political apparatus of the island and did all they could to keep the Jamaican working class landless.

During the fateful month of October 1865, nearly 1,000 Jamaican people were killed or condemned to execution by the government of Governor Edward John Eyre, including the Assemblyman George William Gordon. Eyre was reacting to what he feared was a general uprising of the laboring classes of the island, an uprising that began as a local protest against the enforcement of laws prohibiting people from farming on abandoned plantation land. Angered by the intractability of the planter class both in the local parish governments and in the House of Assembly to address the growing poverty of the island's people, a group of approximately 200 armed men and women marched on the vestry meeting of the parish of St. Thomas in the East, sitting at Morant Bay. A panicked militia fired into the crowd, which erupted in violence. When the dust settled, the parish courthouse was a smoldering ruin and the custos and the entire vestry of the parish of St. Thomas in the East were dead. Eyre's response was swift and brutal. He declared martial law, unleashing the armed forces into the interior of the parish. The soldiers and militia reportedly killed men, women, and children indiscriminately, burning hundreds of houses as they went. Gordon, although no evidence existed to link him to the events in Morant Bay, was arrested at his home in Kingston, brought to Morant Bay, and after a brief military trial, hanged for treason (Heuman 1994).

Like his predecessor Sam Sharpe had done, George William Gordon had sought to find a means to establish a fuller liberation of the Jamaican people. Like Sharpe, Gordon had tried to use the power of reason to attain his goal; again, like Sharpe, Gordon discovered that the deeply entrenched interests of the planter class, as diminished as it was by the 1860s, would not easily acquiesce to the interests of the laboring classes. Although slavery had been abolished for a generation, the ideology of dominance was deeply rooted in the planter psyche. Although they could no longer buy and sell people as commodities, members of the elite classes shared an understanding that the local economy favored by the emancipated workers would not produce the kind of surplus value to which the planters had become accustomed. Although the mode of production had changed with the elimination of enslaved labor, stark differences in the levels of wealth, privilege, and power of the classes remained, as did the deeply seated class conflict between the planters and the workers. However, just as Sam Sharpe's death was an incident that triggered the dialectical change that resulted in the abolition of slavery, George William Gordon's death triggered a dialectical change in which the system of government in Jamaica, in which laws were passed by a House of Assembly representing only a small fraction of the population, was overturned. In the aftermath of the incident at Morant Bay, the British Government revoked the charter of the Jamaica Assembly, the planters on the island lost the right of home rule, and Jamaica would henceforth be ruled from Westminster as a Crown Colony.

The Morant Bay incident occurred at a moment of transition in global capitalism, categorized by some as the emergence of imperialism or the Eurocentric, imperialist world economy (e.g., Brass and Bernstein 1992; Lenin 2010; see Orser 2012 for a discussion of the relationships between imperialism, modernity, Eurocentrism, and historical archaeology), a time when plantation-based agricultural export production expanded exponentially in Latin America, East Africa, the Indian Ocean, Indonesia, Hawaii, the Philippines, and Southeast Asia (e.g., Carter 1992; McCoy 1992; Murray 1992). It is not surprising, therefore, that the home government decided to firm its grip on the sociopolitical world of Jamaica. As had happened in seventeenth-century Virginia and early-nineteenth-century Jamaica, capitalism was experiencing a period of restructuring, this time marked by the concentration of wealth into the hands of agricultural corporations better able to coldly dictate the relations of production than individual plantation proprietors ever could – protected by the ever-increasing military might of the industrialized nation states of Western Europe and North America. Perhaps not coincidentally, the rise of the multinational corporation can be traced to the establishment of the United Fruit Company, which got its start in Jamaica as the Boston Fruit

Company, and which still exists today in its successor company, Chiquita Brands International.

This book has explored Marxist archaeological theory through an examination of plantation landscapes. Through the lens of landscape archaeology, we have examined the diachronic settlement pattern of plantations from the Spanish era through to the end of the plantation mode of production. In so doing, we have seen how the failure of the mercantile capitalist system that had developed in much of the early Spanish Empire failed in Jamaica, largely because there was no mineral wealth to extract given the limitations of sixteenth-century mining technology. Spanish Jamaica settled into a marginal place in the emerging global economy. With little surplus value to be extracted, the settlers of Jamaica were largely left alone by the imperial government, and quickly reverted into a semi-feudal mode of production, where, at least in theory, the native people of Jamaica retained some rights over their labor power, so long as they provided tribute to those in possession of the hatos in which they lived and who controlled the encomienda which tied them to the Spanish imperial economy. Making a modest living by exchanging animal products rendered from the cattle herds that dominated the hato landscape, albeit through illicit trade with enemy privateers, the Spanish settlers of Jamaica lived on the periphery of the emerging capitalist world economy.

When Jamaica was taken from the Spanish by the Penn and Venables expedition of 1655, the English, having failed to conquer the Spanish American Empire, attempted to establish small-scale farming in Jamaica, an enterprise that withered in the shadow of the emergent plantation mode of production, as land consolidation and the introduction of enslaved labor made it difficult for all but the wealthiest colonists to get established in the plantation system, at least initially.

We have examined the nature of that mode of production as it developed in Jamaica. A manifestation of capitalism, the plantation mode of production was based on the establishment of large-scale monocrop agricultural export production (e.g., Genovese 1989). This required the consolidation and privatization of large land-holdings. Those who were able to acquire and mobilize the capital to build the buildings and machinery required for sugar – and later, coffee – production and processing emerged as a powerful and wealthy class of planters. Consistent with capitalism's universal mission to concentrate power and wealth in the hands of the owners of the means of production, the plantation mode of production resulted in the accumulation of great fortunes by those who could control the apparatus of the local government. The planter class accumulated this wealth in several ways. Consistent with the logic of capitalism, the planters extracted surplus value by claiming the products of labor of the working class. Also consistent with the logic of capitalism, the planters did what they could to reduce the costs of production and to control labor. The use of unfree labor in the bodies of enslaved people of African descent served as the means by which labor could be best exploited and surplus value extracted. Simultaneously, the planters came to view their enslaved populations as capital assets against whose value they could acquire credit to consolidate more land and more labor. It should also be remembered that the establishment of the plantation mode of production was but one theater of the imposition of a globalizing Eurocentric political economy that we still refer to as capitalism (Orser 2012).

During their meteoric rise to power and wealth, the Jamaican planters were protected by the conservative government of the ruling Tories. Throughout the eighteenth and well into the nineteenth century, the value of agricultural crops, measured by the price sugar and coffee would fetch on the London market, was tightly controlled by the home government. With price controls in place, the planters avoided much competitive conflict with each other, were buffered from competition from abroad, and developed into a fully conscious class-for-itself. Using both a racialized ideology to subvert the interests of the working class, and the political apparatus of the local and island-wide governments to further their own interests, the small population of white planters created their "egalitarian tyranny" based on white supremacy and class solidarity. Those white men of limited means who could stomach the inequities of the chattel-slavery system had the opportunity to rise in this social system, and thus were aligned with the great planters. Inevitably, social and cultural change occurred as a result of class conflict between this group of largely white planters and the plantation working class, enslaved until the 1830s.

We have also examined the nature of dialectical conflict, contradiction, and change through the lens of landscape archaeology. All modes of production have the potential to develop contradictions in their operating logic, and the plantation mode of production was no exception. In their attempt to limit their costs, and thus to maximize their accumulation of surplus value, Jamaican planters tolerated the development of a system of local production by the enslaved in their kitchen gardens and provision grounds. Although this was an effective way to shift the cost of feeding the enslaved away from the planters, the resulting system in which surplus local production was exchanged locally created a contradiction in the mode of production, as two different approaches to labor and the ownership of the products of labor clashed. The ability of the enslaved class to create an economy independent of the planters, based on local production and market exchange, led to a dialectical conflict within the mode of production that would only be resolved after the great uprising of 1831. As we have seen, the landscapes that the enslaved created within their villages and provision grounds were crucial to the development of the internal economy, and in direct contradiction to the class interests of the planters. These landscapes allowed Jamaica's enslaved working class to accumulate some modest measure of wealth and personal possession, but more importantly, created a class consciousness enlightened by the possibility – and eventuality – of the abolition of slavery, a brutalizing organization of society that the planter class depended on and greatly profited from.

Although some postcolonial and postmodern scholars dismiss the notion, the importation and local development of variants of capitalist modes of production does not contradict capitalism's universalizing mission to establish both capitalized production and the extraction of surplus value through unequal class relations (Chibber 2013; Orser 1996, 2012; Rosenswig 2013). Colonial-era capitalism was inherently a Eurocentric process through which colonial assets were exploited for the benefit of the wealthy classes at home and in the colonies (Orser 2013), and in places like Jamaica, depended on the enslavement of people of African descent.

Marxist theory maintains that capitalism does have a universalizing ambition to incorporate as many loci of production as materially possible; nevertheless the system does provide some measure of flexibility for local variants of modes of production to develop. As we have seen through our comparison case of seventeenth-century Virginia, plantation colonies did not all follow the same socio-historical trajectory. As Orser (2012) has noted, even within the Anglocentric world differences in the practice of African slavery can be historically discerned. Differences similarly existed between various manifestations of the means and relations of production in agricultural colonies, thus multiple variants of the plantation mode of production developed in different time-space contexts. Although influenced by similar global forces, late-seventeenth-century Virginia was not identical to early nineteenth-century Jamaica, although in both contexts the colonial world was shaped by the realities of plantation production of export crops. The framework of Marxist landscape archaeology allows us to perceive and analyze those differences, while simultaneously understanding that key similarities in the organization of production, flow of capital, and dialectical class conflict did exist.

The tragic case of George William Gordon underscores the reality that dialectical change does not by itself establish more just and equitable social systems. When Karl Marx and Fredrick Engels wrote their great works in the middle of the nineteenth century, they hoped that they were establishing a new social science – scientific socialism – that many have interpreted as being an evolutionary framework for analyzing the past and predicting the course of future events. From our vantage point in the early twenty-first century, we can use the power of hindsight to assert that no system of social theory, no matter how complex and elegant, has the power to predict the future. This does not, however, diminish the power that Marxist theory has to structure our interpretations of the past. Because Marxism is, as we have seen, a materialist approach to understanding the construction and reproduction of social relations, it is well suited to archaeology, itself a materialist approach to understanding the past. It is my hope that those who have read this book will not only have gained some understanding about the colonial Caribbean, but will have a better appreciation for the complexity of Marxist theory and the power this approach has for understanding the material remains of the past.

References

Abrams, Elliot M. and David J. Rue (1988) The Causes and Consequences of Deforestation among the Prehistoric Maya. *Human Ecology* 4: 377–395.

Adams, Robert McC. (1966) *The Evolution of Urban Society*. Aldine, Chicago.

Adams, Robert McC. (1965) *The Land Behind Baghdad: A History of Settlement on the Diyala Plains*. University of Chicago Press, Chicago.

Adams, William H. (1990) Landscape Archaeology, Landscape History, and the American Farmstead. *Historical Archaeology* 24(4): 92–101.

Agorsah, E. Kofi (2007) Scars of Brutality: Archaeology of the Maroons in the Caribbean. In *Archaeology of Atlantic Africa and the African Diaspora*, Akinwumi Ogundiran and Toyin Falola, eds. Indiana University Press, Bloomington, pp. 332–354.

Agorsah, E. Kofi (1994) *Maroon Heritage: Archaeological, Ethnographic and Historical Perspective*. Canoe Press, University of the West Indies, Kingston, Jamaica.

Aikman, Alexander (1802) *An Abridgement of the Laws of Jamaica*. Alexander Aikman, St. Jago de la Vega, Jamaica.

Albritton, Robert (1993) Did Agrarian Capitalism Exist? *Journal of Peasant Studies* 20(3): 419–441.

Anderson, Charles A. (1974) *The Political Economy of Social Class*. Prentice Hall, Englewood Cliffs, NJ.

Anonymous (1828) *Slave Law of Jamaica, with Proceedings and Documents Relative Thereto*. James Ridgway, London.

Armstrong, Douglas V. (2003) *Creole Transformation from Slavery to Freedom: Historical Archaeology of the East End Community, St. John, Virgin Islands*. University Press of Florida, Gainesville.

Armstrong, Douglas V. (2011) Reflections on Seville: Rediscovering the African Jamaican Settlements at Seville Plantation, St. Ann's Bay, Jamaica In *Out of Many, One People: The Historical Archaeology of Colonial Jamaica*. James A. Delle, Mark Hauser, and Douglas V. Armstrong, eds. University of Alabama Press, pp. 77–101.

Armstrong, Douglas V. and Kenneth Kelly (2000) Settlement Patterns and the Origins of African Jamaican Society: Seville Plantation, St. Ann's Bay, Jamaica. *Ethnohistory* 7(2): 369–397.

Bagchi, Amlya Kumar (2004) The Axial Ages of the Capitalist World System. *Review* 27(2):93–134.

Bailey, Anne M. and Joseph R. Llobera (1981) *The Asiatic Mode of Production: Science and Politics*. Routledge and Kegan Paul, London.

Bailyn, Bernard (2012) *The Barbarous Years: The Peopling of British North America and the Conflict of Civilizations*, 1600–1675. Alfred A. Knopf, New York.

Barka, Norman (2001) Time Lines: Changing Settlement Patterns on St. Eustatius. In *Island Lives: Historical Archaeologies of the Caribbean*, Paul Farnsworth, ed. University of Alabama Press, Tuscaloosa, pp. 103–141.

Baud, Michiel (1992) Sugar and Unfree Labour: Reflections on Labour Control in the Dominican Republic, 1870–1935. *Journal of Peasant Studies* 19(2): 301–325.

Beaudry, Mary C. (1989) The Lowell Boott Mills Complex and Its Housing: Material Expressions of Corporate Ideology. *Historical Archaeology* 23(1): 19–32.

Beaudry, Mary C., Lauren Cook, and Stephen Mrozowski (1991) Artifacts and Active Voices: Material Culture as Social Discourse. In *The Archaeology of Inequality*, Randall H. McGuire and Robert Paynter, eds. Basil Blackwell, Oxford, pp. 150–191.

Beckford, William (1790) *A Descriptive Account of the Island of Jamaica: With Remarks Upon the Cultivation of the Sugar-Cane, Throughout the Different Seasons of the Year, and Chiefly Considered in a Picturesque Point of View; Also, Observations and Reflections Upon What Would Probably Be the Consequences of an Abolition of the Slave-Trade, and of the Emancipation of the Slaves*. Printed for T. and J. Egerton, London.

Beckles, Hilary McD. (2002) Freedom without Liberty: Free Blacks in the Barbados Slave System. In *Slavery without Sugar: Diversity in Caribbean Economy and Society Since the 17th Century*, Verene A. Shepherd, ed. University Press of Florida, Gainesville, pp. 199–223.

Beckles, Hilary McD. (1995) Sex and Gender in the Historiography of Caribbean Slavery. In *Engendering History: Caribbean Women in Historical Perspective*, Verene Shepherd, Bridget Brereton, and Barbara Bailey (eds.), James Currey, London, pp. 125–140.

Beckles, Hilary McD. (1990) A "Riotous and Unruly Lot": Irish Indentured Servants and Freemen in the English West Indies, 1644–1713. *William and Mary Quarterly* 47(4): 503–522.

Beekman, Christopher S. and William W. Baden, eds. (2005) *Nonlinear Models for Archaeology and Anthropology*. Ashgate Publishing, Burlington, VT.

Benaji, Jairus (1977) Modes of Production in a Materialist Conception of History. *Capital and Class* 1(1): 1–44.

Bender, Barbara (1978) Gatherer-Hunter to Farmer: A Social Perspective. *World Archaeology* 10: 204–222.

Benghiat, Norma (2008) *The World's Finest: Jamaica Blue Mountain Coffee*. Ian Randle, Kingston.

Berlin, Ira and Phillip D. Morgan, eds. (1995) *The Slaves' Economy: Independent Production by Slaves in the Americas*. Frank Cass, London.

Bernhard, Virginia (1992) Men, Women, and Children at Jamestown: Population and Gender in Early Virginia. *Journal of Southern History* 58: 599–618.

Bickel, Richard (1825) *West Indies as They Are; or a Real Picture of Slavery: But More Particularly as It Exists in the Island of Jamaica*. J. Hatchard and Son, London.

Billings, Warren (2004a) *A Little Parliament: The Virginia General Assembly in the Seventeenth Century*. Library of Virginia, Richmond.

Billings, Warren (2004b) *Sir William Berkeley and the Forging of Colonial Virginia.* Louisiana State University Press, Baton Rouge.

Billings, Warren (1968) "Virginia's Deploured Condition" 1660–1676: The Coming of Bacon's Rebellion. PhD Dissertation, Department of History, Northern Illinois University.

Billman, Brian (2002) Irrigation and the Origin of the Southern Moche State in the North Coast of Peru. *Latin American Antiquity* 13(4): 371–400.

Binford, Lewis (2002) *In Pursuit of the Past: Decoding the Archaeological Record.* University of California Press, Berkeley.

Bird, Douglas and James F. O'Connell. 2006. Behavioral Ecology and Archaeology. *Journal of Archaeological Research* 14: 143–188.

Blackburn, Robin (1988) *The Overthrow of Colonial Slavery.* Verso, London.

Blome, Richard (1672) *A Description of the Island of Jamaica; with the Other Isles and Territories in America, to Which the English Are Related.* Dorman Newman, London.

Bourdieu, Pierre (1977) *Outline of a Theory of Practice.* Cambridge University Press, Cambridge.

Braddick, Michael J. (2009) *God's Fury, England's Fire: A New History of the English Civil Wars.* Allen Lane, London.

Brass, Tom and Henry Bernstein (1992) Proletarianisation and Deproletarianisation on the Colonial Plantation. *Journal of Peasant Studies* 3/4: 1–40.

Brathwaite, Kamau (1971) *The Development of Creole Society in Jamaica, 1770–1820.* Clarendon Press, Oxford.

Breen, T. H. (1988) *Tobacco Culture.* Princeton University Press, Princeton, NJ.

Bridges, George Wilson (1828) *The Annals of Jamaica.* John Murray, London.

Brown, Kathleen (1996) *Good Wives, Nasty Wenches, and Anxious Patriarchs: Gender, Race and Power in Colonial Virginia.* University of North Carolina Press, Chapel Hill.

Brown, Maureen (2011) Evidence for Port Royal's British Colonial Merchant Class as Reflected in the New Street Tavern Site Assemblage, Port Royal, Jamaica In *Out of Many, One People: The Historical Archaeology of Colonial Jamaica.* James A. Delle, Mark Hauser, and Douglas V. Armstrong, eds. University of Alabama Press, Tuscaloosa, pp. 56–73.

Brumfiel, Elizabeth (1980) Specialization, Market Exchange, and the Aztec State. *Current Anthropology* 21(4): 459–478.

Burdick, William (2000) GIS Analysis of Jamaican Coffee Plantations. Honors Thesis, Department of Anthropology, Franklin and Marshall College, Lancaster, PA.

Burnard, Trevor (2004) *Mastery, Tyranny, and Desire: Thomas Thistlewood and His Slaves in the Anglo-Jamaican World.* University of North Carolina Press, Chapel Hill.

Burnard, Trevor (2002) Not a Place for Whites? Demographic Failure and Settlement in Comparative Context, Jamaica, 1655–1789. In *A History of Jamaica, From Indigenous Settlement to the Present,* Kathleen Montieth and Glen Richards, eds. University of the West Indies Press, Kingston, Jamaica, pp. 73–88.

Burnard, Trevor (2001) "A Prodigious Mine": The Wealth of Jamaica before the American Revolution Once Again. *Economic History Review* 54(3): 505–523.

Burnard, Trevor (1996) European Migration to Jamaica, 1655–1780. *The William and Mary Quarterly* 53(4): 769–796.

Burnard, Trevor (1994) A Failed Settler Society: Marriage and Demographic Failure in Early Jamaica. *Journal of Social History* 28(1): 63–82.

Bush, Barbara (1990) *Slave Women in Caribbean Society, 1650–1838.* Indiana University Press, Bloomington.

Butler, Kathleen M. (1995) *The Economics of Emancipation: Jamaica and Barbados, 1823–1843.* University of North Carolina Press, Chapel Hill.

Byres, Terence J. (2009) The Landlord Class, Peasant Differentiation, Class Struggle, and the Transition to Capitalism: England, France, and Prussia Compared. *Journal of Peasant Studies* 36(1): 33–54.

Campbell, Mavis C. (1988) *The Maroons of Jamaica, 1655–1796: A History of Resistance, Collaboration, and Betrayal.* Bergin and Garvey, Westport, CT.

Carmichael, Mrs. A. C. (1833) *Domestic Manners and Social Condition of the White, Coloured, and Negro Population of the West Indies.* Whittaker, Treacher, and Co., London.

Carson, Cary (1994) The Consumer Revolution in Colonial America: Why the Demand? In *Of Consuming Interest: The Style of Life in the Eighteenth Century,* C. C. Carson, R. Hoffman, and P. J. Albert, eds. University Press of Virginia, Charlottesville, pp. 444–482.

Carson, Cary, Norman F. Barka, William M. Kelso, Gary Wheeler Stone, and Dell Upton (1981) Impermanent Architecture in the Southern American Colonies. *Winterthur Portfolio* 16(2/3): 135–196.

Carter, Marina (1992) Strategies of Labour Mobilisation in Colonial India: The Recruitment of Indentured Workers for Mauritius. In *Plantations, Peasants, and Proletarians in Colonial Asia,* E. Valentine Daniel, Henry Bernstein, and Tom Brass, eds. Frank Cass, London, pp. 229–245.

Chapdelaine, Claude (2011) Recent Advances in Moche Archaeology. *Journal of Archaeological Research* 19(2): 191–231.

Checkland, S. G. (1957) Finance for the West Indies, 1780–1815. *Economic History Review* 10: 461–469.

Chibber, Vivek (2013) *Postcolonial Theory and the Specter of Capital* Verso, London.

Childe, V. Gordon (1950) The Urban Revolution. *Town Planning Review* 21(1): 3–17.

Childe, V. Gordon (1936) *Man Makes Himself.* Watts and Company, London.

Clement, Christopher (1997) Settlement Patterning on the British Caribbean Island of Tobago. *Historical Archaeology* 31(2): 93–106.

Clement, Christopher and Michael Moseley (1991) The Spring-Fed Irrigation System of Carrizal, Peru: A Case Study of the Hypothesis of Agrarian Collapse. Journal of Field Archaeology 18(4): 425–443.

Collins, Dr. David (1811) *Practical Rules of the Management and Medical Treatment of Negro Slaves in the Sugar Colonies.* J. Barfield, London.

Cook, Lauren, Rebecca Yamin, and John P. McCarthy (1996) Shopping As Meaningful Action: Toward a Redefinition of Consumption in Historical Archaeology. *Historical Archaeology* 30(4): 50–65.

Coombs, John (2011) Beyond the Origins Debate: Rethinking the Rise of Virginia Slavery. In *Early Modern Virginia: Reconsidering the Old Dominion,* Douglas

Bradburn and John Coombs, eds. University Press of Virginia, Charlottesville, pp. 240–278.

Cowie, Sarah (2011) *The Plurality of Power: An Archaeology of Industrial Capitalism.* Springer, New York.

Craton, Michael (1997) *Empire, Enslavement, and Freedom in the Caribbean.* Ian Randle Publishers, Kingston.

Craven, Wesley Frank (1957) *The Virginia Company of London, 1606–1624.* University Press of Virginia, Charlottesville.

Croucher, Karina (2005) Queering Near Eastern Archaeology. *World Archaeology* 37(4): 630–636.

Cundall, Frank (1919) *Jamaica under the Spaniards.* Institute of Jamaica, Kingston, Jamaica.

Curet, L. Antonio and Mark W. Hauser, eds. (2011) *Islands at the Crossroads: Migration, Seafaring, and Interaction in the Caribbean.* University of Alabama Press, Tuscaloosa.

Curtain, Philip (1969) *The Atlantic Slave Trade: A Census.* University of Wisconsin Press, Madison.

Dallas, R. C (1803) *The History of the Maroons.* Longman and Rees, London.

Davis, David B. (1975) *The Problem of Slavery in the Age of Revolution, 1770–1823.* Cornell University Press, Ithaca, NY.

Deetz, James (1977) *In Small Things Forgotten: An Archaeology of Early American Life.* Doubleday, New York.

Delle, James A. (2011) The Habitus of Jamaican Plantation Landscapes. In *Out of Many, One People: The Historical Archaeology of Colonial Jamaica.* James A. Delle, Mark Hauser, and Douglas V. Armstrong, eds. University of Alabama Press, pp. 122–143.

Delle, James A. (2009) The Governor and the Enslaved: Archaeology and Modernity at Marshall's Pen, Jamaica. *International Journal of Historical Archaeology* 12(4): 488–512.

Delle, James A. (2008) An Archaeology of Modernity in Colonial Jamaica. *Archaeologies: The Journal of the World Archaeology Congress,* 4(1): 87–109.

Delle, James A. (2002) Power and Landscape: Spatial Dynamics in Early 19th Century Jamaica. In Maria O'Donovan, ed. *The Dynamics of Power.* Center for Archaeological Investigations, Southern Illinois University, pp. 341–361.

Delle, James A. (2000) The Material and Cognitive Dimensions of Creolization in Nineteenth Century Jamaica. *Historical Archaeology* 34(3): 56–72.

Delle, James A. (1999) The Landscapes of Class Negotiation on Coffee Plantations in the Blue Mountains of Jamaica, 1790–1850. *Historical Archaeology* 33(1): 136–158.

Delle, James A. (1998) *An Archaeology of Social Space: Analyzing Coffee Plantations in Jamaica's Blue Mountains.* Contributions to Global Historical Archaeology. Plenum Press, New York.

Delle, James A. (1996) An Archaeology of Crisis: The Manipulation of Social Spaces in the Blue Mountain Coffee Plantation Complex, 1790–1865. PhD Dissertation, Anthropology, University of Massachusetts, Amherst.

Delle, James A. (1994) The Settlement Pattern of Sugar Plantations on St. Eustatius, Netherlands Antilles. In *Spatial Patterning in Archaeology: Selected Studies of*

Settlement, D.W. Robinson and G.G. Robinson, eds. King and Queen's Press, Williamsburg, VA, pp. 33–61.

Delle, James A. (1989) A Spatial Analysis of Sugar Plantations on St. Eusatius, Netherlands Antilles. MA Thesis, College of William and Mary, Williamsburg, VA.

Delle, James A., Mark P. Leone, and Paul R. Mullins (1999) Archaeology and the Modern State: European Colonialism. In *Routledge Companion Encyclopedia of Archaeology*, Graeme Barker, ed. Routledge, London, pp. 1107–1160.

Delle, James A. and Mary Ann Levine (2004) Excavations at the Thaddeus Stevens/Lydia Hamilton Smith Site, Lancaster, PA: Archaeological Evidence for the Underground Railroad? *Northeast Historical Archaeology* 33: 131–152.

Demarest, Arthur (2005) *Ancient Maya: The Rise and Fall of a Rainforest Civilization*. Cambridge University Press, Cambridge.

Dillehay, Tom S. and Alan L. Kolata (2004) Long-term Human Response to Uncertain Environmental Conditions in the Andes. *Proceedings of the National Academy of Sciences* 101(12): 4325–4330.

Diptee, Audra A. (2010) *From Africa to Jamaica: The Making of an Atlantic Slave Society, 1775–1807*. University Press of Florida, Gainesville.

Dornan, Jennifer L. (2002) Agency and Archaeology: Past, Present, and Future Directions. *Journal of Archaeological Method and Theory* 9(4): 303–329.

Draper, Nicholas (2010) *The Price of Emancipation: Slave-ownership, Compensation, and British Society at the End of Slavery*. Cambridge University Press, Cambridge.

Drescher, Seymour (2004) *The Mighty Experiment: Free Labor versus Slavery in British Emancipation*. Oxford, Oxford University Press.

Dunn, Richard (2000) *Sugar and Slaves; the Rise of the Planter Class in the English West Indies, 1624–1713*. 2nd edition. Published for the Institute of Early American History and Culture at Williamsburg, VA by the University of North Carolina Press, Chapel Hill.

Dunn, Richard S. (1979) *The Age of Religious Wars: 1559–1715*. Norton, New York.

Edwards, Andrew C. (2004) *Archaeology of a Seventeenth-Century Houselot at Martin's Hundred, Virginia*. Colonial Williamsburg Archaeological Reports. Williamsburg, VA, Colonial Williamsburg Foundation.

Edwards, Bryan (1810) *The History Civil and Commercial of the British Colonies in the West Indies*. Levis and Weaver, Philadelphia.

Edwards, Bryan (1798) *The History, Civil and Commercial, of the British Colonies in the West Indies*. Mundell and Son, Glasgow.

Edwards, Bryan (1793) *The History, Civil and Commercial, of the British Colonies in the West Indies*. John Stockdale, London.

Emerson, Thomas E. and Timothy R. Pauketat (2002) Embodying Resistance at Cahokia. In *The Dynamics of Power*, Maria O'Donovan, ed. Center for Archaeological Investigations, Southern Illinois University, Carbondale, pp. 105–125.

Engels, Frederick (2010) *The Origin of the Family, Private Property, and the State*. Penguin, New York.

Engels, Frederick (2007) *Socialism: Utopian and Scientific*. Pathfinder Press, Atlanta.

Engels, Frederick (1979) *Dialectics of Nature*. International Publishers, New York.

Epperson, Terrence (2001) "A separate house for the Christian slaves, one for the Negro slaves": The Archaeology of Race and Identity in Late Seventeenth-century Virginia." In *Race and the Archaeology of Identity*, Charles E. Orser, Jr., ed. Univeristy of Utah Press, Salt Lake City, pp. 54–70.

Epperson, Terrence (2000) Panoptic Plantations: The Garden Sights of Thomas Jefferson and George Mason. In *Lines That Divide: Historical Archaeologies of Race, Class, and Gender*, James A. Delle, Stephen A. Mrosowski, and Robert Paynter, eds. University of Tennessee Press, Knoxville, pp. 58–77.

Epperson, Terrence (1999) Constructing Difference: The Social and Spatial Order of the Chesapeake Plantation. In *"I, Too, Am America": Archaeological Studies of African American Life*. Theresa Singleton, ed. University Press of Virginia, Charlottesville, pp. 159–172.

Evans, Eric J. (1994) *The Great Reform Act of 1832*. 2nd edition. London, Routledge and Kegan Paul.

Evans, Eric J. (2008) *Britain before the Reform Act: Politics and Society 1815–32*. 2nd edition. Longman, London.

Fausz, J. Frederick (1987) The Invasion of Virginia. Indians, Colonialism, and the Conquest of Cant: A Review Essay on Anglo-Indian Relations in the Chesapeake. *Virginia Magazine of History and Biography* 95(2): 133–156.

Fausz, J. Frederick (1977) The Powhatan Uprising of 1622: A Historical Study of Ehtnocentrism and Cultural Conflict. PhD Dissertation, Department of History, College of William and Mary, Williamsburg, VA.

Fausz. J. Frederick (1971) Patterns of Settlement in the James River Basin, 1607–1642. MA Thesis, Department of History, College of William and Mary, Williamsburg, VA.

Foucault, Michel (1979) *Discipline and Punish: The Birth of the Prison*. Vintage Books, New York.

Gailey, Christine and Thomas C. Patterson (1988) State Formation and Uneven Development. In *State and Society: The Emergence and Development of Social Hierarchy and Political Centralization*, John Gledhill, M. Larsen, and Barbara Bender, eds. Unwin Hyman, London, pp. 77–90.

Galle, Jillian (2011) Assessing the Impacts of Time, Agricultural Cycles, and Demography on the Consumer Activities of Enslaved Men and Women in Eighteenth Century Virginia and Jamaica. In *Out of Many, One People: The Historical Archaeology of Colonial Jamaica*. James A. Delle, Mark Hauser, and Douglas V. Armstrong, eds. University of Alabama Press, pp. 211–242.

Gardner, William James (1873) *A History of Jamaica*. Stock, London.

Geggus, David (1993) Sugar and Coffee Cultivation in Saint Domingue and the Shaping of the Slave Labor Force. In *Cultivation and Culture: Labor and the Shaping of Slave Life in the Americas*, Ira Berlin and Philip D. Morgan, eds. University Press of Virginia, Charlottesville, pp. 73–98.

Genovese, Eugene (1989) *The Political Economy of Slavery*, 2nd edition. Wesleyan University Press, Middletown, CT.

Giddens, Antonio (1973) *The Class Structure of Advanced Societies*. Harper and Row, New York.

Gilman, Antonio (1989) Marxism in American Archaeology. In *Archaeological Thought in America*, C. C. Lamberg-Karlovsky, ed. Cambridge University Press, Cambridge, pp. 63–73.

Gilman, Antonio (1984) Explaining the Upper Paleolithic Revolution. In *Marxist Perspectives in Archaeology*, Matthew Spriggs, ed. Cambridge University Press, Cambridge, pp. 115–126.

Gilman, Antonio (1981) The Development of Social Stratification in Bronze Age Europe. *Current Anthropology* 22(1): 1–23.

Gleach, Frederick W. (1997) *Powhatan's World and Colonial Virginia: A Conflict of Cultures*. University of Nebraska Press, Lincoln.

Goucher, Candace and Kofi Agorsah (2011) Excavating the Roots of Resistance: The Significance of Maroons in Jamaican Archaeology In *Out of Many, One People: The Historical Archaeology of Colonial Jamaica*. James A. Delle, Mark Hauser, and Douglas V. Armstrong, eds. University of Alabama Press, pp. 144–162.

Green, William (1976) *British Slave Emancipation: The Sugar Colonies and the Great Experiment 1830–1865*. Oxford University Press, Oxford.

Groover, Mark (2008) *The Archaeology of North American Farmsteads*. University Press of Florida, Gainesville.

Groover, Mark (2003) *An Archaeological Study of Rural Capitalism and Material Life: The Gibbs Farmstead in Southern Appalachia, 1790–1920*. Kluwer/Plenum, New York.

Hakewell, James (1825) *A Picturesque Tour of the Island of Jamaica*. Hurst and Robinson, London.

Hall, Douglas (1989) *In Miserable Slavery: Thomas Thistlewood in Jamaica*. MacMillan, London.

Harris, Marvin (2001) *Cultural Materialism: The Struggle for a Science of Culture*. Updated edition. AltaMira Press, Walnut Creek, CA.

Hart, Richard (2002) *Slaves who Abolished Slavery: Blacks in Rebellion*. University of the West Indies Press, Mona, Jamaica.

Harvey, David (2006a) *Spaces of Global Capitalism*. Verso, London.

Harvey, David (2006b) *The Limits to Capital*, 2nd edition. Verso, London.

Hassan, Fekri A. (1997) Dynamics of a Riverine Civilization: A Geoarchaeological Perspective on the Nile Valley, Egypt. *World Archaeology* 29(1): 51–74.

Hauser, Mark W. (2011a) Linstead Market and the St. Mary's Revolt: Locating Colonial Economies and Local Ceramics.

Hauser, Mark W. (2011b) Routes and Roots of Empire: Pots, Power, and Slavery in the 18th-century British Caribbean. *American Anthropologist* 113(3): 431–447.

Hauser, Mark W. (2008) *An Archaeology of Black Markets: Local Ceramics and Economies in Eighteenth-Century Jamaica*. University Press of Florida, Gainesville.

Hauser, Mark W. (2007) Between Urban and Rural: Organization and Distribution of Local Pottery in Eighteenth-Century Jamaica. In *Archaeology of Atlantic Africa and the African Diaspora*, Akinwumi Ogundiran and Toyin Falola, eds. Indiana University Press, Bloomington, pp. 292–310.

Hauser, Mark W. (2001) Peddling Pots: Determining the Extent of Market Exchange in Eighteenth Century Jamaica through the Analysis of Local Coarse Earthenware. PhD Dissertation, Department of Anthropology, Syracuse University, Syracuse, NY.

Hauser, Mark W. and Douglas V. Armstrong (2012) The Archaeology of Not Being Governed: A Counterpoint to a History of Settlement of Two Colonies in the Eastern Caribbean. *Journal of Social Archaeology* 12(3): 310–333.

Headlee, Sue E. (1991) *The Political Economy of the Family Farm: The Agrarian Roots of American Capitalism.* Praeger Publishers, New York.

Hegel, G. W. F (1977) *Phenomenology of Spirit.* Oxford University Press, Oxford.

Heuman, Gad (1994) *The Killing Time: The Morant Bay Rebellion in Jamaica.* MacMillan, London.

Heuman, Gad (1981) *Between Black and White: Race, Politics, and the Free Coloureds of Jamaica, 1792–1865.* Greenwood Press, Westport, CT.

Hicks, Dan and Audrey Horning (2006) Historical Archaeology and Buildings. In *The Cambridge Companion to Historical Archaeology,* Dan Hicks and Mary C. Beaudry, eds. Cambridge University Press, Cambridge, pp. 273–292.

Higman, Barry W. (2005) *Plantation Jamaica, 1750–1850: Capital and Control in a Colonial Economy.* University of the West Indies Press, Kingston, Jamaica.

Higman, Barry W. (2002) The Internal Economy of Jamaican Pens, 1760–1890. In *Slavery without Sugar: Diversity in Caribbean Economy and Society since the 17th Century,* Verene A. Shepherd, ed. University Press of Florida, Gainesville, pp. 63–81.

Higman, Barry W. (1998) *Montpelier, Jamaica: A Plantation Community in Slavery and Freedom, 1739–1912.* Press University of the West Indies, Mona, Jamaica.

Higman, Barry W. (1995) *Slave Population and Economy in the British Caribbean, 1807–1834.* Kingston, Jamaica, UWI Press.

Higman, Barry W. (1991) Jamaica Port Towns in the early Nineteenth Century. In *Atlantic Port Cities: Economy, Culture, and Society in the Atlantic World, 1650–1850,* F. W. Knight and P. K. Liss, eds. University of Tennessee Press, Knoxville, pp. 117–148.

Higman, Barry W. (1988) *Jamaica Surveyed: Plantation Maps and Plans of the Eighteenth and Nineteenth Centuries.* University of the West Indies Press, Mona, Jamaica.

Higman, Barry W. (1987) The Spatial Economy of Jamaican Sugar Plantations: Cartographic Evidence from the 18th and 19th Centuries. *Journal of Historical Geography* 13(1): 17–19.

Higman, Barry W. (1986) Jamaican Coffee Plantations 1780–1860: A Cartographic Analysis. *Caribbean Geography* 2: 73–91.

Higman, Barry W. (1976) *Slave Population and Economy in Jamaica, 1807–1834.* Cambridge University Press, New York and Cambridge.

Hobsbawn, Eric (1999) *Industry and Empire: The Birth of the Industrial Revolution.* Penguin, London.

Hobsbawn, Eric (1996) *The Age of Revolution, 1789–1848.* Random House, New York.

Holt, Thomas (1992) *The Problem of Freedom: Race, Labor, and Politics in Jamaica and Britain, 1832–1938.* Johns Hopkins University Press, Baltimore.

Hood, J. Edward (1996) Social Relations and the Cultural Landscape. In *Landscape Archaeology: Reading and Interpreting the American Historical Landscape,* edited by Rebecca Yamin and Karen Metheny, pp. 121–146. University of Tennessee Press, Knoxville.

Horn, James (2006) *A Land as God Made It: Jamestown and the Birth of America.* Basic Books, Boston.

Hudgins, C. L. (1990) Robert "King" Carter and the Landscape of Tidewater Virginia in the Eighteenth Century. *In Earth Patterns: Essays in Landscape*

Archaeology, edited by William Kelso and Rachel Most, pp. 59–70. University Press of Virginia, Charlottesville.

Hudson, Brian J. (1997) Houses in the Caribbean: Homes and Heritage. In *Self-help Housing, the Poor, and the State in the Caribbean*, edited by Robert B. Potter and Dennis Conway, pp. 12–29. Knoxville, University of Tennessee Press.

Jamaica Almanac (1788) The New Jamaica Almanack and Register. Bennett & Dickson, Kingston, Jamaica.

Jamaica Almanac (1789) The New Jamaica Almanack and Register. Bennett & Dickson, Kingston, Jamaica.

Jamaica Almanac (1800) The New Jamaica Almanack and Register. Bennett & Dickson, Kingston, Jamaica.

James, Lawrence (2000) *Raj: The Making and Unmaking of British India*. Little, Brown, and Company, London.

Johnsen, Harald and Bjornar Olsen (1992) Hermeneutics and Archaeology: On the Philosophy of Contextual Archaeology. *American Antiquity* 57(3): 419–436.

Johnson, Matthew (1996) *An Archaeology of Capitalism*. John Wiley and Sons, London.

Judd, Denis (2004) *The Lion and the Tiger: The Rise and Fall of the British Raj*. Oxford University Press, Oxford.

Keegan, William F. and Leslie-Gail Atkinson (2006) The Development of Jamaican Prehistory. In *The Earliest Inhabitants: The Dynamics of the Jamaican Taino*, edited by Leslie-Gail Atkinson, pp. 13–33. University of the West Indies Press, Mona, Jamaica.

Kelly, Kenneth G. and M. D. Hardy,eds. (2011) *French Colonial Archaeology in the Southeast and Caribbean*. University Press of Florida, Gainesville.

Kelso, Willam (2008) *Jamestown: The Buried Truth*. University Press of Virginia, Charlottesville.

Kelso, William (1990) Landscape Archaeology at Thomas Jefferson's Monticello. In *Earth Patterns: Essays in Landscape Archaeology*, William Kelso and Rachel Most, eds. University Press of Virginia, Charlottesville, pp. 7–22.

Kelso, William (1989) Comments on the 1987 Society for Historical Archaeology Landscape Symposium. *Historical Archaeology* 23(2): 48–49.

Kelso, William and Rachel Most, eds. (1990) *Earth Patterns: Essays in Landscape Archaeology*. University of Virginia Press, Charlottesville.

Klein, Terry H. (1991) Nineteenth-Century Ceramics and Models of Consumer Behavior. *Historical Archaeology* 25(2): 77–91.

Kohl, Philip (1987) The Use and Abuse of World Systems Theory: The Case of the Pristine West Asian State. *Archaeological Method and Theory* 2: 1–31.

Kohl, Philip (1981) Materialist Approaches in Prehistory. *Annual Review of Anthropology* 10: 89–110.

Konnert, Mark (2008) *Early Modern Europe: The Age of Relgious War, 1559–1715*. University of Toronto Press, Toronto.

Kozák, Jan and Vladimír Čermák (2010) *The Illustrated History of Natural Disasters*. Springer, Dordecht.

Kryder-Reid, Elizabeth (1994) "As Is the Gardener, So Is the Garden": The Archaeology of Landscape as Myth. In *The Historical Archaeology of the Chesapeake*, P. Shackel and B.J. Little, eds. Smithsonian Institution Press, Washington, DC, pp. 131–148.

Kulikof, Alan (1986) *Tobacco and Slaves*. University of North Carolina Press, Chapel Hill.

Kupperman, Karen (2007) *The Jamestown Project*. Harvard University Press, Cambridge, MA.

Kurlansky, Mark (1993) *A Continent of Islands: Searching for the Caribbean Destiny*. De Capo Press, Boston.

Kus, James (1984) The Chicama-Moche Canal: Failure or Success? An Alternative Explanation for an Incomplete Canal. *American Antiquity* 49(2): 408–415.

Laborie, P. J. (1798) *The Coffee Planter of Saint Domingo*. Cadell and Davies, London.

Laumann, Edward O. and David Knoke (1987) *The Organizational State: Politics and Government, 1977–1981*. University of Wisconsin Press, Madison.

Laycock, Henry (1999) Exploitation via Labor Power in Marx. *Journal of Ethics* 3(2): 121–131.

Lees, Susan H. (1994) Irrigation and Society. *Journal of Archaeological Research* 2(4): 36–78.

Lefebvre, Henri (1991) *The Production of Space*. Blackwell, Malden, MA.

Lenin, Vladimir Ilyich (2010) *Imperialism, the Highest Stage of Capitalism*. Penguin Classics, New York.

Leone, Mark P. (2005) *The Archaeology of Liberty in an American Capital: Excavations in Annapolis*. University of California Press, Berkeley.

Leone, Mark P. (1999) Ceramics from Annapolis Maryland: A Measure of Time Routines and Work Discipline. In *Historical Archaeologies of Capitalism*, Mark P. Leone and Parker B. Potter, Jr., eds. Kluwer, New York, pp. 195–216.

Leone, Mark P. (1995) Historical Archaeologies of Capitalism. *American Anthropologist* 97(2): 251–268.

Leone, Mark P. (1988) The Georgian Order as the Order of Merchant Capitalism in Annapolis, Maryland. In *The Recovery of Meaning: Historical Archaeology in the Eastern United States*, Mark P. Leone and Parker B. Potter, Jr., eds. Smithsonian Institution Press, Washington, DC, pp. 219–229.

Leone, Mark P. (1984) Interpreting Ideology in Historical Archaeology: The William Paca Garden in Annapolis, Maryland. In *Ideology, Power and Prehistory*, D. Miller and C. Tilley, eds. Cambridge University Press, Cambridge, pp. 25–35.

Leone, Mark P., Parker B. Potter, Jr., and Paul A. Shackel (1987) Toward a Critical Archaeology. *Current Anthropology* 28(3): 283–302.

Leslie, Charles (1740) *A New History of Jamaica*. J. Hodges, London.

Lewis, Kenneth (1985) Plantation Layout and Function in the South Carolina Lowcountry. In *The Archaeology of Slavery and Plantation Life*, Theresa Singleton, ed. Academic Press, San Diego, CA, pp. 35–66.

Lewis, Kenneth (1984) *The American Frontier: An Archaeological Study of Settlement Pattern and Process*. Academic Press, New York.

Lobdell, Richard A. (1972) Patterns of Investment and Sources of Credit in the British West Indian Sugar Industry. *Journal of Caribbean History* 4: 31–53.

Long, Edward (1774) *The History of Jamaica; or, General Survey of the Ancient and Modern State of That Island: With Reflections on Its Situations, Settlements, Inhabitants, Climate, Products, Commerce, Laws, and Government*. T. Lowndes, London.

Loftfield, Thomas C. (2001) Creolization in Seventeenth-Century Barbados. In *Island Lives: Historical Archaeologies of the Caribbean*. P. Farnsworth, ed. University of Alabama Press, Tuscaloosa, pp. 207–233.

Lowndes, John (1807) *The Coffee Planter*. C. Lowndes, London.

Luccketti, Nicholas (1990) Archaeological Excavations at Bacon's Castle, Surry County, Virginia. In *Earth Patterns: Essays in Landscape Archaeology*, William Kelso and Rachel Most, eds. University Press of Virginia, Charlottesville, pp. 23–42.

Lucero, Lisa J. (2002) The Collapse of the Classic Maya: A Case for the Role of Water Control. *American Anthropologist* 104(3): 814–826.

Lukacs, Georg (1972) *History and Class Consciousness*. MIT Press, Cambridge, MA.

Lull, Vincente and Rafael Mico (2011) *Archaeology of the Origin of the State: The Theories*. Oxford University Press, Oxford.

Mackeson mss. Letters of John Mackeson, Kent County Library, Kent, United Kingdom.

Mahoney, James (2010) *Colonialism and Postcolonial Development: Spanish America in Comparative Perspective*. Cambridge University Press, Cambridge.

Malios, Seth (2000) *At the Edge of the Precipice: Frontier Ventures, Jamestown's Hinterland, and the Archaeology of 44JC802*. Association for the Preservation of Virginia Antiquities, Richmond, VA.

Mallios, Seth (1999) *Archaeological Excavations at 44JC568, the Reverend Richard Buck Site*. Association for the Preservation of Virginia Antiquities. Richmond, VA.

Martin, Ann Smart (1996) Frontier Boys and Country Cousins: The Context for Choice in Eighteenth-Century Consumerism. In *Historical Archaeology and the Study of American Culture*, Lu Ann De Cunzo and Bernard L. Herman, eds. Henry Francis du Pont Winterthur Museum, Winterthur, DE, pp. 71–102.

Martin, Ann Smart (1994) "Fashionable Sugar Dishes, Latest Fashion Ware": The Creamware Revolution in the Eighteenth-Century Chesapeake. In *Historical Archaeologies of the Chesapeake*, Paul A. Shackel and Barbara J. Little, eds. Smithsonian Institution Press, Washington, DC, pp. 169–187.

Marx, Karl (2000) *Theories of Surplus Value*. Prometheus Books, Amherst, NY.

Marx, Karl (1993) *The Grundrisse: Foundations of the Critique of Political Economy*. Penguin Classics, New York.

Marx, Karl (1992) *Capital, Volume 1*. International Publishers, New York.

Marx, Karl (1984) *Capital, Volume 3*. International Publishers, New York.

Marx, Karl (1979) *A Contribution to the Critique of Political Economy*. International Publishers, New York.

Marx, Karl (1976) *The German Ideology*. Progress Publishers, Moscow.

Marx, Karl (1975) *The Eighteenth Brumaire of Louis Bonaparte*. International Publishers, New York.

Marx, Karl (1964) *Pre-Capitalist Economic Formations*. International Publishers, New York.

Marx, Karl (1961) *Economic and Philosophic Manuscripts of 1844*. Foreign Language Publishing House, Moscow.

Marx, Karl (1902) *Wage Labor and Capital*. New York Labor News Company, New York.

MacGregor, John (1847) *The Progress of America, from the Discovery by Columbus to the Year 1846*. Whittaker and Co., London.

Matthews, Christopher (2005) Public Dialectics: Marxist Reflection in Archaeology. *Historical Archaeology* 39(4): 26–44.

Mays, Simon (1989) Marxist Perspectives on Social Organization in the Central European Bronze Age. In *Domination and Resistance*, Daniel Miller, Michael Rowlands, and Christopher Tilley, eds. Unwin Hyman, London, pp. 215–226.

McCartney, Martha (2011) *Jordans Point Virginia: Archaeology in Perspective, Prehistoric to Modern Times*. University Press of Virginia, Charlottesville.

McCoy, Alfred W. (1992) Sugar Barons: Formation of a Native Planter Class in the Colonial Philippines. In *Plantations, Peasants, and Proletarians in Colonial Asia*, E. Valentine Daniel, Henry Bernstein, and Tom Brass, eds. Frank Cass, London, pp. 106–141.

McFadden, Leslie, Phillip Levy, David Muraca, and Jennifer Jones (1999) *Interim Report: The Archaeology of Rich Neck Plantation*. Colonial Williamsburg Foundation, Williamsburg, VA.

McGuire, Randall H. (2008) *Archaeology as Political Action*. University of California Press, Berkeley.

McGuire, Randall H. (1993) Archaeology and Marxism. *Archaeological Method and Theory* 5: 101–157.

McGuire, Randall H. (1992) *A Marxist Archaeology*. Academic Press, San Diego.

McGuire, Randall H. (1991) Building Power in the Cultural Landscape of Broome County, New York, 1880 to 1940. In *The Archaeology of Inequality*, Randall H. McGuire and Robert Paynter, eds. Basil Blackwell, Oxford, pp. 102–124.

McGuire, Randall H. and Paul Reckner (2002) The Unromantic West: Labor, Capital, and Struggle. *Historical Archaeology* 36(3): 44–58.

McKee, Lawrence (1996) The Archaeology of Rachel's Garden. In *Landscape Archaeology: Reading and Interpreting the American Historical Landscape*, Rebecca Yamin and Karen B. Metheny, eds. University of Tennessee Press, Knoxville, pp. 70–90.

McKendrick, N., J. Brewer, and J. H. Plumb (1982) *The Birth of a Consumer Society: The Commercialization of Eighteenth Century England*. Indiana University Press, Bloomington.

M'Mahon, Benjamin (1839) *Jamaica Plantership*. Effingham Wilson, London.

Middlekauf, Robert (2007) *The Glorious Cause: The American Revolution, 1763–1789*. Oxford University Press, Oxford.

Mills, C. Wright (2000) *The Power Elite*, new edition. Oxford University Press, Oxford.

Montieth, Kathleen (2002a) The Labor Regimen on Jamaica Coffee Plantations during Slavery. In *Jamaica in Slavery and Freedom: History, Heritage, and Culture*, Kathleen Montieth and Glen Richards, eds. University of the West Indies Press, Mona, Jamaica pp. 259–273.

Montieth, Kathleen (2002b) Planting and Processing Techniques on Jamaican Coffee Plantations during Slavery. In *Working Slavery, Pricing Freedom: Perspectives from the Caribbean, Africa, and the African Diaspora*, Verene A. Shepherd, ed. Palgrave, New York, pp. 112–129.

Montieth, Kathleen (1991) The Coffee Industry in Jamaica, 1790–1850. MA Thesis, University of the West Indies, Mona, Jamaica.

Morgan, Edmund (1975) *American Slavery, American Freedom: The Ordeal of Colonial Virginia*. W. W. Norton, New York.

Morgan, Jennifer (2004) *Laboring Women: Reproduction and Gender in New World Slavery*. University of Pennsylvania Press, Philadelphia.

Morgan, Tim, Nicholas Luccketti, Beverly Straube, S. Fiona Bessey, and Annette Loomis (1995) *Archaeological Excavations at Jordan's Point* (2 volumes). Virginia Company Foundation, Williamsburg VA.

Moseley, Michael (1983) The Good Old Days Were Better: Agrarian Collapse and Tectonics. *American Anthropologist* 85(4): 773–799.

Mintz, Sidney W. (2010) *Three Ancient Colonies: Caribbean Themes and Variations*. Harvard University Press, Cambridge, MA.

Mintz, Sidney W. and Douglas Hall (1960) *The Origins of the Jamaican Internal Marketing System*. Yale University Publications in Anthropology, New Haven, CT.

Mrozowski, Stephen A. (2006) *The Archaeology of Class in Urban America*. Cambridge University Press, Cambridge.

Mrozowski, Stephen A. (1991) Landscapes of Inequality. In *The Archaeology of Inequality*, Randall H. McGuire and Robert Paynter, eds. Basil Blackwell, Oxford, pp. 79–101.

Mrozowski, Stephen, A. Stephen and Mary Beaudry (1990) Archaeology and the Landscape of Corporate Ideology. In *Earth Patterns: Essays in Landscape Archaeology*, William M. Kelso and Rachel Most, eds. University Press of Virginia, Charlottesville, pp. 191–208.

Morzowski. Stephen A., Grace H. Zeising, and Mary Beaudry (1996) *Living on the Boott: Historical Archaeology at the Boott Mills Boardinghouses Lowell, Massachusetts*. University of Massachusetts Press, Amherst, MA.

Mullin, Michael (1995) Slave Economic Strategies: Food, Markets, and Property. In *From Chattel Slaves to Wage Slaves* Mary Turner, ed. Ian Randle, Kingston, Jamaica, pp. 68–79.

Mullins, Paul (1999a) Race and the Genteel Consumer: Class and African American Consumption, 1850–1930. *Historical Archaeology* 33(1): 22–38.

Mullins, Paul (1999b) "A Bold and Gorgeous Front": The Contradictions of African America and Consumer Culture. In *Historical Archaeologies of Capitalism*, Mark P. Leone and Parker B. Potter, Jr., eds. Kluwer, New York, pp.169–194.

Muraca, David (1993) Martin's Hundred: A Settlement Study. MA Thesis, College of William and Mary, Williamsburg, VA.

Murray, Martin J. (1992) "White Gold" or "White Blood"? The Rubber Plantations of Colonial Indochina, 1910–40. In *Plantations, Peasants, and Proletarians in Colonial Asia*, E. Valentine Daniel, Henry Bernstein, and Tom Brass, eds. Frank Cass, London, pp. 41–67.

Neiman, Fraser D. (2008) The Lost World of Monticello: An Evolutionary Perspective. *Journal of Anthropological Research* 64: 161–193.

Neiman, Fraser D. (1980) *Field Archaeology of the Clifts Plantation Site, Westmoreland County, Virginia*. Robert E. Lee Memorial Association, Stratford, VA.

Neiman, Fraser D. (1978) Domestic Architecture of the Clifts Plantation Site: The Social Context of Early Virginia Building. *Northern Neck Historical Magazine* 28: 3096–3128.

Noël Hume, Ivor and Audrey Noël Hume (2001) *The Archaeology of Martin's Hundred*. University of Pennsylvania Press, Philadelphia.

Noël Hume, Ivor (1982) *Martin's Hundred*. Knopf, New York.

O'Laughlin, Karen Fay and James F. Lander (2003) *Caribbean Tsunamis: A 500-year History from 1498–1998*. Kluwer, New York.

Oldfield, J. R. (1995) *Popular Politics and British Anti-slavery: The Mobilization of Public Opinion against the Slave Trade*. Manchester University Press, Manchester.

Oldfield, J. R. (1992) The London Committee and Mobilization of Public Opinion against the Slave Trade. *Historical Journal* 35(2): 331–343.

Orser, Charles E., Jr. (2012) An Archaeology of Eurocentrism. *American Antiquity* 77(4): 737–755.

Orser, Charles E., Jr. (2007) *The Archaeology of Race and Racialization in Historic America*. University Press of Florida, Gainesville.

Orser, Charles E., Jr. (2004) *Race and Practice in Archaeological Interpretation*. Philadelphia, University of Pennsylvania Press.

Orser, Charles E., Jr. (1999) Archaeology and the Challenges of Capitalist Farm Tenancy in America. In *Archaeologies of Capitalism*, Mark P, Leone and Parker B. Potter, Jr. eds. Kluwer/Plenum, New York pp. 143–168.

Orser, Charles E. Jr. (1996) *A Historical Archaeology of the Modern World*. Plenum Publishers, New York.

Orser, Charles E. Jr. (1992) *In Search of Zumbi: Preliminary Archaeological Research in Serra Da Barriga, State of Alagoas, Brazil*. Illinois State University.

Orser, Charles E., Jr. (1991) The Continued Pattern of Dominance: Landlord and Tenant on the Postbellum Cotton Plantation. In *The Archaeology of Inequality*, Randall H. McGuire and Robert Paynter, eds. Basil Blackwell, Oxford, pp. 40–54.

Orser, Charles E., Jr. (1988) *The Material Basis of the Postbellum Tenant Plantation: Historical Archaeology in the South Carolina Piedmont*. University of Georgia Press, Athens.

Orser, Charles E., Jr. and Pedro Funari (2001) Archaeology of Slave Resistance and Rebellion. *World Archaeology* 33(1): 61–72.

Orser, Charles E. Jr. and A. M. Nekola (1985) Plantation Settlement from Slavery to Tenancy: An Example from a Piedmont Plantation in South Carolina. In *The Archaeology of Slavery and Plantation Life*, Theresa Singleton ed. Academic Press, San Diego, pp. 67–94.

Outlaw, Alain Charles (1990) *Governor's Land: Archaeology of Early Seventeenth Century Virginia Settlements*. Department of Historic Resources, Richmond, VA.

Padron, Francisco Morales (2003) *Spanish Jamaica*. Ian Randle Press, Kingston, Jamaica.

Pares, Richard (1950) *A West-India Fortune*. Longmans, Green, and Co., New York.

Paterson, Robert (1843) *Remarks on the Present State of Cultivation in Jamaica; the Habits of the Peasantry; and Remedies Suggested for the Improvement of Both*. W. Burness, Edinburgh.

Patterson, Thomas C. (2008) A Brief History of Landscape Archaeology in the Americas. In *Handbook of Landscape Archaeology*, Bruno David and Julian Thomas, eds. Left Coast Press, Walnut Creek, CA, pp. 77–84.

Patterson, Thomas C. (2003) *Marx's Ghost: Conversations with Archaeologists*. Berg, Oxford.

Patterson, Thomas C. (1997) *Inventing Western Civilization*. Monthly Review Press, New York.

Patterson, Thomas C. (1991) *The Inca Empire: The Formation and Disintegration of a Pre-Capitalist State*. Berg, New York.

Patterson, Thomas C. (1990) Processes in the Formation of Ancient World Systems. *Dialectical Anthropology* 15(1): 1–18.

Patterson, Thomas C. (1986) Ideology, Class Formation, and Resistance in the Inca State. *Critique of Anthropology* 6(1): 75–85.

Pawson, Michael and David Buisseret (2002) *Port Royal, Jamaica*. University of the West Indies Press, Mona, Jamaica.

Paynter, Robert (1999) Epilogue: Class Analysis and Historical Archaeology. *Historical Archaeology* 33(1): 184–195.

Paynter, Robert (1989) The Archaeology of Equality and Inequality. *Annual Review of Anthropology* 18: 369–399.

Paynter, Robert (1985) Surplus Flow between Frontiers and Homelands. In *Archaeology of Frontiers and Boundaries*, Stanton Green and Steven M. Perlman, eds. Academic Press, Orlando, FL, pp. 163–211.

Paynter, Robert (1983) Expanding the Scope of Settlement Analysis. In *Archaeological Hammers and Theories*, J. Moore and A. Keene, eds. Academic Press, Orlando, FL, pp. 233–275.

Paynter, Robert (1982) *Models of Spatial Inequality*. Academic Press, New York.

Paynter, Robert (1981) Social Complexity in Peripheries: Problems and Models. In *Archaeological Approaches to the Study of Complexity*, S. E. v. d. Leeuw, ed. A. E. van Giffen Institute, Amsterdam, Netherlands, pp. 118–141.

Paynter, Robert and Randall McGuire (1991) The Archaeology of Inequality: Material Culture of Domination and Resistance. In *The Archaeology of Inequality*, R. H. McGuire and R. Paynter, eds. Basil Blackwell, Oxford, pp. 1–27.

Pearson, Mike and Michael Shanks (2001) *Theatre/Archaeology*. Routledge, London.

Pergrine, P. and Gary Feinman (1996) *Pre Columbian World Systems*. Prehistory Press, Madison WI.

Phillippo, James (1843) *Jamaica: Its Past and Present State*. John Snow, London.

Phillips, John A. and Charles Wetherell (1995) The Great Reform Act of 1832 and the Political Modernization of England. *American Historical Review* 100(2): 411–436.

Pluckhahn, Thomas J. (2010) Household Archaeology in the Southeastern United States: History, Trends, and Challenges. *Journal of Archaeological Research* 18(4): 331–385.

Pogue, Dennis (1996) Giant in the Earth: George Washington, Landscape Designer. In *Landscape Archaeology: Reading and Interpreting the American Historical Landscape*, Rebecca Yamin and Karen B. Metheny, eds. University of Tennessee Press, Knoxville, pp. 52–69.

Polanyi, Karl (2001) *The Great Transformation: The Political and Economic Origins of Our Time*. 2nd paperback edition. Beacon Press, Boston.

Pogue, Dennis (2001) The Transformation of America: Georgian Sensibility, Capitalist Conspiracy, or Consumer Revolution? *Historical Archaeology* 35(2): 41–57.

Porter, Anthony (1990) *Jamaica, a Geological Portrait*. Institute of Jamaica Press, Kingston.

Price, Barbara (1982) Cultural Materialism: A Theoretical Review. *American Antiquity* 47(4): 709–741.

Price, Richard (1996) *Maroon Societies: Rebel Slave Communities in the Americas.* Johns Hopkins University Press, Baltimore.

Prucell, Robert (2006) *Archaeological Semiotics.* Blackwell, Malden, MA.

Purkiss, Diane (2007) *The English Civil War: A People's History.* Harper Collins, New York.

Reckford, Mary (1968) The Jamaica Slave Rebellion of 1831. *Past and Present* (40): 108–125.

Reddick, Rhoda E. (1985) Women and Slavery in the Caribbean: A Feminist Perspective. *Latin American Perspectives* 44(12): 63–80.

Reeves, Matthew (2011) Household Market Activities among Early Nineteenth-Century Jamaican Slaves: An Archaeological Case Study from Two Slave Settlements. In *Out of Many, One People: The Historical Archaeology of Colonial Jamaica*, James A. Delle, Mark Hauser, and Douglas V. Armstrong, eds. University of Alabama Press, Tuscaloosa, pp. 183–210.

Reeves, Matthew (1997) "By Their Own Labor": Enslaved Africans' Survival Strategies on Two Jamaican Plantations. PhD Dissertation, Anthropology, Syracuse University, Syracuse, New York.

Rice, James D. (2012) *Tales from a Revolution: Bacon's Rebellion and the Transformation of Early America.* Oxford University Press, Oxford.

Roberts, George W. (1957) *The Population of Jamaica.* University of Michigan, Ann Arbor.

Robertson, James (2005) *Gone Is the Ancient Glory: Spanish Town, Jamaica 1534–2000.* Ian Randle Publishers, Kingston.

Robertson, James (2002) Re-writing the English Concept of Jamaica in the Late 17th-Century. *English Historical Review* 117(473): 813–839.

Roseberry, William (1997) Marx and Anthropology. *Annual Review of Anthropology* 26: 25–46.

Rosenswig, Robert M (2012) Materialism, Mode of Production, and a Millennium of Change in Southern Mexico. *Journal of Archaeological Method and Theory* 19: 1–48.

Roughley, Thomas (1823) *The Jamaica Planter's Guide.* Longman, Hurst, Rees, Orme, and Brown, London.

Rouse, Irving (1992) *The Tainos: Rise and Decline of the People who Greeted Columbus.* Yale University Press, New Haven, CT.

Saitta, Dean (2007) *The Archaeology of Collective Action.* University Press of Florida, Gainesville.

Sanders, William T. (1956) The Central Mexican Symbiotic Region: A Study in Prehistoric Settlement Patterns. In *Prehistoric Settlement Patterns in the New World*, G. R. Willey, ed. Viking Fund Publications in Anthropology, New York, pp. 115–127.

Sanders, William T., J. R. Parsons and R. S. Santley (1979) *The Basin of Mexico: Ecological Processes in the Evolution of a Civilization.* Academic Press, New York.

Sandweiss, Daniel H., Ruth Shady Solis, Michael E. Moseley, David K. Keefer, and Charles R. Ortloff (2009) Environmental Change and Economic Development in Coastal Peru between 5800 and 3600 Years Ago. *Proceedings of the National Academy of Sciences* 106(5): 1359–1363.

Satchell, Vernon (1990) *From Plots to Plantations: Land Transactions in Jamaica, 1866–1900*. Institute of Social and Economic Research, Kingston, Jamaica.

Sayers, Daniel (2003) Glimpses into the Dialectics of Antebellum Landscape Nucleation in Agrarian Michigan. *Journal of Archaeological Method and Theory* 10(4): 369–432.

Sen, Asok (1984) Transition from Feudalism to Capitalism. *Economic and Political Weekly* 19(30): 51–69.

Shennan, Stephen (2008) Evolution in Archaeology. *Annual Review of Anthropology* 37: 43–65.

Shepherd, Verene A. (2009) *Livestock, Sugar, and Slavery: Contested Terrain in Colonial Jamaica*. Ian Randle Publishers, Kingston.

Shepherd, Verene A. (2002) Land, Labor, and Social Status: Non-sugar Producers in Jamaica in Slavery and Freedom. In *Working Slavery, Pricing Freedom: Perspectives from the Caribbean, Africa, and the African Diaspora*, Verene A. Shepherd, ed,. Palgrave, New York, pp. 153–178.

Shepherd, Verene A. and Kathleen E. A. Montieth (2002) Pen-Keepers and Coffee Farmers in a Sugar-Plantation Society. In *Slavery without Sugar: Diversity in Caribbean Economy and Society Since the 17th Century*, Verene A. Shepherd, ed. University Press of Florida, Gainesville, pp. 82–101.

Sheridan, Richard B. (2000) *Sugar and Slavery: An Economic History of the British West Indies, 1623–1775*. 2nd edition. University of the West Indies Press, Mona, Jamaica.

Sheridan, Richard B. (1974) *Sugar and Slavery: An Economic History of the British West Indies, 1623–1775*. Caribbean University Press, Eagle Hall, Barbados.

Sheridan, Richard B. (1971) Simon Taylor, Sugar Tycoon of Jamaica, 1740–1813. *Agricultural History* 45(4): 285–296.

Simmonds, L. E. (2004) The Afro-Jamaican and Internal Marketing System: Kingston, 1780–1834. In *Jamaica in Slavery and Freedom: History, Heritage, and Culture*, K. Montieth and G. Richards, eds. University of the West Indies Press, Mona, Jamaica, pp. 274–290.

Siskind, Janet (1978) Kinship and Mode of Production. *American Anthropologist* 80(4): 860–872.

Smith, S. D. (2002) Coffee and the "Poorer Sort of People" in Jamaica During the Period of African Enslavement. In *Slavery without Sugar: Diversity in Caribbean Economy and Society Since the 17th Century*, Verene A. Shepherd, ed. University Press of Florida, Gainesville, pp. 102–128.

Smith, S. D. (1996) Accounting for Taste: British Coffee Consumption in Historical Perspective. *Journal of International History* 27(2): 183–214.

Spriggs, Matthew (1984) *Marxist Perspectives in Archaeology*. Cambridge University Press, Cambridge.

Steward, Julian (1990) *Theory of Culture Change: The Methodology of Multilineal Evolution*. University of Illinois Press, Urbana.

Stewart (1808) *An Account of Jamaica and Its Inhabitants*. Longman, Hurst, Rees, and Orme, London.

Stewart (1823) *A View of the Past and Present State of the Island of Jamaica*. Oliver and Boyd, Edinburgh.

Stinchcombe, Arthur L. (1995) *Sugar Island Slavery in the Age of Enlightenment: The Political Economy of the Caribbean World*. Princeton University Press, Princeton, NJ.

Tarter, Brent (2011) Bacon's Rebellion, the Grievances of the People, and the Political Culture of Seventeenth-Century Virginia. *Virginia Magazine of History and Biography* 119: 4–41.

Thorner, Alice (1982) Semi-feudalism or Capitalism? Contemporary Debate on Classes and Modes of Production in India. *Economic and Political Weekly* 17(49): 1961–1968.

Tomich, Dale W. (2004) *Through the Prism of Slavery: Labor, Capital, and World Economy*. Rowman and Littlefield, Lanham, MD.

Tomich, Dale W. (1990) *Slavery in the Circuit of Sugar: Martinique and the World Economy, 1830–1848*. Johns Hopkins University Press, Baltimore, MD.

Torres, Joshua M. and Reniel Rodriguez Ramos (2008) The Caribbean: A Continent Divided by Water. In *Archaeology and Geoinformatics: Case Studies from the Caribbean*, Basil A. Reid, ed. University of Alabama Press, Tuscaloosa, pp. 13–29.

Tosi, Maurizio (1976) Dialectics of State Formation in Mesopotamia, Iran, and Central Asia. *Dialectical Anthropology* 1: 173–180.

Trigger, Bruce (1993) Marxism in Contemporary Western Archaeology. *Archaeological Method and Theory* 5: 159–200.

Trigger, Bruce (1989) *A History of Archaeological Thought*. Cambridge University Press, Cambridge.

Trouillot, Michel-Rolph (1988) *Peasants and Capital: Dominica in the World Economy*. Johns Hopkins Studies in Atlantic History and Culture. Johns Hopkins University Press, Baltimore.

Upton, Dell (1984) White and Black Landscapes in Eighteenth-century Virginia. *Places* 2(2): 59–72.

Upton, Dell (1982) The Origins of Chesapeake Architecture. In *Three Centuries of Maryland Architecture*, Maryland Historic Trust and the Society for the Preservation of Maryland Antiquities, eds. Maryland Historical Trust, Annapolis, pp. 44–57.

van Binsbergen, Wim and Peter Geschiere, eds. (1985) *Old Modes of Production and Capitalist Encroachment: Anthropological Explorations in Africa*. Routledge and Keegan Paul, London.

Vlach, John (1993) *Back of the Big House: The Architecture of Plantation Slavery*. University of North Carolina Press, Chapel Hill.

Voss, Barbara (2000) Feminisms, Queer Theories, and the Archaeological Study of Past Sexualities. *World Archaeology* 32(2): 180–192.

Wallerstein, Immanuel (1989) *The Modern World System III: The Second Era of Great Expansion of the Capitalist World Economy, 1730–1840*. Academic Press, San Diego.

Wallerstein, Immanuel (1980) *The Modern World System II: Mercantilism and the Consolidation of the European World Economy, 1600–1750*. Academic Press, New York.

Wallerstein, Immanuel (1979) *The Capitalist World Economy*. Cambridge University Press, Cambridge.

Wallerstein, Immanuel (1976) *The Modern World-System: Capitalist Agriculture and the Origins of the European World-Economy in the Sixteenth Century*. Academic Press, New York.

Walsh, Lorena (2010) *Motives of Honor, Pleasure, and Profit: Plantation Management in the Colonial Chesapeake, 1607–1763*. University of North Carolina Press, Chapel Hill.

Walvin, James (2008) *Britain's Slave Empire*. Tempus Publishing, Stroud, UK.

Walvin, James (1997) *Fruits of Empire: Exotic Produce and British Taste, 1660–1800*. New York University Press, New York.

Washburn, Wilcomb E. (1957) *The Governor and the Rebel: A History of Bacon's Rebellion in Virginia*. University of North Carolina Press, Chapel Hill.

Watts, David (1990) *The West Indies, Patterns of Development and Change since 1492*. Cambridge University Press, Cambridge.

Webb, Stephen Saunders (1984) *1676: The End of American Independence*. Harvard University Press, Cambridge, MA.

Weber (1996) The Greenhouse Effect: Gender-related Traditions in Eighteenth-century Gardening. In *Landscape Archaeology: Reading and Interpreting the American Historical Landscape*, R. Yamin and K. B. Metheny, eds. University of Tennessee Press, Knoxville, pp. 32–51.

Wertenbaker, Thomas Jefferson (1940) *Torchbearer of the Revolution: The Story of Bacon's Rebellion and its Leader*. Princeton University Press, Princeton, NJ.

Wesson, Cameron B. (2008) *Households and Hegemony: Early Creek Prestige Goods, Symbolic Capital, and Social Power*. University of Nebraska Press, Lincoln.

Wilkie, Laurie (2001) Methodist Intentions and African Sensibilities: The Victory of African Consumerism over Plantation Paternalism at a Bahamian Plantation. In *Island Lives: Historical Archaeologies of the Caribbean*, Paul Farnsworth, ed. University of Alabama Press, Tuscaloosa, pp. 272–300.

Wilkie Laurie and Paul Farnsworth (2005) *Sampling Many Pots: An Archaeology of Memory and Tradition at a Bahamian Plantation*. University Press of Florida, Gainesville.

Wilkie, Laurie and Paul Farnsworth (1999) Trade and the Construction of Bahamian Identity: A Multiscalar Exploration. *International Journal of Historical Archaeology* 3(4): 283–320.

Wilkie, Laurie A. and Kevin M. Bartoy (2000) A Critical Archaeology Revisited. *Current Anthropology* 41(5): 747–777.

Willey, Gordon (1953) *Prehistoric Settlement Patterns in the Viru Valley, Peru*. Bureau of American Ethnology, Washington, DC.

Williams, Eric (1944) *Capitalism and Slavery*. University of North Carolina Press, Chapel Hill.

Wilmot, S. (1984) Not "Full Free": The Ex-Slaves and the Apprenticeship System in Jamaica 1834–1838. *Jamaica Journal* 17: 2–10.

Wilson, Samuel M. (2007) *The Archaeology of the Caribbean*. Cambridge University Press, Cambridge.

Wolf, Eric (1982) *Europe and the People Without History*. Berkeley: University of California Press.

Woodward, Robyn (2011) Feudalism or Agrarian Capitalism? The Archaeology of the Early 16th Century Spanish Sugar Industry. In *Out of Many, One People: The Historical Archaeology of Colonial Jamaica*, James A. Delle, Mark Hauser, and Douglas V. Armstrong, eds. University of Alabama Press, Tuscaloosa, pp. 23–40.

Wright, Irene A. (1930) The Spanish Resistance to the English Occupation of Jamaica, 1655–1660 *Transactions of the Royal Historical Society* Fourth Series, Vol. 13, pp. 117–147.

Wright, Philip, ed. (2002) *Lady Nugent's Journal of Her Residency in Jamaica from 1801 to 1805*. University of the West Indies Press, Mona, Jamaica.

Wurst, LouAnn (2011) "Human Accumulations": Class and Tourism at Niagara Falls. *International Journal of Historical Archaeology* 15(2): 254–266.

Wurst, LouAnn (2006) A Class All its Own: Explorations of Class Formation and Conflict. In *Historical Archaeology*, Martin Hall and Stephen Silliman, eds. Blackwell, Malden, MA, pp. 190–206.

Wurst, LouAnn (1999) Internalizing Class in Historical Archaeology. *Historical Archaeology* 33(1): 7–21.

Wurst, LouAnn (1991) "Employees Must Be of Moral and Temperate Habits": Rural and Urban Elite Ideologies. In *The Archaeology of Inequality*, Randall H. McGuire and Robert Paynter, eds. Basil Blackwell, Oxford, pp. 125–149.

Yamin, Rebecca and Karen B. Metheny (1996) *Landscape Archaeology: Reading and Interpreting the American Historical Landscape*. University of Tennessee Press, Knoxville.

Index

259

For EU product safety concerns, contact us at Calle de José Abascal, 56–1°,
28003 Madrid, Spain or eugpsr@cambridge.org.

www.ingramcontent.com/pod-product-compliance
Ingram Content Group UK Ltd.
Pitfield, Milton Keynes, MK11 3LW, UK
UKHW020335140625

459647UK00018B/2152

* 9 7 8 0 5 2 1 7 4 4 3 3 1 *